Christians under Covers

Christians under Covers

EVANGELICALS AND SEXUAL PLEASURE
ON THE INTERNET

Kelsy Burke

UNIVERSITY OF CALIFORNIA PRESS

University of California Press, one of the most distinguished university presses in the United States, enriches lives around the world by advancing scholarship in the humanities, social sciences, and natural sciences. Its activities are supported by the UC Press Foundation and by philanthropic contributions from individuals and institutions. For more information, visit www.ucpress.edu.

University of California Press
Oakland, California

Library of Congress Cataloging-in-Publication Data

Burke, Kelsy, 1985– author.
    Christians under covers : evangelicals and sexual pleasure on the Internet / Kelsy Burke.
        pages   cm
    Includes bibliographical references and index.
    ISBN 978-0-520-28632-0 (cloth : alk. paper)
    ISBN 978-0-520-28633-7 (pbk. : alk. paper)
    ISBN 978-0-520-96158-6 (ebook)
    1. Christians—Sexual behavior—United States.   2. Sex—Religious aspects—Christianity.   3. Internet—Religious aspects—Christianity.
4. Sex in mass media.   I. Title.
    HQ63.B87   2016
    233'.5—dc23
                                                                    2015031933

Manufactured in the United States of America

24   23   22   21   20   19   18   17
10   9   8   7   6   5   4   3   2

To Jody, my first writing coach

CONTENTS

LIST OF FIGURES AND TABLES

FIGURES

TABLES

ACKNOWLEDGMENTS

"Acknowledgments" is such a detached and formal word. "My desperately sincere thanks" would be a more apt way to express my gratitude to the many people who have supported this project at its various stages.

Writing this book would not have been possible without the help of those who use and create what I collectively call Christian sexuality websites. I owe thanks to the many research participants who took time to complete my survey and participate in interviews and to the business owners, bloggers, and other website administrators who talked to me and helped me recruit participants for the study. If you find yourself reading this book, I hope that you find my depictions fair, even if you may disagree with my conclusions.

When this project was a dissertation, I was able to pursue research fulltime and pay for expenses that accompanied online and offline research thanks to fellowships and grants. These included a University of Pittsburgh Andrew W. Mellon Predoctoral Research Fellowship, a University of Pittsburgh Social Sciences Doctoral Dissertation Fellowship, an Association for the Sociology of Religion Fichter Research Grant, and a University of Pittsburgh Women's Studies Graduate Student Research Grant. The Kinsey Institute at Indiana University allowed me to use their archives for preliminary research. I was fortunate to attend Harvard Divinity School's 2011 Debates on Religion and Sexuality, where I met Mark Jordan and fellow participants, who provided smart, challenging dialogue that got my writing off the ground.

At the University of Pittsburgh, Kathy Blee supported this quirky project from the beginning. Her guidance, questions, careful editing, and countless conversations (all of which continued long after I graduated) have made me a better writer and scholar. Thanks also to Mohammed Bamyeh, Nicole

Constable, and Rachel Kutz-Flamenbaum for offering helpful and encouraging feedback at several crucial stages in my progress. I am indebted to my writing workshop and grad student comrades at Pitt—especially to Kim Creasap and Amy McDowell—for their thoughtful feedback and much-needed support.

My colleagues at St. Norbert encouraged and eased the transition from dissertation to book. Faculty development summer grants supported my writing, and my fellow faculty friends gave encouragement and insight— Tom Bolin, Ben Chan, Karlyn Crowley, Reg Kim, Ty Meidl, Katie Ries, and Drew Scheler. I owe thanks to two SNC students: Greg Grohman, who helped with editing, and Cameron Stefanowski, who volunteered his time to create one of the photographs used in the book. I am especially grateful for my discipline colleagues, Cheryl Carpenter-Siegel, Alexa Trumpy, and Jamie Lynch. Special thanks to Alexa for her always-smart suggestions and for reading so many drafts of paragraphs and chapters and to Jamie for his eye for visualizing data—my graphs wouldn't have been the same without his help.

Thanks to Bernadette Barton, Ashley Currier, Susie Meister Butler, Dawne Moon, and Lisa Ruchti—friends and mentors who generously offered their time and ideas. Jill Peterfeso diligently maintained our writing exchange no matter the season. Orit Avishai and Lynne Gerber always said yes when I asked them to read yet another draft and kept pushing me to think bigger and write more clearly. At the University of California Press, I have benefited from an amazing team: Ally Power, Will Vincent, Dore Brown, and Naomi Schneider. I feel immensely grateful for Naomi, my editor, who took an early interest in the book and supported it through production. Thanks also to the anonymous reviewers of the manuscript, to Genevieve Thurston for copyediting, to Lisa DeBoer for indexing, and to Gretchen Panzer for her careful reading.

Finally, I am incredibly thankful for my amazing and supportive family: to John and Kitty for helping me finish the dissertation by offering babysitting and a quiet writing space stocked with chocolates; to my parents, Alan and Jody, for three decades of unwavering encouragement; to Sylvie, who made writing a bit more difficult to accomplish but also made life more thoroughly filled with joy; and to Maggie for putting up with my research for this project for the majority of our relationship, encouraging time and space for me to write, listening to me read chapters aloud during our baby's naps, cooking dinners and brewing a lot of coffee, and for the million other ways she helped bring the book into being.

A NOTE TO READERS ON QUOTING ONLINE CONTENT

Expectations about privacy are different in online environments than in public physical spaces. Much of the data I present in this book are publicly accessible—the majority of websites in my study do not require any log-in information or membership. Yet individuals who contribute to websites that deal with unique and sensitive issues, like sex from a Christian perspective, generally do not expect that their comments will be used for anything other than the online dialogue in which they are generated. Although the people I interviewed understood that their posts could be seen by virtually anyone, I believe that posting to an online message board or commenting on a blog is more similar to sharing a story in a semipublic space—like a Bible study or an Alcoholics Anonymous meeting—than in a public space—like a park or busy town center. Even though strangers could plausibly enter these semipublic groups, there is general consensus among qualitative researchers that it is unethical for a researcher to invade these spaces without permission and use what they hear or observe as data. I realize this comparison only goes so far—a stranger would surely be noticed and questioned upon entering a Bible study, for example, whereas people using online spaces must generally expect the undetected presence of strangers, since lurkers can read online content without ever disclosing their presence.

I attempt to find middle ground in understanding the Internet as both public and private. While I did not request permission from website administrators to collect data from online content that is publicly viewable, I take seriously the privacy of website users and have done my best to protect their identities. I have quoted and described content as anonymously as possible, changing details that may reveal the online identity of the author and using pseudonyms for all website users and names of websites.

I have further edited quotes to make them easier to read by outsiders to this online community by making changes to avoid what I deem to be distracting and excessive jargon of computer-mediated communication. Generally, I have spelled out acronyms and shorthand and added punctuation where appropriate. When referencing scripture that is quoted by website users, I adhere to the translation they themselves used. Typically, this is the New International Version (NIV).

Introduction

Samantha's is an online store that specializes in sex toys for women. Customers interact virtually with the owner and namesake, though Samantha insists they get a "personal touch" through the detailed product descriptions and reviews she writes to help them pick out toys that are just right: the perfect vibrator, massage oil, or fuzzy handcuffs. For unsuspecting visitors to the site, Samantha's funny and confident writing style may conjure up the image of the *Sex and the City* character with the same name, who loved to talk about sex almost as much as she loved to have it. However, disrupting this Hollywood image is the story of how her website began, with Samantha asking for prayers from an online community of conservative Christians about whether or not God wanted her to start a sex toy business. God's answer, the website users unanimously agreed, was yes.

I followed Samantha online for about a year before I interviewed her. I was one of thousands who encountered her virtual presence—the stories of her personal struggles and her advice to other message board members. No one online, including me, knew what Samantha really looked like, who she *really* was. Samantha wasn't her real name; it was a username she created for online activity. Her profile picture for the message board where I met her—a single red rose with a long thorny stem—gave no hints of her physical appearance. Yet Samantha's story was similar to those of many evangelical women using Christian sexuality websites. Just a few years before she started her business, she had never used a sex toy or even experienced an orgasm. Samantha grew up in an evangelical church that spoke very little about sexuality. For years after she got married, she enjoyed the "closeness" she felt to her husband during sex but never felt deep sexual pleasure or desire.

She finally shared some of these sexual troubles with a close friend, who told Samantha about a website "where people talk about sex in a really frank but respectful way and from a Christian worldview." Samantha followed her friend's advice, got on her computer, and typed the URL: www.Between TheSheets.com.[1] There she discovered a virtual world of over 30,000 registered members—engaged and married Christians—talking frankly and explicitly about sexuality through a series of message board threads.

> I was just so floored—I mean, in a happy way—that people were talking about really specific things like "try this technique" or "lean forward or lean backwards," like really practical advice. I could really tell that people had a heart for God and their spouse and for wanting to help people. So I started posting and getting a lot of encouragement. I just needed to learn so many things. I mean, topics on orgasm and oral sex and how do you do this and how do you do that.

Samantha had found an online community of people who, just like her, had a "heart for God" but were not focusing on the sins of sexuality that they were used to hearing about from Christian leaders. Instead, they were insisting that God wanted married (heterosexual) couples to have active and satisfying sex lives. Thanking God for great sex, these website users insisted, was not a flippant vulgarity but rather a sincere form of praise.

A year after Samantha discovered BetweenTheSheets.com (BTS), her sex life had radically transformed. Following the advice of other members, she experimented with sex toys and learned that she liked sex and wanted to share her story to inspire others. She posted frequently to the BTS message boards and developed a reputation as someone who could offer advice. And so she posted to the site asking for prayers from other members about a crazy idea she had: "you know people are asking me all the time to recommend toys—I wonder if I should start a business. Just pray for this as something that I'm thinking about." Within twenty-four hours, the message boards on BTS were buzzing with enthusiastic support for Samantha's start-up.

Samantha's story is surprising because God and sex seem to occupy distinct and separate spaces within our communities and our psyches. Queer theorist Michael Warner, reflecting on his Pentecostal upbringing, describes them as two ecstasies that seem an "excruciating alternative" to one another.[2] Indeed, religious pleasures and sexual pleasures are often pitted against each other in debates over contentious social issues like homosexuality, premarital sex, and pornography. Conservative Christian leaders frequently lament that succumbing to sinful sexual desires voids the desire for eternal salvation. Given this reality, conservative Christians today face a dilemma, what Warner describes as the "the agony" of "choosing between orgasm and religion."[3] From their religious leaders, they hear a constant refrain of negative messages about sex. But the wider culture encourages them to see sex as pleasurable and desirable. How do they reconcile these conflicting ideas? For some, like Samantha, the answer is found in online communities that are both Christian and sex-positive. This book examines what happens when conservative religion and sexuality meet on the Internet—when public and private spaces converge in a virtual reality that has a new set of opportunities, expectations, and sanctions for discourse.

American evangelicals have a rich history when it comes to promoting sexual pleasure within marriage, having drawn upon multiple mediums— like books, workshops, and radio shows—since the 1970s.[4] Today, evangelicals encourage sexual expression through all of these channels, as well as through a wide range of digital media, including online sex toy stores, online message boards, blogs, podcasts, and virtual Bible studies that discuss a plethora of topics related to marital sex. The content of these digital resources reflects the ideas presented in print literature written by well-established and respected evangelical authorities, but unlike a book that is already written, the internet is like a book that is constantly being *rewritten* by a collective of ordinary believers, each with unique experiences and perspectives. These spaces also allow non-evangelical religious collaborators who buy into the parameters set forth by evangelicalism (that sex is intended only within heterosexual, monogamous matrimony) to contribute to online religious dialogue. The Internet allows creators and users of Christian sexuality websites to draw from existing religious doctrine while also talking about God in personal and sometimes unorthodox and unprecedented ways.

Website users portray their marital beds as crowded. Their choices appear to be (or at least attempt to be) influenced by God, who celebrates sexual pleasure for married Christians; Satan, who thwarts sexual pleasure for married Christians; and the websites themselves, which act as what sociologist Erving Goffman calls "reference groups" that monitor these desires and behaviors through feedback, providing credibility for some sex acts while condemning others.[5] Indeed, the Internet does more than reflect broader cultural and religious messages about sex: the Internet is a space to *perform* and sometimes *reimagine* these messages. Christian sexuality websites shape the idea of what Christian sex should be. While users of these websites continually emphasize their individual relationships with God, these online communities offer collective interpretations of this relationship. Central to *Christians under Covers* is how individuals use the Internet to interpret and make meaning of both their religious faith and their sexual pleasure. I trace how website creators and users establish a sense of credibility by relying on familiar evangelical Christian tropes that justify talk of sex within a religious setting. Drawing from popular evangelical authors who write about sex, they establish new guidelines for sexual behavior. This sexual logic, what I call the logic of godly sex, combines traditional and modern ideas: belief in an uncompromising truth about who can have sex (only married, monogamous heterosexuals) and in subjective sexual experiences that depend upon individual choice and taste.

Although many scholars and cultural critics claim that conservative Christian messages about sexuality simply reproduce gender inequality and homophobia, I show how online discussions about Christian sexuality enable *and* limit women's agency and reinforce *and* challenge heteronormativity.[6] On Christian sexuality websites, women's discussions of sexual pleasure and men's discussions of gender-deviant sex practices move beyond hegemonic understandings of men as dominant penetrators and women as submissive actors. Website users find ways to integrate women's multiple experiences of pleasure and men's interest in non-normative sex into a religious framework. They maintain beliefs that privilege men and heterosexuality while simultaneously incorporating feminist and queer language into their talk of sex: they encourage sexual knowledge, emphasize women's pleasure, and justify marginal sexual practices within Christian marriages. These findings suggest that Christian sexuality website users present themselves as sexually modern rather than prudish, distancing themselves from stereotypes about conservative religion and sex.

When it comes to stereotypical attitudes against sex, the Religious Right appears to be fighting a losing battle. Recent survey data suggest that religious conservatives who support abstinence-only sex education, restrictions on marriage for gay couples, and bans on women's access to abortion are outnumbered by a majority of Americans who oppose these views.[7] Today, conservative religion seems to be losing cultural relevance as Americans are less strictly devout and are increasingly progressive when it comes to sexual attitudes and practices. On primetime television, for example, we are more likely to see a gay family (however tokenized) than an explicitly religious one. With some exceptions, conservative religious characters have been mostly relegated to reality television. Programs like *19 Kids and Counting* and *Duck Dynasty* portray conservative Christian piety as spectacle—wholesome and endearing at times but just as often strange and extreme. Those who hold onto the Moral Majority platform of thirty years ago seem out of touch with today's reality. This is perhaps why the issue of religion is largely absent in scholarship on contemporary heterosexuality.[8] Religious conservatives are marginalized not only in mainstream society but also in the academic fields that theorize heterosexuality. Scholars in critical heterosexuality studies have long noted the ways in which religion *historically* contributed to heterosexuality, yet they tend to leave out religion as one of the *modern* forces of heterosexuality's power. This book explains how, perhaps counterintuitively, religion remains deeply attached to modern-day heterosexuality.

Changing attitudes about sex and sexuality in the larger secular culture, coupled with some evangelicals' bold online declarations about sexual pleasures, force an inexorable link between religion and the heterosexual ideal.[9] As Christian sexuality website users push the boundaries of gender and sexual norms, they lose the ability to rely on those norms to justify heterosexuality as normal and natural. As they write about sexuality in an era in which monogamous, married lifestyles are not the sole territory of heterosexuals, they lose the ability to rely on monogamy and marriage to define heterosexuality's exclusivity. What is left to define heterosexuality when contemporary representations of sexuality dissociate opposite-sex attraction from gender roles, sex practices, marriage, and family? For users of Christian sexuality websites, all that remains is a belief in Jesus Christ as Lord and Savior, trust in the Bible as the ultimate source of truth, and an intimate relationship with God. The normative power of contemporary heterosexuality can be garnered through a religious faith that maintains heterosexuality's exclusivity without needing additional rationale.[10]

DOING SEX, DOING GENDER, DOING RELIGION

Though it may seem like a contradiction, studying the heterosexual sex lives presented on Christian sexuality websites can be a feminist and queer project. As a critical sociologist, I bring to this book two theoretical assumptions: (1) interactions shape social realities—people together make meaning of their own and others' identities; and (2) interactions are bound within regulatory systems of power and inequality.[11] Thus, I examine how social (online) interaction shapes and disrupts gender and sexuality within the overlapping regulatory systems of gender hegemony, heteronormativity, and evangelical Christianity. I offer an analytical model that uses religion to, in the words of Annamarie Jagose, "dramatise incoherencies in the allegedly stable relations between chromosomal sex, gender, and sexual desire."[12]

Most of us grew up believing that every person is born with genitals that, though hidden to the social world, make that individual either male or female, man or woman. Yet, as sociologists Candace West and Don Zimmerman famously argue, gender is a process that we continually *do,* not something that we inherently *are.*[13] The belief that people are cisgendered, or cissexual, (that their gender presentation aligns with some biological reality) is actually based on how we present our gender to the rest of the world (for example, the way we dress, talk, and move). We assume that biological sex causes gender, but we base this assumption only on social observations of gender presentations (i.e., we see only the effect, not the cause). This is circular logic, and it exposes the ways in which this gender binary reflects *social* norms rather than *natural* facts.

"Doing gender" means that we perform masculinity and femininity in the *right* way so that we are recognized according to a gender binary. Yet getting this performance right can include a range of actions, behaviors, and appearances, since each of us exhibit some qualities that are, at least some of the time, contradictory and inconsistent. A woman cannot possibly exude submissiveness in all of her speech, action, and gestures at every moment of the day. Similarly, a man can engage in some behaviors not typically defined as masculine without having onlookers question his gender identity. Sociologist Judith Lorber asks her readers to imagine a man on a subway holding an infant in a sling on his chest. Would other subway passengers question his manhood? Probably not, since notions of fatherhood today are more flexible than they were fifty years ago, and also because other signifiers, like his clothing, could confirm his "manliness."[14] Some gender ideals are broad and adjustable. Other gender norms, especially those that violate expectations regarding heterosexuality, are less so.

Sexual acts are physical, but they absorb meaning in social contexts. This is partly evident by the infiltration of sexuality into multiple levels of social life: from the ways in which high school boys tease one another to immigration policy that penalizes homosexuality.[15] We rely on social knowledge to interpret bodies, thoughts, desires, and actions associated with sex. Sociologists John H. Gagnon and William Simon use the term *sexual social scripts* to explain how we learn a sexual common sense: what is the right progression of sexual acts, what we can likely expect and not expect of our partners, what is considered erotically appealing and what is not, and how we link nonsexual emotions (like romance and love) to sexual encounters. These scripts vary depending on the actor (man or woman, for example) and the setting (fraternity party versus honeymoon, for instance), but they rely on a shared social knowledge rather than on intuition.[16]

Just as gender and sexuality are created through actions, speech, and behaviors, religion is socially constructed through practice and discourse. The term *lived religion* emphasizes how individuals re-create, transform, and challenge religious institutions in everyday experiences and talk—in other words, how individuals experience religion within or beyond church walls.[17] Sociologist Orit Avishai calls this "doing religion"—how people actively construct their religious identity through "a mode of conduct and being, a performance of identity."[18] In the same way that gender and sexuality are constructed through interaction, religion does not exist prior to or outside of the ways in which people practice it. Like gender and sexuality, religion is *embodied.* Religious practice happens cognitively, through a belief system and moral framework; emotionally, through a sense and feeling of the divine; and physically, through religious rituals that require the body to move, shape, and express devotion.[19]

Although gender, sexuality, and religion are socially constructed through interaction, each is regulated by specific and intertwined social controls. The ways in which we perform the traits associated with being a man or woman are based on social norms that reflect *gender hegemony.*[20] Hegemony refers to the implicit ways in which forms of privilege regulate social life, or in the words of Michel Foucault, how power manifests "without the king." Claims of gender equality, despite ongoing gender imbalances, are indicative of a trend some scholars call *postfeminism.* Postfeminist culture merges anti- and pro-feminist ideas, giving women a sense that they control their sexuality while at the same time sending messages that their sexuality should be heterosexual and submissive/available to men. For example, stereotypes about how young white women perform sexuality (à la *Girls Gone Wild*) have become synonymous with sexual pleasure, leaving few alternatives for the women involved. As journalist Ariel Levy describes, "What we once regarded as a *kind* of sexual expression we now view *as* sexuality."[21] Gender hegemony captures the ways in which postfeminist society continues to naturalize beliefs about gender and sexuality that tend to privilege the choices available to men, not women.[22]

Central to gender hegemony and postfeminism is *heterosexual hegemony*—what Adrienne Rich calls "compulsory heterosexuality," Gayle Rubin calls "obligatory heterosexuality," and Judith Butler calls the "heterosexual matrix."[23] Doing gender implies not only who you should be, according to normative standards about femininity and masculinity, but also whom you should want or desire sexually. Heterosexuality depends upon and ensures an asymmetrical relationship between men and women; it provides the "scaffolding" for uneven relationships.[24] Even though the act of sex is what ostensibly defines heterosexuality—a man and a woman showcasing their sexual attraction to one another—sex acts are often not the focus of critical heterosexuality studies. Because heterosexuality is an organizing principle of much of our nonsexual life, we find evidence of its power without needing to look to the bedroom. For example, at a structural level, heteronormativity influences laws that give privileges to employed heterosexual men and women. At a cultural level, heteronormativity influences values and beliefs that normalize a nuclear, heterosexual family. At the level of everyday practices, heteronormativity influences the way we perceive strangers, as we tend to assume people are straight unless proven otherwise.[25]

Feminist and queer theory situates sex within the social world rather than outside of it, but feminist and queer theorists disagree on how heteronormativity influences (or may be influenced by) the act of sex. Sexuality is both "pleasure and danger," in the words of Carol Vance, "simultaneously a domain of restriction, repression, and danger as well as a domain of exploration, pleasure, and agency."[26] On the one hand, radical feminists argue that sex is always (and especially) reflective of and contributing to men's dominance and women's oppression. On the other hand, pro-sex feminists distinguish between sex acts that reproduce systems of power and "queer" sex that may actually challenge and dismantle those systems.[27] Cultural anthropologist Margot Weiss finds a mediating perspective in these debates through an ethnography of San Francisco's pansexual BDSM community. Weiss examines how practitioners of BDSM work to construct boundaries between real world inequalities and a "scene" that may evoke those inequalities—male heterosexual dominants coupled with female submissives, for example. As both "performative" *and* "material," these scenes work as "circuits" to connect sexuality with the broader world. Weiss considers sexuality to be "a conduit between domains that appear divided from each other: those conceptualized as subjective or private, and those understood as social or economic."[28] In other words, transgressive sex like BDSM is always linked to—though not necessarily determined by—the oppressions that mark social life.

Despite heteronormativity's stronghold, what is considered "normal" sexuality in the contemporary United States has shifted throughout history and today incorporates a wider range of practices and identities than in the past. Nonetheless, certain criteria of normal sex persist, what Rubin calls the "charmed circle" of sexuality. In the circle there is love, commitment, and monogamy; the exclusion of those who are very young or very old; clear distinction between male and female bodies; privacy; and acts that are genitally centered. Outside the circle, there is promiscuity, pornography, and sex that happens casually, in groups, or in public.[29] Increasingly, gays and lesbians have found space within the charmed circle. Lisa Duggan calls this phenomenon *homonormativity*, describing gays' and lesbians' pursuits of sexual decency by highlighting qualities of gender conformity, monogamy, and domesticity. Despite a wide range of circumstances, individuals may construct their gendered and sexual lives as "normal" by emphasizing their qualities that align with social norms and hiding or overlooking those qualities that fall outside these norms.[30]

Like gender and sexual identities, religion is constructed and enacted within systems of power—what we can consider *Christian hegemony*. American society is most accommodating of religions within or close to Protestant Christianity since Protestantism acts as a regulating, albeit unseen, force in "secular" America. Beliefs and practices associated with Protestantism have been taken for granted as normal and acceptable and are the standard by which dominant culture judges social issues, especially those related to gender and sexuality. Protestant beliefs about sex are synonymous with "good old American values."[31] As sociologist Bernadette Barton describes in her (auto)-ethnographic work on being gay in the American South, there are numerous implicit and explicit pressures to affiliate oneself with conservative Christianity (and its belief system regarding sexuality). What Barton describes as the "Bible Belt panopticon" works through symbols, language, and interaction—"cross rings, fish key chains, Christian T-shirts, bumper stickers, tote bags, and verbal references to one's Christian identity"—to normalize Bible Belt Christianity.[32] Normalizing this version of Christianity serves to further normalize heterosexuality and normative gender identities, which together construct a sense of wholesome American life.

Religion, of course, cannot be generalized to such an extent that all faiths and practices universally support traditional gender roles and heterosexuality to the exclusion of gender nonconformity and non-heterosexuality.[33] The Protestant denomination the United Church of Christ, for example, has ordained openly gay ministers since 1972, and the first Metropolitan Community Church, which explicitly ministers to a gay and lesbian congregation, was founded in 1968. Today, there exist movements in virtually every Christian denomination, from liberal to conservative, to openly accept LGBT members.[34] As sociologist of religion Melissa Wilcox points out, many LGBT Christians join these affirming groups and churches "not to integrate their sexual or transgender identities with their Christian beliefs but to gain support for an already integrated identity."[35] Much like users of Christian sexuality websites, Wilcox finds that LGBT Christians make sense of their religious beliefs in individualized ways so that they contribute to, rather than take away from, a holistic sense of self that includes their sexual desires and identities.

Yet as an ideology (i.e., the prevailing notions that construct our "common sense") Protestant Christianity dominates the American imagination to promote values that exalt heterosexuality and a gender binary.[36] Even those who do not adhere to strict religious beliefs are affected by conservative Christianity's message. This is how ideology works. The presence and proliferation of LGBT Christians, for example, shows how those who want to exist comfortably as Christian *and* queer must work against the prevailing definition of American religion. They must challenge a ruling ideology with their own oppositional one.[37] This suggests that religion continues to be a primary place where the terms and conditions of "normal" sexuality are contested, as it has been throughout American history. Religion has been there all along in the construction of heterosexuality, and it doggedly persists. Christian sexuality websites are one space where we see this complicated and contradictory construction unfold.

The interacting hegemonies of heterosexuality, gender, and religion do not construct a single, coherent definition of "normal." Rather, they produce a contradictory and complex notion of sanctioned and valued gendered and sexual expressions. Sexual norms are often implicit and difficult to pinpoint because normal behavior receives little societal scrutiny and doesn't require explanation or justification. Yet what counts as normal and acceptable sexuality must actually be continually defined and defended. This is because, as Judith Butler observes, "gay is to straight *not* as copy is to original, but, rather, as copy is to copy."[38] Although Protestant ideals of heterosexuality appear to be the "original," or the grounds on which all other sexual identities are situated, they are in fact social constructions—a copy for which there is no original.

CONNECTING THE INTERNET

The proliferation of digital media has transformed the ways in which people relate to their own and to others' bodies—gendered, sexual, religious, and otherwise. In one sense, new technologies cause a "fading away," since our awareness of our physical bodies can be forgotten momentarily as we immerse ourselves in digital environments.[39] Health psychologist Michael Ross distinguishes *typing* from *doing* and *being,* suggesting that Internet communication offers possibilities that real-life exchanges do not: an online performance that exists somewhere between "fantasy and action."[40] In the case of sexuality, Ross argues that users can experiment with desires and interests online without the consequences that may accompany acting on them. Yet what digital immersion makes possible may be disrupted and confined as users of these technologies return to their physical bodies and physical lives. Aimee Carrillo Rowe and her coauthors call this "virtual migration," writing about Indian call-center workers who are trained to speak with American accents and spend their shifts talking to American customers. The intensive time these workers spend in virtual realities leads to ambivalence. They express feelings of empowerment due to their access to the Western world and the relatively high compensation they receive, yet their job unsettles their sense of their own culture, time, and space. Identities that are "split and then split again" situate these workers in a virtual borderland without a firm sense of belonging in any of the spaces they occupy.[41]

Although we may interact with others through digital technologies without the physical presence of their bodies, online interactions do not eliminate or transcend social difference. Studies on virtual reality consistently suggest that even though these spaces are distinct from the physical world, new technologies often reflect the values of "real" life, creating online environments that reinforce regulations of the body and marginalize minority groups. In one such example, danah boyd examines how youth describe their decisions to leave the social networking site MySpace for the increasingly dominant Facebook. She argues that the Internet fosters a kind of segregation that is much like "good and bad neighborhoods," where users believe that certain sites attract dubious characters (implying uneducated users and users of color) while other sites are clean and safe (dominated by a white middle class).[42] In examining Christian sexuality websites, I consider how inequalities rooted in gender and sexuality are cemented through online exchanges. Users' identities are firmly centered within America's sense of "normal" sexuality and therefore limit their expressions. At the same time, gender, sexuality, and religion as social constructions must also be continually reproduced (and therefore potentially changed). This book considers how the Internet makes gender, sexuality, and religion both restrained *and* malleable.

A SHORT HISTORY OF HETEROSEXUALITY
AND EVANGELICALS

Contrary to the assumption that heterosexuality is universal and eternal, Protestantism predates it by more than three centuries. How did heterosexuality come to be? And how have both the desire for and the act of sex and religion influenced how heterosexuality has manifested itself? The answers to these questions reveal that, at different historical moments, religion and sexuality may appear glued together or entirely unglued. Tracing this history helps explain why some evangelicals, rather than members of other Christian groups, have established Christian sexuality websites and other forms of sex advice.[43]

Prior to the nineteenth century, being sexually "normal" in America depended largely upon adhering to strict gender roles. Idealized definitions of manhood and womanhood depended upon certain sex acts (procreative coitus) as well as familial arrangements (marriage), but neither marriage nor sex was connected to a sexual identity as we know it today.[44] Protestantism propelled this definition of normality by solidifying marriage and monogamy as markers of it. Debates over defining marriage in the late 1800s, for example, centered around the marital practices of the emerging Mormon Church. The result was that a strictly *Protestant* definition of marriage became constituted as the *American* definition of marriage. As Mormons settled in the territory of Utah, their communal practices involving polygamy gained the attention of both popular culture and the courts. The Supreme Court eventually declared polygamy to be unconstitutional, and today the Church of Jesus Christ of Latter-day Saints does not condone the practice. Sarah Baringer Gordon, a historian of American religion, argues that the court outlawed polygamy in order to solidify a Protestant notion of American ideals—a nuclear family in which each man is entitled to one wife.[45]

Religious discourse preoccupied sexual attitudes and knowledge until the nineteenth century, but the invention of "the heterosexual" offered an alternative way to think about sexual categories. Historian Jonathan Ned Katz ascribes the origin of the term *heterosexual* to when late nineteenth-century psychiatrist Richard von Krafft-Ebing wrote of male-female sex as fueled by passion rather than the desire to procreate. This description of heterosexuality, according to Katz, marked "different-sex eroticism" as a new and nonreligious way of imagining sexuality.[46] As the twentieth century progressed, the relationship between sexuality and religion continued to transform. Medical doctors, in addition to priests, prescribed what was healthy and normal sexually; capitalist consumerism fostered a pleasure ethic that was removed from family relationships; and heterosexual identity came to encompass sexual pleasures (including but not limited to procreation) and other organizations of social life.[47]

Combined with these new ways of understanding sexual relationships came new ideas that further threatened Protestant Christianity. Science, immigration, and the industrial revolution challenged the religious ideology surrounding marriage and family. As a reaction to these monumental shifts at the turn of the twentieth century, a new sect of strict American Protestantism developed. Fiercely opposed to the "dangerous" traits of modernity, diversity, and secularism, these "fundamentalists" followed a doctrine of biblical literalism and inerrancy and adhered to what they insisted were traditional American values that were fast becoming obsolete: marriage, childrearing, and national pride. In the decades that followed, fundamentalist groups split to become what social scientists today call *conservative Protestant evangelicals,* an umbrella term for a broad movement that shares a similar theology despite being, as sociologists Robert Putnam and David Campbell describe, "amorphous" with "blurry boundaries."[48] In general, evangelicals emphasize repentance for humans' sinful nature, salvation through Jesus Christ alone, and a belief that the Bible is the literal word of God. While fundamentalists distinguish themselves from secular culture by creating separate churches, schools, and social events, evangelicals of the late twentieth and early twenty-first centuries engage *with* secular culture, drawing from popular trends while simultaneously critiquing them. Negotiating an identity that is "in the world" but not "of the world," evangelicals are deeply connected to salient cultural values but have made them their own. As culture shifts, so do the activities and practices of evangelicals.[49]

The changing cultural values of the twentieth century included a decline in organized religion and a proliferation of sexuality. The 1950s were a notable time in twentieth-century history, during which American culture appeared to align with many evangelical attitudes. Evangelical preacher Billy Graham was a household name and widely celebrated for his preaching that linked Christianity to the nuclear family, America, and capitalism. At the same time, however, America's first sexologist, Alfred Kinsey, made his way into household conversations. Even though strict sexual mores remained in place, Kinsey's dry, scientific language allowed people to talk about sex independent of religion and morality.[50] Popular marriage manuals began to emphasize the pleasurable aspects of sex in addition to the importance of procreation. Gender and sexual norms and attitudes gradually became more progressive throughout the last half of the twentieth century, resulting in what media and communications scholar Feona Attwood calls *sexualized culture*.[51] Sexualized culture is a culture obsessed with sex in all of its multiple manifestations, from politicians' adulterous scandals to bikini models selling sports cars. Beyond the "sex sells" mantra, sexualized culture impacts everyday life by promoting the idea that all Americans should strive to have personally fulfilling sex lives and that their sexuality—when fulfilled—produces overall happiness.

The idea that good sex is an important part of achieving personal fulfillment is evidence of what scholars call *therapeutic culture,* which rose to prominence during the twentieth century.[52] Improving the "self" became definitive of a prioritized emotional, physical, and spiritual well-being. Since the 1960s, Americans no longer rely solely on the religious identities shaped *for them* (by family, friends, religious leaders, etc.). Instead, they create their own religious identities that can be aligned with other aspects of their "selves." What Robert Wuthnow calls *dwelling-oriented spirituality*—or a spirituality defined by sacred spaces in physical buildings—has transformed to *seeker-oriented spirituality,* one that is based on personal experiences rather than predetermined times and places.[53] This emphasis on individualism and voluntarism (the seeker) rather than established, compulsory religion (the dwelling) makes individuals feel like they are creating a spirituality on their own terms. Successful American religions must accommodate this sense of individualism and make meaning of individuals' ordinary and unique experiences.

Evangelicals combine their religious message with many topics related to personal lifestyle—such as dieting, getting out of debt, raising children, and even marital sex.[54] They find ways to connect their faith in God with the idiosyncratic joys and toils of daily life. A job promotion, the safe travels of a family member, and financial savings are all a part of God's interventions. Beginning in the 1950s, evangelicals started to develop a sense that they could talk about sex without appearing obscene and indeed that they *should* talk about sex in order for believers to achieve happiness in their Christian marriages.[55] Evangelical psychologists, medical doctors, and pastors published sex manuals that challenged and competed with secular sex advice, instructing Christians how to have God-sanctioned, pleasurable sex within their marriages. In the 1970s, these sex manuals became the foundation of a booming industry that continues today.

Evangelicals have easily adapted to the cultural value of self-improvement because their beliefs grant much authority and autonomy to individual believers. Like Protestantism in general, evangelicals believe that God communicates directly with them through the Holy Spirit. Their relationships with God may be assisted by, but are not dependent upon, a church body or preacher. Their relationship to clergy also varies. Many evangelicals have limited relationships with actual clerics but are authoritatively shaped by a range of lay leaders, both men and women, including Bible study and small group leaders. Individuals themselves shape their religious experiences in profound ways, for it is one's own relationship with God that acts as the primary religious authority in one's life. This relationship gives some believers the sense that they have the authority to give an evangelical perspective on those issues that are important to them. Even without formal training or the input of clergy, some individual evangelicals confidently assert their beliefs as representative of a Christian perspective.

In an age of spiritual "seekers," different media forms have made visible the religious and spiritual options available to them. As of 2010, one in three Americans has used the Internet for information regarding religion or spirituality.[56] Evangelicals have historically used new media as they have emerged—from early radio broadcasting to the World Wide Web. This has allowed evangelical leaders, to a greater extent than those of other Christian groups, to be what sociologists Shayne Lee and Phillip Luke Sinitiere label "cultural innovators" while simultaneously promoting traditional religious values.[57] Highly mediated forms of evangelical expression—like Christian television, music, radio, and virtual Bible studies—thrive in today's technology-obsessed society, and Christian sexuality websites are but one of many examples of evangelical institutions that use digital media to convey their religious message.[58]

Digital media changes not only religion but also sexuality. Online representations of sexuality portray a certain version of "how identities work." As anthropologist Mary Gray points out in her study of queer youth in rural America, media depictions of gays and lesbians give these youth a narrative for their identities that connects with a broader culture that is largely missing in their small hometowns.[59] With the proliferation of gays and lesbians in TV and movies, the nationwide legalization of gay marriage, and a general mainstreaming of gay acceptance through efforts like the *It Gets Better Project,* heterosexuality must now contend with non-heterosexuality more than ever. In what James Joseph Dean calls a "post-closeted culture," "straights can neither assume the invisibility of gays and lesbians, nor count on others to always assume their heterosexuality. In this context, straights also cannot assume that other straights are homophobic or intolerant of gays and lesbians."[60] Although heterosexuality maintains its dominant status, it must be continually defined and defended in new, culturally relevant ways.

Evangelical messages about sex are changing, as believers struggle to hold on to the pillars that define the faith while keeping up with contemporary culture. It appears that many evangelicals are gradually aligning themselves with the rest of the American population in appearing tolerant of homosexuality and supporting same-sex marriage. Between 2003 and 2013, evangelicals have doubled their support for gays and lesbians having the right to marry, though their support remains lower than any other major religious group.[61] Consider the Southern Baptist Convention's 2014 conference, The Gospel, Homosexuality, and the Future of Marriage. Though the official stance of Southern Baptists is staunch opposition to same-sex marriage and homosexual sex, organizers of the conference recognized the need to update their denomination's message. As the conference objectives describe, evangelicals are acutely aware of the need to "prepare for the moral revolution surrounding homosexuality and same-sex marriage happening across America." The questions guiding the conference were politically savvy and potentially LGBT-affirming: How do we effectively minister to those who identify as lesbian, gay, bisexual, and transgender? How can Christians show the love of Christ to gay family members or neighbors? A journalist covering the event described "advances in tone," like one speaker who declared that Christians must "repent of anti-gay rhetoric."[62]

One possible conclusion to be drawn from the historical trajectory of sexuality and religion that make possible the stories told in this book—stories about conservative Christians who love sex and love to talk about it—is that evangelicals are on their way toward acceptance of multiple kinds of sexual expressions and identities. Indeed, the very *illogicality* of what I call the logic of godly sex may appear to make inevitable an inclusive understanding of godly sexuality—wherein the sense of permissiveness afforded to straight, married Christian couples may extend to non-straight, non-married, and non-Christian couples. Alternatively, it is possible that evangelicals will continue to defend heterosexuality's exclusivity even in a post-closeted culture. The logic of godly sex is a circular and incorrigible proposition that allows heterosexuality to rest not on its former pillars—marriage, monogamy, and binary gender—but upon religion. Which prediction will come true? Christian sexuality websites are one place where this future is unfolding.

THE STUDY

Cyberspace has the power to both reflect the larger world's norms and values and shape and reimagine these norms and values, creating new realities for its participants. Through in-depth analysis of websites and their content, observations of online activity in real time, and online interviews with website creators and users, *Christians under Covers* shows how religious conservatives use the Internet as both a producer and a product of their faith. Together, these methods constitute a "virtual ethnography" in which I immersed myself for almost two years.[63] Unlike traditional ethnographers, I did not identify a population within spatial boundaries, nor did I travel to any specific location to live for an extended period of time. Instead, as I conducted my fieldwork, my life went on mostly as normal. I lived at my home, shopped at my usual grocery store, and met up with friends for dinner. Yet I would disrupt my familiar life to sit in front of my laptop and enter the "field"—a community whose insiders had a particular way of talking and interacting, creating an online culture that was, at first, quite unfamiliar to me.

BetweenTheSheets.com, LustyChristianLadies.com, LovingGroom.com, AffectionateMarriage.com, StoreOfSolomon.com, and MaribelsMarriage.com are all examples of Christian sexuality websites—sites that are easily recognizable as Christian with content focused specifically and explicitly on positive expressions of sex/sexuality within marriage.

My study includes thirty-six websites in total—sixteen blogs, eighteen online stores, and two message boards—which informants told me was an exhaustive list at the time of my research (as much as that is possible when studying the ever changing and expanding Internet). There are also many Christian websites dedicated to broad forms of marriage support that also mention sex—websites catering to couples considering divorce or struggling with child rearing, for example. I exclude these sites from this study so as to get right to the heart of the matter: how explicit talk about sex (both the act of and the desire for) is linked to the construction of gender and sexual norms alongside religious faith.

Although it is difficult to gauge how many people use Christian sexuality websites and who these users are, the sites are easy to find for anyone looking for online discussions about Christian sexuality. Creators of LustyChristian Ladies.com reported that their site receives over 400,000 hits per month. The owner of StoreOfSolomon.com told me that her business grows each year. And statistics gathered for BetweenTheSheets.com message boards between March 2004 and June 2011 indicate that over 31,000 unique members posted almost 300,000 comments on nearly 15,000 threads. I found these sites and others by performing basic Google searches for phrases like "Christian sex advice" or "Christian sexuality." The sites brought up by these searches allowed me to find other relevant sites. For example, BetweenTheSheets.com's creators encourage couples to experiment with sex toys, like vibrators, and they advertise StoreOf Solomon.com on their site as a Christian-owned sex toy store, where customers can be sure to avoid pornographic images. And StoreOfSolomon.com includes a "Recommended Links" list that points users to several Christian sexuality blogs and message boards.

To conduct research, I spent an enormous amount of time on my computer, often checking the most active websites in my study multiple times each day. I followed lively debates on discussion threads, read about struggles and triumphs on personal blogs, and went through product description after product description on Christian-owned sex toy stores, all while scribbling field notes and taking screenshots to save to my hard drive. I analyzed about 12,000 online comments on the most active website in my study, BetweenTheSheets.com, and thousands of additional posts on eleven other sites. For the most part, I "lurked" on these websites—my presence was not explicitly known by other users and I never posted comments. Administrators of some of the websites generously advertised my research on my behalf, asking users of their sites to volunteer to participate in an online survey or online interview. The survey that I designed, the Christianity, Sexuality, and the Internet Survey (referred to throughout this book as the CSIS), asked questions about demographics, religious affiliation and participation, Internet use, sexual history, and sexual attitudes. It was completed by 768 website users of seven different sites. I also conducted fifty interviews, most of which took place in a private online chat room to preserve the original form of social interaction being studied. I interviewed forty-four users and administrators of the two most active sites in my study, BetweenTheSheets.com and LustyChristianLadies.com; three bloggers on other Christian sexuality sites; two owners of online sex toy stores; and one author of a popular Christian sex advice book.

The websites I analyzed took great measures to moderate their sites, which made it less likely that I encountered content posted by so-called trolls or people who used the sites maliciously. All of the bloggers I interviewed screened comments to their blogs before posting them, and BTS required membership in order to post content, which was then closely monitored by administrators and fellow members. As one of the creators explained to me, "we've developed this sense of community and people are aggressive in protecting that." Members flag inflammatory or off-topic comments that are then investigated by a team of administrators. One administrator told me that he takes this job seriously and regularly deactivates members for violating the site's terms of use. I am fairly confident that the people I interviewed were Christians and regular website users; most of the interviews lasted at least two hours, and I likely would have suspected deception in responses to detailed questions related to their website use, religious faith, and sexuality. The data I gathered from responses to the CSIS further confirms patterns among website users that align with the stated beliefs of the sites. If the stories included in this book were told by individuals intending to deceive, they did so convincingly enough that their social performance went unnoticed by me and other website users, suggesting that the performance itself merits analysis and inclusion in this project.[64]

While studying websites and their users, I also identified print literature and real-life events whose authors and speakers promoted beliefs similar to those found online. I read dozens of published evangelical sex advice books, and I traveled to three cities in the Midwest and the South to observe Christian sexuality workshops: one geared toward single and married women, one for married couples, and one for any Christian—single or married, man or woman—who wanted to learn about sexuality from a well-known evangelical pastor. For all of these events, I requested to attend as a researcher and observer.

Perhaps ironically, I gained access to the virtual world of Christian sexuality websites by attending a real-life conference, an event organized for members of BTS. Meeting me in person likely made the administrators and creators of the site more comfortable with me and my project, and once the conference ended, they gave me permission to use the BTS website to collect data and recruit interview and survey respondents. The other websites that helped with recruitment for my study agreed to do so in part because of my access to BTS, a well-known and respected site. Like many ethnographers, I likely gained access to my research because of my appearance and familiarity with the culture I studied. As a teenager, I was actively involved in multiple evangelical churches, organizations, and programs, and I later attended a Baptist college. Research participants were also able to see a photo of me (a white cisgender woman) on a website I created for the study. They likely made assumptions about my sexual identity and current religious beliefs, which I neither confirmed nor denied.[65]

CHRISTIAN SEXUALITY WEBSITES AND THEIR USERS

Recent surveyors of American religion have faced a peculiar dilemma of classifying evangelicals, since many who fall under the category do not embrace the term.[66] Instead, many people who attend evangelical denominations, as well as many who attend *non*denominational churches and espouse evangelical beliefs, prefer to identify simply as "Christian." This broad identification, along with beliefs about gender and sexuality, links evangelicals to other conservative religious traditions in America. Collectively, these groups present an ideology that conflates American and Christian identity, purporting "Christian" and "American" values based on religious beliefs related to heterosexuality, marriage, and family. Melinda Bollar Wagner calls this "generic panconservative Christianity," which deemphasizes doctrinal differences in favor of a few core values.[67] We increasingly see evidence of this in political activism. For example, a coalition of Christian organizations representing Catholics, evangelical Protestants, and Latter-day Saints (LDS or Mormons) sent an amicus brief to the Supreme Court in 2015 to support a ban on same-sex marriage.[68]

In this book, I write frequently about those I label explicitly as evangelical, since it is this specific religious movement of mostly white evangelical Protestants that dominates Christian sexuality websites. I also use the broader label of "conservative Christians" to describe others who use these websites, since mainline Protestants, Catholics, and Latter-day Saints use the websites, too. Mark Chaves, a sociologist of American religion, proposes that instead of using the designations "liberal" and "conservative" to categorize religious groups, we should ask if they "adapt their religion to a changing world" or if they are "inclined to resist such adaptation."[69] This, however, can be misleading, especially in the context of my research, since the Christianity described in this book is both adaptive *and* resistant, depending on the cultural change. Even when it comes to gender and sexuality, Christian sexuality websites reveal a story full of contradictions, in which individuals remain committed to their "conservative" beliefs that sex is permissible only for monogamous, married, heterosexual couples while embracing certain "liberal" ideas like support for sexual experimentation and women's pleasure. I use the word "conservative" to describe the Christians in this book because I think there is no better term. "Conservative" and "Christian" are two words that I came across online far more often than specific denominational labels like evangelical, Catholic, Methodist, and Mormon. I only learned about these differences in religious affiliation from the survey I conducted with website users (the CSIS)—this was not a topic that was discussed commonly in these particular online forums. Instead, users emphasize what they have in common: a belief in Jesus Christ, the Bible, and the importance of good sex in Christian marriages.

All of the websites in my study include content that supports evangelical Protestant tenets, including an emphasis on repentance, salvation by Jesus Christ alone, and biblical inerrancy. Yet Christian sexuality websites attract users who attend various types of churches. Some affiliate with mainline Protestant denominations—such as Methodists and Episcopalians—while others identify as Latter-day Saints. A few identify as Catholic. Whereas about 25 percent of the American population can be identified as evangelical, I coded 72 percent of CSIS respondents and 93 percent of website users I interviewed as evangelical (see table 1; for more details on the interview sample, see Appendix B). These respondents were either affiliated with denominations within the evangelical tradition, self-identified as evangelical, or self-identified as "Christian."[70]

The website users in my study who identified as non-evangelical shared many similarities with evangelicals. Table 2 presents the demographic information of the four prominent religious traditions represented in the CSIS compared with national data.[71] CSIS respondents varied in age, but they were predominantly white, college educated, and married with children. Following national trends, the evangelical Protestants were most likely to reside in the U.S. Midwest and South, whereas most LDS respondents resided in the West (predominantly in Utah).[72] Not surprisingly, CSIS

TABLE 1 Religious traditions represented in the CSIS

	Number of respondents	Percentage of total sample
Evangelical Protestant		
Nondenominational	265	34.6
Baptist	144	18.6
Pentecostal	46	6.0
Holiness	20	2.6
Reformed	12	1.6
Adventist	4	0.5
Other denomination	46	6.0
Evangelical or unspecified Christian	19	2.5
Subtotal	556	72.4
Mainline Protestant	91	11.9
Catholic	25	3.3
Latter-day Saint	89	11.6
Jewish	1	0.1
None	5	0.6
Total	767	100

NOTE: Because of rounding, some totals do not equal 100 percent.

respondents were much more likely to be married than their national counterparts. Out of those who responded to the CSIS, the evangelicals, mainline Protestants, and Catholics tended to be older and have been married longer than Latter-day Saints, the majority of whom were between eighteen and twenty-nine. As indicated in figure 1, there were very few newlyweds who completed the CSIS, and many respondents reported that they had been married more than fifteen years.

When it comes to the focus of this book (in survey terms: religiosity, internet use, and sexual attitudes), CSIS respondents were remarkably similar across religious lines. The population sampled in the CSIS attended church at a higher rate than evangelicals nationally and the overall public, suggesting that users of Christian sexuality websites do not use these sites to replace real-life religious communities. The majority attended religious services at least once a week, ranging from 64 percent of Catholics to 96 percent (eighty-five out of eighty-nine respondents) of LDS respondents (figure 2). Evangelicals, mainline Protestants, Catholics, and Latter-day Saints respondents reported spending slightly more time online than evangelicals nationally and Americans overall. On average, the CSIS sample spent seven to twelve hours per week

TABLE 2 Demographic characteristics by religious tradition, CSIS and national samples (GSS and Pew)

	Evangelical Protestants (%)		Mainline Protestants (%)		Catholics (%)		Latter-day Saints (%)	
	CSIS	*GSS*	*CSIS*	*GSS*	*CSIS*	*GSS*	*CSIS*	*Pew*
Gender								
Men	49	38	48	47	52	46	27	47
Women	51	62	52	53	48	54	73	53
Age								
18–29	25	12	28	18	20	19	64	11
30–49	56	35	40	38	44	37	32	29
50–64	18	28	30	25	32	24	3	29
65 and older	1	26	3	19	4	20	1	31
Race								
White	91	65	96	80	92	79	94	92
Nonwhite	9	35	4	20	8	21	6	8
U.S. region								
West	22	12	12	26	19	27	81	83
Midwest	27	20	27	25	33	24	6	5
Northeast	10	10	16	19	24	24	2	2
South	41	59	46	30	24	25	11	10
Education								
College degree	59	20	81	31	64	74	72	44
No degree	41	80	19	69	36	26	28	56
Marital status								
Married	94	50	94	44	96	47	94	73
Not married	6	50	6	56	4	53	6	27
Children								
Has children	79	81	74	70	80	75	72	86
Has no children	21	19	26	30	20	25	28	14

NOTE: Because of rounding, some totals do not equal 100 percent. Also, due to the fact that some CSIS respondents did not answer all survey questions, some of the totals given are less than the total number of survey respondents. Respondents were included in analyzed data if they completed 90 percent of the survey.

online. As figure 3 shows, they are about twice as likely as evangelicals nationally and Americans overall to use the Internet an average of seven to eighteen hours per week, but they are not more likely to be high users (more than eighteen hours per week). When it comes to sexual attitudes, CSIS respondents report more conservative attitudes about homosexuality (figure 4) and premarital sex (figure 5) than their national counterparts.

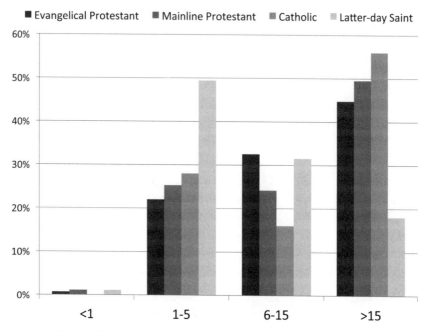

Evangelical Protestant Mainline Protestant Catholic Latter-day Saint

FIGURE 1. Number of years married by denomination, CSIS married sample.

The survey group that showed the biggest difference in sexual attitudes from their national counterparts was mainline Protestants, who were about twice as likely to oppose homosexuality than mainline Protestants nationally and four times more likely to oppose premarital sex. Mainline Protestants who responded to the CSIS appear to support those beliefs usually associated with evangelicals rather than the moderate to liberal beliefs represented by many mainline Protestant denominations. This may be explained by the fact that the mainline Protestants who responded to the CSIS were more likely to reside in the South than mainline Protestants nationally. What Barton describes as "Bible Belt Christianity," regardless of denominational difference, is overwhelmingly conservative when it comes to sexuality.[73]

The CSIS data suggest that Christian sexuality website users are different from the "typical" Christian American, if we can even say there is such a thing. They attend church and go online more often than their national counterparts and have more restrictive sexual attitudes when it comes to who is allowed to have sex. In many ways, Christian sexuality websites are peculiar and particular. They do not represent evangelicals everywhere, and my findings cannot be applied to evangelicalism or conservative Christianity as

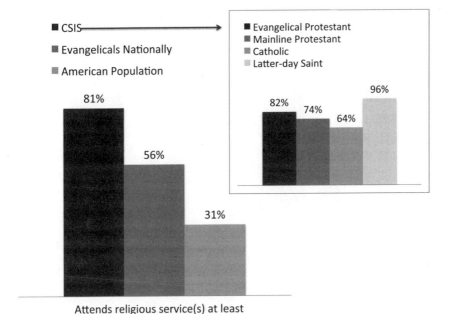

CSIS ⟶

■ Evangelical Protestant
■ Mainline Protestant
■ Catholic
■ Latter-day Saint

■ Evangelicals Nationally

■ American Population

81%

82% 74% 64% 96%

56%

31%

Attends religious service(s) at least
once a week.

FIGURE 2. Frequency of attendance at religious services, CSIS and GSS sample.

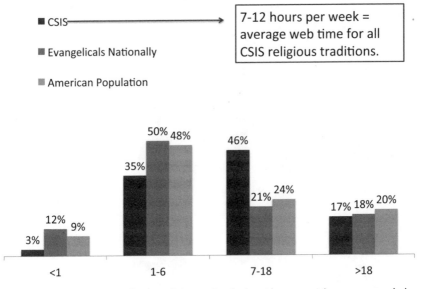

■ CSIS ⟶

7-12 hours per week =
average web time for all
CSIS religious traditions.

■ Evangelicals Nationally

■ American Population

50% 48%

46%

35%

12% 9%

21% 24%

17% 18% 20%

3%

<1   1-6   7-18   >18

"Not counting time spent for your job or school, about how many hours per week do
you use the Web?"

FIGURE 3. Internet use by denomination, CSIS and GSS sample.

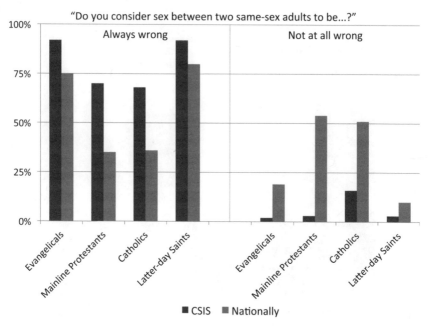

FIGURE 4. Attitudes about sex between same-sex adults by denomination, CSIS and GSS sample.

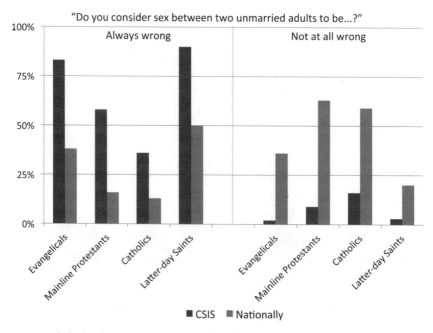

FIGURE 5. Attitudes about sex between unmarried adults by denomination, CSIS and GSS sample.

a whole. I do not pretend to know the "truth" about what most evangelicals are doing in the bedroom or what most of them believe about sex. Instead, I examine Christian sexuality websites as a space where religion is made. Website users bring religion to life as they use it to ask questions for which there are few easy answers—questions about bodies, desires, restraint, and negotiation. I examine online talk about sex in these online religious spaces to show the complex and sometimes contradictory ways in which sexuality manifests in social life.

ORGANIZATION OF THE BOOK

Website users and creators shape what religion looks like, how it is practiced, and how religious beliefs might affect daily life. Chapter 1 examines how some evangelicals draw from existing religious doctrine to talk about sex in strikingly different ways from evangelicals in the past, constructing a new sexual logic for what counts as "godly sex." On the one hand, they draw from evangelical beliefs that the Bible is the literal word of God and that His instructions for how to live a Christian life are straightforward and black and white, with no exceptions. This sets the boundaries for who is allowed to be sexual—only married, heterosexual, monogamous couples. On the other hand, these evangelicals draw from salient cultural ideas that emphasize individuality, personal choice, and distinguished tastes in order to make claims about what is sexually possible for those with permission to be sexual. In doing so, they uphold the major tenets of their evangelical faith but also keep up with contemporary secular values about sex.

Chapters 2 and 3 examine how Christian sexuality websites become context and culture for the online communities that work to reconcile religion and sexuality. I investigate how website creators and users take up the logic of godly sex to justify creating and participating in anonymous virtual spaces that endorse frank talk about sex. Chapter 2 tells the stories of website creators and examines how they use their religious faith to explain why they create the sites they do and why they are the "right kind" of Christians to do it. Chapter 3 details how website users get to know each other and trust that they are among a community of like-minded believers. Central to both chapters are how these Christians confront concerns about using the Internet for information related to sexuality at a time when evangelical leaders describe pornography as a nearly ubiquitous presence online. Viewing pornography, according to these evangelicals, is unequivocally a sin. Creators and users of the sites establish themselves as insiders within these communities by creating online personas that resonate with other conservative Christians—they use familiar tropes that incorporate commonly held evangelical Protestant beliefs into their discussions. They justify anonymous online interaction by citing their belief that God knows who someone "really is" and that everyone who finds and uses the sites does so for a God-led purpose.

The logic of godly sex plays out differently for the men and women who use Christian sexuality sites. Chapter 4 examines how women frame talk of their own pleasure by telling *sexual awakening* stories. Like classic evangelical conversion narratives, these website users tell tales of overcoming sin and suffering by turning to their relationships with Jesus Christ. Their religious commitment transforms their sexual bodies and therefore their overall lives—their marriages, attitudes, and faith. These stories suggest that women's bodies and the pleasure they experience are deeply connected to others—God and their husbands—and that they must balance their own needs with selfless acts that prioritize their marital and spiritual relationships.

Markedly different from the restraints women face in talking about sexual pleasure are the stories of men who are interested in non-normative, or kinky, sex. Chapter 5 focuses on men who take the advice given in evangelical print literature to a logical extreme—extending the emphasis on mutual pleasure and sexual permissiveness within marriage so as to justify sex acts that are seemingly inappropriate within an evangelical context. Men who are interested in two gender-subversive sex acts—pegging (the anal penetration of a man by a woman) and erotic cross-dressing—justify their interest by relying on the *gender omniscience* of their spouse and God. Secure in the knowledge that both God and their spouse *know* that they are gender normal, these men uphold standards of their faith related to gender and (hetero)sexuality and ensure their masculine status.

Together, these chapters detail how the logic of godly sex is contradictory yet resilient. Conservative Christians endorse a bounded sense of proper sexuality, but they use the Internet to expand and reshape those borders. In the final chapter, I offer some conclusions about the implications of this construction of godly sex, considering how Christian sexuality website creators and users create openings and closures for religious beliefs, sexual bodies, and the boundaries that surround what it means to be "normal."

ONE

Godly Sex

A NEW EVANGELICAL SEXUAL LOGIC

In 1976, Pastor Tim LaHaye and his wife, Beverly, ventured into what was firmly secular territory within the publishing industry to produce a sex advice manual written from a Christian perspective. Their book, as they explained in its introduction, was intended to fill a gap in existing literature, both secular and religious: "Most Christian books [about sex] skirt the real issues and leave too much to the imagination [...]. Secular books, on the other hand, often go overboard telling it like it is in crude language repulsive to those who need help. [...] Convinced that God meant lovemaking to be enjoyed by both partners, we prayed that He would lead us to make this work fully Biblical and highly practical."[1] *The Act of Marriage: The Beauty of Sexual Love* is as its authors describe: an extremely practical book about sex that constantly references the Bible and the authors' interpretation of it. It combines the tone of a spirited sermon with the kinds of anatomical drawings and descriptions of male and female bodies that make teenagers blush in sex education courses. It is simultaneously a book about biology, relationships, and religion. The authors outline in great detail what a couple's first sexual encounter may be like, providing step-by-step instructions on how to engage in foreplay and have sexual intercourse. This includes tips for communicating—"the husband should proceed" with "verbal expressions of love"—and practical advice—"it is a rare bride who will be able to provide sufficient natural vaginal lubricant on her honeymoon."[2] It mimicked other sex advice books of the era by acknowledging the realistic and often unglamorous side of sex while simultaneously highlighting the grandiose elements of love and romance.[3] Yet unlike secular books that positioned sexual satisfaction as the ultimate goal, the LaHayes insisted that couples should pursue sexual satisfaction for a higher good. Their book departed from others at the time by making God an important character in a couple's sexual story.

The Act of Marriage sold 500,000 copies by 1979 and 1.5 million copies by 1993.[4] The LaHayes promoted the book in several Christian venues, like the Focus on the Family radio broadcast, and also appeared on the mainstream TV program the Phil Donahue show. According to its authors in an updated edition published in 1998, it has been used in premarital counseling by ministers more "than any other" book on sex.[5]

Before they published *The Act of Marriage,* the LaHayes hosted a radio program about Christian married life that touched upon some of the book's themes. Following its publication, Tim became well known for his involvement in the conservative Christian political organization the Moral Majority, along with Jerry Falwell, and later for the publication of the dispensationalist fiction series *Left Behind*.[6] He was named one of the top twenty-five most influential evangelicals in America by *Time* magazine in 2005. Beverly participated in conservative politics alongside her husband, founding the conservative women's organization Concerned Women for American in 1979. She also wrote various nonfiction publications related to Christian womanhood.

In *The Act of Marriage,* the LaHayes confront a tension within their evangelical beliefs: they believed that while God designed pleasure to be a part of sex, Christian couples likely could not achieve that pleasure on their own. Good and mutually satisfying sex does not happen intuitively; couples need advice and guidance in order to achieve it. And herein lies a problem: on the surface, evangelical beliefs actually suggest the contrary—that believers should be able to consult the Bible for instructions about sex and all other aspects of everyday life. Of course, the Bible is silent on many of the idiosyncrasies of modern life (smartphones and traffic jams, for example).[7] Similarly, when it comes to sex, the Bible lacks direct answers on a range of topics, from the preferable frequency of sex within marriage to the appropriateness of acts other than penile-vaginal intercourse.

The information about sex that most Americans receive from a wide array of sources—such as morning TV talk shows, popular newspapers and magazines, and schools—is largely off-limits to, or at least treated with harsh skepticism by, evangelicals. Evangelicals must filter through secular messages about sex—which, according to many evangelical spokespersons, tend to disregard God's messages—in order to determine how to have a sexual life that aligns with Christian values. Lorraine Pintus, coauthor of the best-selling Christian sex advice book *Intimate Issues: Answers to 21 Questions Christian Women Ask about Sex,* explained to me that Christians today are inundated by what she and others call the "world's perspective" when it comes to sexuality: "When you turn on the TV, you don't see lifelong commitments, privacy, or even one man, one woman anymore." Authors Ed and Lisa Young call this a "hijacking" of sex; they believe sex was designed by God but that it has taken on a secular bent in its near-ubiquitous presence in popular culture.[8] Such blatant disregard for Christian values, according to these evangelicals, means that secular advice or information about sex should be treated critically or avoided altogether. This opens up a need and a market for advice that is distinctly Christian. Evangelicals must look to interpreters who bridge the gaps between secular messages that are relevant in modern life but have the wrong values and biblical messages that have the right values but seem to be irrelevant to modern life.

Today, Christian sex advice is well integrated into evangelical culture. While authors of evangelical sexual manuals, like the LaHayes, are not representative of all evangelicals, they are easily recognized within mainstream evangelicalism. The coauthors of *Intimate Issues,* Linda Dillow and Lorraine Pintus, have appeared on Focus on the Family's radio show and Pat Robertson's TV program, *The 700 Club.* Shannon Ethridge, author of *The Sexually Confident Wife: Connecting with Your Husband Mind, Body, Heart, Spirit,* is a spokesperson for Teen Mania, one of America's largest evangelical youth organizations. Ed and Lisa Young's *Sexperiment: 7 Days to Lasting Intimacy with Your Spouse* started as a church program and later became a New York Times best-selling book. Pastor Ed Young founded a nondenominational mega-church in Texas that now has eight satellite churches. He has over 170,000 likes on Facebook and nearly 820,000 followers on Twitter. Far from being on the margins of evangelical culture, these authors share beliefs and speaking platforms with many of today's leading evangelicals. This gives their messages about sex respectability and fuels a growing interest (and industry) in evangelical sex advice.[9]

Thirty-five years after *The Act of Marriage* was originally published, Mark Driscoll wrote what may be its contemporary counterpart—*Real Marriage: The Truth about Sex, Friendship, and Life Together,* which he coauthored with his wife, Grace. Mirroring what the LaHayes wrote in their introduction about the need for a book like theirs, Mark and Grace begin *Real Marriage* by explaining why they chose to write it. They describe the book as "Biblically faithful, emotionally hopeful, practically helpful, sociologically viable, and personally vulnerable." Physical intimacy is central to the book's philosophy and, according to its authors, key to a good marriage. For example, the Driscolls make connections between physical intimacy, sexual appeal, and the quality of a marriage, telling couples to "sleep together naked. Undress in front of your spouse. [...] Dress in clothes that fit and flatter your figure or build." They claim that doing these things and maintaining an active sex life ensures that husband and wife "are literally bonded together as one."[10] Just as he was to the LaHayes' narrative, God is central to the story the Driscolls tell. Anyone can find temporary gratification from sex, they assert, but it is following God's rules for sex that ensures long-term satisfaction both in one's marriage and, ultimately, in the afterlife.

Like Tim LaHaye, Mark Driscoll is a celebrity among conservative Christians. He founded and formerly pastored the Seattle-based megachurch Mars Hill, and he gained recognition by using modern technology to promote his conservative religious message. He has spoken at conferences with other well-known evangelical leaders, including John Piper and Tim Keller, given a guest sermon at the church of the famous evangelical pastor Rick Warren, and been interviewed on *The 700 Club*. His sermons are downloaded on iTunes approximately seven million times per year. While LaHaye had a radio program, Driscoll has podcasts, online videos, virtual Bible studies, and an extensive following on Facebook and Twitter. He merges traditional beliefs with a contemporary, hip aesthetic, making his outspoken conservative views on sexuality and relationships seem cool and relevant to the modern world. He does not shy away from secular culture but rather engages with it head on. For example, he has publicly debated Ron Jeremy (a famous porn star from the seventies) about the perils of pornography and sexualized culture. Driscoll and his wife, Grace, promoted *Real Marriage* on TV and radio, appearing on programs like *Loveline with Dr. Drew* and *The View*. They insist that the values the book promotes—such as friendship and intimacy in marriage—appeal to a broad audience of Christian Americans.[11]

On the surface, both *The Act of Marriage* and *Real Marriage* support similar beliefs. They state that sexual intimacy is to be enjoyed by couples only if they are heterosexual, married, and monogamous. Both unequivocally condemn homosexuality. The LaHayes and Driscolls support complementarianism, or the belief that God created men and women to fulfill different and balancing roles, wherein a husband practices headship and a wife submission. Both sets of authors talk about gender in essentialist terms and use their roles as coauthors and husband and wife to portray what they believe to be male and female perspectives. Tim LaHaye, for example, writes that his wife brings a "delicate sense of balance" to the book. Both books include separate chapters for women and for men. As Mark Driscoll states in the introduction to a chapter specifically written for men, "were I writing to women [in this chapter], my tone would be considerably different. So while women are welcome to read this chapter, they are also forewarned that it may get a little rough." The authors emphasize the opposing sexual roles and needs of men and women and therefore offer members of both genders different advice.[12]

Yet as similar as they are, *The Act of Marriage* and *Real Marriage* are different books, written in different times. In the words of the Driscolls, "The questions today are different." As Mark told an interviewer for the online magazine *Christianity Today,* "A lot of Christian teaching about sex is answering the questions of a previous generation."[13] The Driscolls wrote their book in order to deal with the monumental shifts that have happened in American society when it comes to sexual attitudes and discourse. As they put it, the book will help a Christian "be a good missionary in this sexualized culture."[14] And while this may seem as if the Driscoll perspective on sex is one of "us versus them," they actually complicate the relationship between their Christian values and the values of the secular world.

Comparing *Real Marriage* to *The Act of Marriage* shows the ways in which it, far from being diametrically opposed to contemporary sexualized culture, actually embodies and aligns with it in many ways. For example, the LaHayes advised against engaging in oral sex, masturbation, anal sex, and using sex toys. Though they do not believe that the Bible forbids oral sex, they write that they "do not personally recommend or advocate it." They warn couples that very few ministers advocate for oral sex within marriage and that the practice should never "be used as a substitute for coitus." *Real Marriage,* on the other hand, tells couples to experiment sexually to find practices that optimize their pleasure, even if they include oral or anal sex or sex toys. In answering the question, "Does oral sex help a couple's marriage in bringing them closer together?" the Driscolls reply simply, "Yes. Many husbands and wives enjoy oral sex." They even go so far as to engage in a scriptural exegesis that favors oral sex, interpreting the Song of Solomon as biblical support for a range of sexual acts, including "kissing (1:2), oral/fellatio—her initiative (2:3), manual stimulation—her invitation (2:6), erotic striptease (6:13–7:9), and new places and positions, including outdoors—her initiative (7:11–13)."[15] In discussing oral sex and other sexual desires and activities, the Driscolls replace the caution, skepticism, and prescriptive advice of the LaHayes with open encouragement to experiment to better understand individual tastes and personal satisfaction.

Evangelicals who write about sex, both in print and online, navigate their religious beliefs in a secular culture. Indeed, this is at the crux of the evangelical movement of the last half-century: to be in the world but not of it. When it comes to sex, the result is a new evangelical sexual logic, what I call the *logic of godly sex*, reflecting traditional beliefs about gender and sexuality but accommodating a contemporary understanding of sexual identities, practices, and desires. At the heart of this twenty-first century sexual logic is the ability, and indeed the prerogative, of married Christians to have "good" sex. This "goodness" incorporates dual meanings—"good" meaning normal, allowed, and sanctioned by God and "good" in the sense of feelings of pleasure and satisfaction. Both dimensions are important in constructing the logic of godly sex; the former instructs who is allowed to have sex, and the latter tells couples how they can enjoy sex. Yet these dimensions draw from what seem to be contradictory philosophies: on the one hand, religious beliefs that are objective and about non-negotiable truths, and on the other hand, liberal and nonreligious ideas about free will, autonomy, and personal taste. Conservative Christians, especially when using the Internet, merge these philosophies, allowing them to align their specific sexual interests—so long as they are married, monogamous, and heterosexual—with their moral framework.

SEX MATTERS: THE INHIBITION PARADOX

Throughout their history, evangelicals have effectively conveyed the importance of sex by both speaking and not speaking about it. There have always been Christian conversations about God's purpose for sexuality, and indeed, preaching against certain kinds of sex has become a key marker of the Christian tradition. As historian of religion Mark Jordan argues, Christian discussions of sexual sins have always been "a part of a general program for ordering Christian moral teaching." Christian thought has long maintained that a person's sexual purity—or sexual sinfulness, as it may be—tells the story of a person's morality (or immorality) perhaps better than any other indicator. Christian leaders have spoken little in support of sexual enjoyment, even within heterosexual marriage. Jordan notes that sexual sins have included "every erotic or quasi-erotic action that can be performed by human bodies except penile-vaginal intercourse between two partners who are not primarily seeking pleasure and who do not intend to prevent conception."[16] What has been *allowed* sexually has, for much of Christian history, been an extremely narrow category. It is a relatively recent historical phenomenon for conservative Christians to claim sexual pleasure as part of their religious framework, and many leaders and writers in this tradition still avoid the topic. Reflecting this long history of negatively portraying sexuality, churches still tend not to emphasize God-sanctioned sexual pleasure as much as they do Satan-tempted sexual sins.

The website creators and users in this study describe sexual inhibitions—once required to live a godly life—as hard to shed on or after one's wedding day. Evangelical sex advice illustrates the paradox of these inhibitions as couples struggle to achieve the sexual pleasure they believe God wants for their marriages. Messages about the perils of sexuality are a part of how evangelicals understand marital sex. For instance, Leia, a member of the online message board BetweenTheSheets.com, described to me how she grew up with a sense that sexuality was bad: "I never learned much about sex from church. [. . .] I never felt like it would be okay for me to date or have sex ever. I mean, intellectually I knew that my parents would be happy if I got married, but it didn't seem to make sense in my head." Leia grew up without space to acknowledge her dual identities as both a sexual person and a Christian. The church did not provide an environment in which she felt allowed to acknowledge her sexual feelings, even though she knew they were appropriate within marriage.

All evangelicals who write about sexual pleasure have to contend with a religious tradition that simultaneously encourages and condemns sexuality. Premarital sex is a prominent example. Evangelicals believe that what some have called sexual "soul ties" permanently and physically link one person to all of his or her past sexual partners.[17] One member of BTS, FatherMoses, describes this as scientific fact and "Pavlovian." He writes that "there is biological evidence in the form of the effects of the orgasmic release of oxytocin (women) and vasopressin (men). There is little more than simple Pavlovian conditioning in that there IS a distinct effect on the brain that occurs when we orgasm with our partners (married or not)." FatherMoses emphasizes a chemical response that becomes entrenched in our physical bodies and attaches us to sexual partners.[18] This claim reduces humans to basic animal reflexes and drives—in this case bringing up the example of Pavlov's dog, who physically reacts to what it associates with food—yet it also draws from religion to make sense of our physical reality. The profound physical connection that results from sex should happen only between a husband and wife, and Christians must protect their marriages by constraining sexual activity to within that relationship. This inhibition paradox points to the power of the past over married evangelicals' sexuality. According to these evangelical beliefs, a sinful sexual history may impede the sexual pleasure that God created for married couples to enjoy.

Given how much silence surrounds positive expressions of sexuality within conservative Christian culture, there was palpable nervousness at the opening of the Intimate Issues conference I attended. It was a Friday night, and I sat with five hundred other women in the pews of an evangelical megachurch, all of us having come to hear two women talk about sex. The conference was based on the best-selling book by the same name, written by Linda Dillow and Lorraine Pintus. The authors led two days of sessions dedicated to explaining God's plan, as they believe it, when it comes to single and married women's sexuality. On this first night, the hum of uneasy chatter quieted as two women stepped out into the sanctuary. They sat in two chairs and acted as if they were putting on makeup and fixing their hair. We realized that the scene was meant to portray a young woman's wedding day and that the older woman was the mother. The mother began to speak, starting a conversation likely to be familiar to many of the mothers and adult daughters in the audience: "My lovely daughter, this is the most important day of your life." The daughter smiled in affirmation. The mother continued: "And as your mother, I think it's time that I talk to you about something that mothers and daughters should talk about, when it is the right time, at a time like this, on today, that is your wedding day." The comedic energy grew as the mother rambled on, and we, the audience, began to sense what was coming. "I think it is time," the mother began again, "for us to talk about ssss . . ." The audience started a quiet laughter as the *ssss* sound persisted, the mother unable to add any connecting vowels or syllables to form a word, *the* word. "It's time for us to talk about sssss," she tried once again. More laughter. "It's time for us to talk about sseee, sssss, ssss . . . " The audience's laughter grew into a roar. Before the mother could try again, the daughter interjected, "Mom, why is it so hard for you to say the word *sex?*" The older woman expressed exaggerated surprise and then both stood and took a quick bow before exiting the stage. They were quickly replaced by the speakers, Linda and Lorraine, as the audience continued to laugh and applaud.

"We're going to be real here, this weekend," Lorraine began. "We're going to talk about some things that you probably haven't heard talked about in church before." And then they said it—confidently, seriously, and in unison: "We're going to talk about sex." Linda took over: "Why is it important for us, a group of Christian women, to talk about sex? I'm going to give you three reasons. First, because God thinks it's important." Murmurs of assent from around the sanctuary. "Second, because Satan thinks it's important." I heard women muttering "Mm hmm," and one, under her breath, said "Amen." Linda continued, "And third, because *you* know it's important." A woman from the audience called out, "That's right!" as all of the women around me seemed to nod emphatically. Linda went on to state that sex matters for devout Christians because of its personal, spiritual, and cultural contestations. Sex is never neutral. In explaining why sex is important, Linda set up the inherent conflict that exists when it comes to Christians and sexuality. Pitted against one another are God and Satan, each with competing perspectives on sexuality. Somewhere in between them are those women attending the conference, ordinary believers who inevitably commit sins (since Christians believe that sin is an inherent part of the human condition) yet strive to live in a way that praises and pleases God.

Evangelicals constantly work to ease frictions that stem from their beliefs about sex. God made sex to be something good, but Satan and the secular world make it something bad. God created sex to be enjoyed between a husband and wife, but men and women are naturally quite different from one another. Sex is to be celebrated within marriage, but it is to be condemned in any other context. At another Christian sexuality conference, organized for members of BetweenTheSheets.com, the audience was given a message similar to Linda's from Intimate Issues. At this conference, David, a church pastor, told us emphatically,

> Sex means war. Your spouse is not the enemy of your sex life. Satan is the enemy of your sex life. God created sex to showcase His great design for men and women in marriage, and there's a party being thrown in heaven when married Christians have sex. Just by having sex you are winning a battle in the war against Satan. Sex should be spiritually comforting, spiritually connecting, and spiritually productive for the two most important relationships in your life: God and your spouse.

David presented the stakes of sexuality as reaching far beyond the walls of the bedroom. By having sex in the way that God designed, he insisted that Christians engage in a war with the devil and make progress toward victory over him. He advised couples: "Use weapons to fight to keep your marriage out of Satan's hands." These weapons include praying before, during, and after sex and making sure to have sex as often as possible.

Part of what makes Linda's and David's messages so compelling is that they frame godly sex as spiritually unique and exceptional. Titles of evangelical sex advice books—*A Celebration of Sex, The Gift of Sex, Holy Sex*—prominently display the belief that God creates sex as an extraordinary form of intimacy.[19] Authors, bloggers, and married couple Tony and Alisa DiLorenzo suggest that marriage and one's relationship with God are mutually affirming—if one is strong, it is likely that the other will be, as well. In their book *Stripped Down: 13 Keys to Unlocking Intimacy in Your Marriage,* they share the story of a challenge they made to have sex every day for thirty days.[20] Weeks into the challenge, Tony and their children got sick, and Alisa wrote about how the couple struggled to preserve their commitment to everyday intimacy:

> The idea of being intimate was the furthest thing from my mind, and yet I made a promise to Tony that we would be intimate every day or night that we could. I decided to do something I had never done before, not knowing whether it was okay. I prayed during sex. Not out loud, just in my heart. It was an honest request to God to help me "get in the mood." [. . .] Was my prayer answered? Yes! My desire for my husband was aroused, and we were able to enjoy another night of intimacy.[21]

With the help of God, Alisa and Tony were able to maintain physical closeness in their marital relationship. According to Alisa, God directed her feelings of sexual arousal, making her sex life literally a part of the divine. She later reflected on her decision to pray and why it had made her uneasy: "It had always seemed like that [sex] was one area where God shouldn't be. But God formed Adam and Eve and created sex. The Bible even has an entire book (Song of Songs) dedicated to sex. In spite of all that, most of us exclude Him from this portion of our lives."[22] Alisa's lesson, she believes, is that Christian couples should actively involve God in their sexual lives, for the benefits are great. She and Tony concluded that the challenge led to a more intimate and fulfilling marital relationship, which in turn led to a more intimate and fulfilling relationship with God.

GOOD SEX: WHO'S ALLOWED?

According to evangelicals who write about sex, what God makes possible when it comes to sex depends upon following God's rules about who's allowed to have it. All of the Christian sexuality websites in this study indicate that God permits sexual intimacy only between married, monogamous, heterosexual couples. These criteria for who is allowed to have sex highlight a trio of behaviors that conservative Christians believe God forbids: *un*married, *non*-monogamous, or *homo*sexual sex. I asked Christianity, Sexuality, and the Internet Survey (CSIS) respondents their attitudes about unmarried sex and sex between two adults of the same sex—whether they consider these acts to be always wrong, almost always wrong, wrong only sometimes, or not wrong at all.[23] To measure the stance of evangelicals on one of the nuances of monogamy that preoccupies them, I also asked respondents about whether it is wrong for a married couple to view pornography together, since pornography is the most frequently mentioned sin of adultery (through thought and fantasy). Figure 6 shows their responses. About nine out of ten survey participants reported that homosexual sex is always wrong; eight out of ten said that unmarried sex is always wrong; and six out of ten responded that it is always wrong for a married couple to view pornography. These responses are typical of the attitudes presented on Christian sexuality sites, where there is overwhelming opposition to these practices.[24]

What unites many conservative Christian faith groups is the belief that sex should only take place within legal marriages.[25] Evangelical groups that promote abstinence until marriage, like True Love Waits and Silver Ring Thing, exemplify this belief. Evangelical authors who promote sexual pleasure are therefore careful to always specify their intended audience.[26] For example, in their book *Sexperiment,* authors Ed and Lisa Young write, "The Sexperiment [a challenge for couples to have sex every day for seven consecutive days] isn't for everyone. It's reserved for those who are married, because God designed sex to be enjoyed within the marriage bed."[27] All of the books and websites included in my study emphasize the importance of remaining a virgin until one's wedding night. To be sure, many sex advice books and online discussions talk at length about sex taking place outside of marriage, but words like *destruction, sadness, emptiness,* and *danger* are used to describe it. Author Shannon Ethridge writes candidly about her own promiscuous history and says bluntly about agreeing to have sex with a boyfriend, "I lost big-time—my heart, my dignity, my self-esteem."[28] Although most stories of extramarital sex are about lustful teenagers engaging in premarital sex, Christian sexuality website users are adamant that these rules also apply to older adults. On the topic of sex after divorce, Samantha, owner of the eponymous online sex toy shop, insists that any sex outside of marriage is a sin: "I don't think God is changing the rules just because you're thirty-five." Because they believe there are no exceptions to this holy rule, BetweenTheSheets.com

■ Always wrong ■ Almost always wrong ■ Wrong only sometimes ■ Not at all wrong

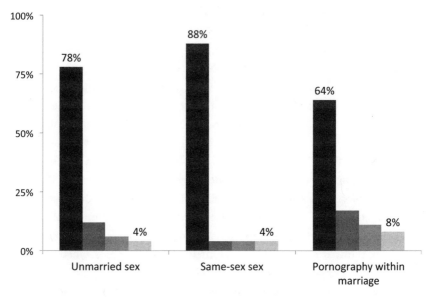

FIGURE 6. Attitudes about sex between unmarried adults, sex between same-sex adults, and a married couple viewing pornography together, CSIS sample.

members often suggest that an engaged couple struggling to remain chaste should consider moving their wedding date forward.

Although it is common for some authors and website users to disclose a past that involved sinful sexual behavior, most married website users who completed the CSIS reported having only a single sexual partner in their lifetime. As table 3 shows, married CSIS respondents engaged in extramarital sex less often than evangelicals nationally and the general population. They were also much more likely than married evangelicals nationally to report having had a single sexual partner.[29] It is possible that they have more conservative practices than evangelicals overall because they are actively interested in applying their religious beliefs to their sexual lives. Members of the overall evangelical population may not apply their religious beliefs to their sexual lives, and this may influence why they have sexual histories that, at least when it comes to the number of sexual partners, more closely resemble those of the broader public.

For evangelicals, God's rules about monogamy must be observed through deed and also through thoughts and fantasies. Though the Hebrew Bible frequently references God's forbiddance of adultery (most notably in the Ten

TABLE 3 Total number of consensual adult sex partners for married respondents, CSIS and GSS samples

	CSIS respondents (%)	Evangelicals nationally (%)	Overall population (%)
0	0	2.9	1.3
1	61.4	35.7	29.8
2–4	21.5	32.7	31.1
5–9	10.3	16.4	16.9
10 or more	6.7	12.3	20.9

NOTE: Because of rounding, some totals do not equal 100 percent.

Commandments, found in Exodus and Deuteronomy), evangelicals often reference a verse found in the New Testament (Matthew 5:28, NIV) instead: "But I tell you that anyone who looks at a woman lustfully has already committed adultery with her in his heart." Many evangelicals believe that pornography is the form of adultery that most frequently tempts believers, especially men. Some describe the problem of porn as an epidemic in contemporary culture.[30] Nearly all Christian sexuality websites in this study contain at least some information warning their users about the perils of pornography use (or addiction, as many evangelicals term habitual viewing of porn). One online Christian sex toy store, GardenFruit.com, claims that "pornography is the number one reason for failed marriages." The Driscolls dedicate an entire chapter in *Real Marriage* to porn and its problems, and they explicitly state that "sinful sex includes […] erotica, […] sinful lust, [and] pornography."[31] According to most respondents in this study, viewing someone else having sex is a clear violation of godly sexuality.[32] About three in four CSIS respondents reported that they never view pornography, which is actually comparable to the overall U.S. population.[33]

The final violation of godly sexuality that is undisputed on Christian sexuality websites is homosexuality, or more specifically, *having sex* with someone of the same sex.[34] Conservative Christians who write about sex suggest repeatedly and emphatically that God only approves of sex if it takes place between a man and a woman. Some message board threads debate the origins of homosexuality: A faulty gene akin to alcoholism? Socialization gone wrong? A selfish choice? For instance, one blogger on LustyChristianLadies.com wrote, "Homosexuality is a sin that is chosen, not genetically infused in you when you were born. God doesn't wire us to sin and he doesn't make any faulty wires … we choose to sin. God made marriage to be between man and wife. There is no other choice, unless you choose to sin." Most authors of sex advice books also agree that acting on homosexual desires is a choice that should be avoided, and some go so far as to offer readers who may be struggling with same-sex attraction advice on ways to avoid sin and strengthen their (heterosexual) marriages.[35] Popular authors and website users who choose not to talk much about homosexuality likely rely on the fact that there are many conservative Christian resources already addressing homosexuality. Many Christian sexuality website users and popular authors speak definitively and curtly on the topic, like Mark Driscoll did when he told an audience during a speaking tour, "the Bible repeatedly forbids homosexual sex," and then did not address the topic again.

By naturalizing heterosexuality, Christian sex advice bolsters beliefs that gender differences between men and women are natural and directed by God. At the BetweenTheSheets.com conference, creators of the site explained God's intentionality in designing men, women, and their union in marriage. "Men and women are like apples and oranges," BTS cocreator John told us. "We are all designed by the same creator, but men and women are very different from one another." Evangelical beliefs about gender typically fall into one of two camps: complementarianism or mutual submission. The former refers to the belief that men and women were created to fulfill different but equally important roles within marriage, families, and social life. It is the belief system that is endorsed officially by most evangelical leaders and denominations, most Christian sexuality websites, and nearly all of the authors of sex advice books in my sample. Mutual submission refers to the belief that both men and women should submit to God and to one another; marital relationships should focus on acts of service and compassion and no household leader should be determined. This approach, according to many studies on the everyday lives of married evangelicals, is the one most often practiced by most evangelicals, even if they publicly support an ideology of men's headship and women's submission.[36]

Regardless of whether or not they support complementarianism, mutual submission, or something in-between, conservative Christian commentators on marriage, family, and sexuality treat differences between men and women as natural and innate. Combining loose references to popular science and biblical scripture, bestselling books in this genre make direct connections between biology and characteristics associated with masculinity and femininity.[37] Authors of the sex advice book *Intimacy Ignited: Conversations Couple to Couple,* for example, state as a matter of fact, "Your husband craves your respect," and then ask their female readers: "Does it surprise you that your husband's deepest need is for respect, not love?" They go on to explain, "When God created the first man and woman, He wired subtle differences in their maleness and femaleness as to their basic needs. God wove into the fabric of a man's being a basic need for respect."[38] Differences between men and women, according to these authors, are rooted in physiology (they are "wired"), which God designed. Similarly, authors Ed and Gaye Wheat write in *Intended for Pleasure* that God made men and women to be naturally different so that they would be sexually compatible: "If men and women both were satisfied with a short period of arousal, the sex act would become a brief, mechanical experience. If both took a very long time to become aroused, the experience could become boring and monotonous. [...] The differences between men and women provide ground for creative, interesting interaction and enrich the sexual relationship in marriage."[39] According to these authors, a divine creator predetermined differences between men and women to cause distinct physical responses to sex.

Taken together, the requirements for who is allowed to have sex create specific conditions that frame the logic of godly sex. These conditions root this logic firmly within an evangelical tradition. Reflecting a long Christian history in which religious leaders have traditionally preached an anti-sex message, evangelicals who write about sexual pleasure continue to condemn certain sexual practices. Laying the foundation for the logic of godly sex, they firmly prohibit sexual unions between anyone other than heterosexual, monogamous, married people. Without these strict requirements, evangelicals would have little theological grounds, according to the major tenets of their conservative faith, for their messages about sexual pleasure. Relying on this fundamental understanding of godly sex, Christians online then extend this logic. They use their theological foundations to justify participating in some of the spoils of sexualized secular culture. Conservative Christians believe they can indulge in their sexual desires in order to achieve personal, marital, and spiritual fulfillment.

GOOD SEX: WHAT'S ALLOWED?

The idea that God created sex to be pleasurable is foundational to Christian sexuality websites and sex advice books. As author and medical doctor Ed Wheat writes in the introduction to *Intended for Pleasure,*

As a Christian physician, it is my privilege to communicate an important message to unhappy couples with wrong attitudes and faulty approaches to sex. The message, in brief, is this: You have God's permission to enjoy sex within your marriage. He invented sex; He thought it up to begin with. You can learn to enjoy it. [. . .] When we discover the many intricate details of our bodies that provide so many intense, wonderful physical sensations for husbands and wives to enjoy together, we can be sure that He intended us to experience full satisfaction in the marriage relationship.[40]

Here, Dr. Wheat writes confidently about *God's* intentions in creating our bodies to enjoy sexual intimacy. Though he writes of "God's permission," it is actually *he,* as a medical authority and respected Christian leader, who gives Christian husbands and wives permission to enjoy sex. Thirty-five years after Dr. Wheat and his wife, Gaye, published *Intended for Pleasure,* Pastor Mark Driscoll echoed this sentiment much more simply to an audience at his LoveLife conference: "The reason sex is so fun is because God made it." Focusing on sexual pleasure allows Christian website users to justify a wide range of sexual practices based on their specific and personalized "tastes." Acknowledging individual choice, which is highly interpretable and subjective, opens up vast possibilities within heterosexual, monogamous, conjugal sex.

Evangelical authors almost always rely on exegesis of scripture to reveal what they believe is God's support for sexual pleasure. Most frequently referenced is the Song of Solomon, often called the Song of Songs, a book from the Hebrew Bible that details Solomon and his new bride consummating their relationship. A close reading of this book, according to some evangelicals, reveals that God approves not only of sexual pleasure but also of sex acts other than penile-vaginal intercourse. Coauthors Joseph and Linda Dillow and Peter and Lorraine Pintus claim in their book, *Intimacy Ignited,* that the Song of Solomon has been their "sex manual" for years: "Heat rises from the pages as we view the steamy, yet appropriate, exchange of endearments and caresses."[41] Similarly, in *Real Marriage,* Mark and Grace Driscoll call the Song of Solomon "the most erotic section of the entire Bible" and explain, verse by verse, their interpretation of the sexual acts being described. Citing Tremper Longman III, a "widely respected Old Testament scholar," they suggest that the word *naval* that appears in most translations of the book actually is better translated as *vulva.* They quote Longman, who writes, "Whether literally navel or vulva, the image evokes a comparison that is based on taste. The description of the woman's aperture as containing wine implies the man's desire to drink from the sensual bowl. Thus, this may be a subtle and tasteful allusion to the intimacies of oral sex."[42] Christians who support a literal interpretation of the Bible find support in its pages for the belief that God wants couples to experience sexual pleasure and permits sexual alternatives to traditional coitus.

However, the Bible does not speak of the wide range of sex acts available to married couples, and even evangelical writers and speakers cannot present an exhaustive list of possible biblically sanctioned sexual activities. Instead, they present what are usually brief, biblically based criteria that can be applied by couples to their specific situations.[43] For example, at their Intimate Issues conference, Linda Dillow and Lorraine Pintus instructed their audience that once they establish that sex falls within God's design of heterosexual, monogamous marriage, they need only ask a single question to determine what sexual activities are permissible for them: *is it beneficial?* Dillow and Pintus contribute to a larger discussion common among evangelicals that attempts to untangle behaviors that count as sin and those that simply make for poor choices for certain people. In *Real Marriage,* the Driscolls categorize behaviors into three types, "lawful," "helpful," and "enslaving," drawing from 1 Corinthians 6:12 (NIV): "'I have the right to do anything,' you say—but not everything is beneficial."[44] Consuming alcohol is one example. Most evangelicals believe that although God does not prohibit an adult from drinking a beer (it is not "unlawful"), it may not be "helpful" for some individuals and may even be "enslaving" for an alcoholic. Applying this idea to marital sex, evangelicals emphasize that even if a particular sex act is not forbidden by scripture, all sex that takes place within a marriage should strengthen that marriage and bring the husband and wife closer to God. This means that what is appropriate for some couples will not be for others.

Blogger Maribel told me that the question her readers ask her most often is if the sex they desire is "okay" according to God's design. "People ask a lot of questions like, 'Do you think it's okay if I do this . . . ?' Asking my opinion of what they do and whether or not it is acceptable. Or just about if the dynamics of their sex life are 'normal.' I think people just want validation." Maribel recognizes that sexuality is a high-stakes issue in the Christian faith tradition and that her readers have few outlets to openly discuss their sexual lives. She is amused at the fact that she—a stay-at-home mom who blogs—is asked to provide the validation these Christian couples seek. "I mean, I can offer them support. I try to address different topics on the blog, but really I just try to encourage people to do what works in their marriage and quit worrying about what other people are doing." She attempts to convey the message that these couples—assuming they are straight, married, and monogamous—do not need validation from *her;* they already have validation from *God,* the highest authority, to enjoy sexually "what works in their marriages."

Drawing from the guidelines presented by Dillow and Pintus, the Driscolls, and others who write about godly sex, Christian sexuality website users appear to be more comfortable making claims about who can have sex than making judgments about what they can do sexually. Figure 7 summarizes the attitudes of CSIS respondents regarding four specific sexual practices within marriage: masturbation, anal sex, oral sex, and the use of vibrators.[45] The vast majority of respondents agreed that oral sex and using a vibrator are "not wrong at all." And even for anal sex and masturbation, only 20 and 10 percent, respectively, of CSIS respondents overall reported that those acts are "always wrong." LDS respondents were the most restrictive—39 percent said masturbation and anal sex are always wrong—but no religious group reported a consensus on these two acts. Instead, most respondents believed that there are circumstances in which both acts *may* be acceptable within marriage. Although the vast majority of CSIS respondents reported that sex between an unmarried or same-sex couple is "always wrong" (78 and 88 percent, respectively), their attitudes about other sexual acts were less straightforward.

All of the website users I interviewed also completed the CSIS, and so I asked them about any sexual attitude question in which their responses were ambiguous. I wanted to know for those acts that were considered "almost always wrong," when are they okay? And for acts that were considered "wrong only sometimes," when are they *not* okay? One respondent, Jess35, who follows the LustyChristianLadies blog, said that she reported that viewing pornography is only "almost always wrong" because it is so hard to define: "There is sometimes a fine line between art and porn. I don't know that it's wrong to ever feel aroused by these things that are borderline—I think that might be natural." For Jess35, there may be ambiguous "things" that skirt the line between respectable depictions of sexual bodies (art) and obscene depictions (porn). Therefore, she does not feel comfortable making judgments about those who view pornography. Another LustyChristianLadies.com reader, Junebug, explained why she answered that it is "almost always wrong" for a married person to masturbate (she was among 53 percent of respondents who responded this way): "Well, 'a person' is pretty general, I guess, haha. I guess it is grey for me. [...] I don't think it's the best

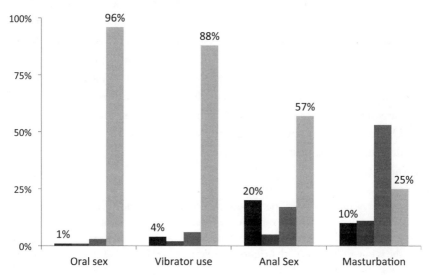

FIGURE 7. Attitudes about oral sex, the use of vibrators, anal sex, and a married man or woman masturbating, CSIS sample.

scenario, but I don't think it's wrong in a marriage as long as it is something that helps the relationship." Junebug hesitated about making judgments about specific sexual acts without knowing the relational context in which those acts occur. Echoing the criteria set forth by Dillow and Pintus, Junebug believes that masturbation is permissible in a marriage if it benefits that relationship.

BTS member Chloe explained to me why she skipped the survey question asking about her attitude toward anal sex within marriage, a practice that 57 percent of CSIS respondents reported is "not at all wrong" and 20 percent reported is "always wrong":

> I am undecided. I guess I haven't "researched" it sufficiently. It is not something DH [dear husband] and I are interested in. Of course, there can be negative health consequences related to it, [and] the little I've heard about women experiencing it is that they don't like it. Those things would probably cause me to shy away from it in general. If DH were really interested in it, I'd be willing to look into it from a Biblical and health standpoint and hope we could reach some common ground on it. I don't know that I'd say across the board that "it is wrong," but again I don't know that if I gave it time and thought that I wouldn't say it was wrong. I might. ???

Chloe refused to take a stand about whether she considered anal sex to be right or wrong. She talked through some of the reasons for her reservations: she wasn't personally interested in it and it could be medically risky. Then she admitted that if her husband were interested in anal sex, she would consider it more thoroughly, do more "research." Chloe's concluding question marks ("???") suggested that she was unable to make universal judgments about whether anal sex is appropriate for all couples and that she doesn't have a definitive answer because it's not an act in which she or her husband wish to engage.

One contributor to BetweenTheSheets.com used the analogy of a carnival to describe what is possible when it comes to sex within marriage. At the carnival there are

> a great number of rides (sex acts) that a couple may enjoy if they so desire. What each couple enjoys varies just as preferences at the carnival vary. If he gets dizzy and sick on things that spin, the tilt-a-whirl is not a good choice. If she is uncomfortable with heights, that Ferris wheel is a bad idea. If they both enjoy him driving the bumper car, but neither is big on her driving, that's just fine. Start with a few rides and over time test out others.

Within marriage (the carnival), couples are free to determine what kinds of sex (different rides) bring them the most pleasure. The sexual repertoire of couples may differ based on personal preference. Just as the Ferris wheel is not any better than the roller coaster, varying sex acts do not contain inherent value that make them good or bad.

This carnival of sexual possibilities reflects what sociologist of religion Lynne Gerber explains are some of the "most central values" that define contemporary evangelicalism. She argues that, "because of their explanatory power, choice and free will become powerful concepts in the evangelical imaginary."[46] In her study of evangelical ex-gay and dieting movements, Gerber finds that participants centralize the ability to choose to do right or wrong in order to make their commitments to change meaningful rather than coerced. Choice is framed within a level playing field so that those who choose to commit sins can be held accountable for their actions. These choices proliferate so long as couples live according to God's design. Emphasizing what couples *choose* to do within monogamous, heterosexual matrimony means that discussions about *what's* allowed sexually emphasize individualized preference and taste, unlike discussions about *who's* allowed to have sex, in which evangelicals emphasize an unambiguous interpretation of the Bible.

Using the logic of godly sex allows conservative Christians to dance between senses of permissiveness and restrictiveness related to sexuality. In my interview with Lisa, who writes the blog WeddingNights.com, she described her beliefs about sex as straightforward:

> I usually follow two basic guidelines when it comes to my opinion as to what is "okay" in bed. Number one: no third parties. Sex is meant to be exclusive between a husband and a wife, so this would mean no actual third parties participating, no affairs, nobody watching the couple have sex, [and] no viewing of pornographic material (print or video). Number two: no one is getting hurt. So this would mean no one is physically getting hurt or is being abused or is forced to do something that they don't want to do or feel is morally wrong. If those two rules are met, then I think a couple has tremendous freedom.

Lisa summarizes the logic of godly sex, noting the requirements for who is allowed to have it (a husband and wife, without "third parties") and what they can do (anything, so long as no one "gets hurt," either figuratively or literally). The latter depends largely on the circumstances, tastes, and dispositions of individual couples. If sex takes place within the context she outlines, Lisa declares that couples have "tremendous freedom" within their sexual lives.

The freedom that Lisa describes in defining godly sex offers new possibilities for understanding gender roles within the sexual relationships of conservative Christians. In prioritizing sex acts that benefit a marriage relationship, evangelicals also prioritize mutuality and consent on the part of both husband and wife. This gives women, as well as men, a clear voice within a marriage, even among those Christians who support complementarianism. For instance, authors Ed and Gaye Wheat write at length about the importance of wives submitting to their husbands: "Submission is the most important gift a wife can give her husband. A responsive and receptive wife willingly demonstrates that she surrenders her freedom for his love, adoration, protection, and provision." Yet they go on to state that women are entitled to experience sexual pleasure: "If you [directed toward women] desire to have an orgasm, [it is] *because you know it is your right,* your provision from God. [. . .] Your goal, now, is satisfaction given by a loving husband, and achieving the fulfillment of orgasm."[47] According to these evangelical authorities, women must submit to their husbands, but this gender arrangement can and should exist alongside the right to be sexually pleased by their husbands.

Emphasizing individual taste and mutual pleasure allows these religious conservatives to discuss the natural differences between men and women while simultaneously using gender-equal language when talking about sex. In this way, they confirm existing studies on evangelical life that show how individuals make sense of their gendered beliefs and everyday practices by combining ideas about complementarianism and mutual submission.[48] Evangelicals who write about sex make several generalized claims about what men and women are like sexually. They assert that women have more difficulty reaching orgasm than men, that men physically require sexual release but that women do not, that sex for women is largely emotional rather than physical, and that women are less flexible in their sexual repertoires than men are. A common theme in these generalizations is that women are less sexual than men—that they don't like sexual variation, that they don't physically need sex in the ways in which men do, and that the emotional connections sex offers them may easily be replaced with a cup of coffee and a long conversation with their spouse. Men, however, are considered to be much more sexual than women—they can experiment with different types of sexual play with confidence and pleasure, and they physically require sex to live happy, productive lives. Yet, as Kevin Leman writes about such generalizations, "every stereotype will be proven false by somebody, which is why individual communication is so crucial in marriage. I can give you advice about what most men like, but that very advice might really turn your husband off."[49] Although Christian sex advice perpetuates gender stereotypes, authors tell individual couples that they can disregard these stereotypes, depending on their unique circumstances and desires.

Website users' sexual attitudes and practices, as reported in the CSIS, illuminate this contradictory message about gender. As figure 8 shows, the majority of married respondents reported their spouse as their only sexual partner. Yet men were more likely than women to report having had multiple sexual partners. These data appear to confirm evangelicals' general belief that men have stronger and harder-to-control sexual urges than women. When it came to sexual practices in marriage, however, men and women who responded to the CSIS reported similar levels of activity. For example, figure 9 shows that men and women both reported that they perform and receive oral sex at comparable rates. Men are slightly more likely to "never" perform oral sex than women (7 percent, compared to 4 percent), and women are slightly more likely than men to "always" receive it (16 percent, compared to 15 percent). Regarding attitudes about different sexual acts, results for questions about acts performed by a woman are nearly identical to questions about acts performed by a man. The greatest difference—and it is really

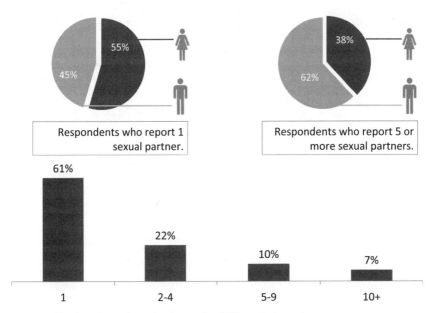

Respondents who report 1 sexual partner.

Respondents who report 5 or more sexual partners.

FIGURE 8. Number of sexual partners by gender, CSIS married sample.

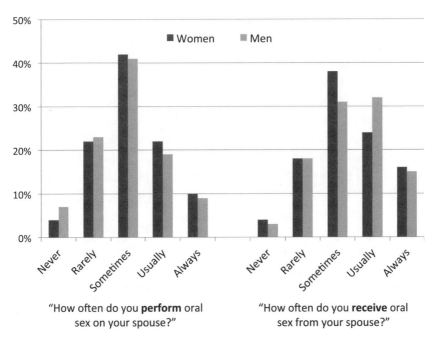

"How often do you **perform** oral sex on your spouse?"

"How often do you **receive** oral sex from your spouse?"

FIGURE 9. Frequency of oral sex in marriage by gender, CSIS married sample.

barely a difference at all—was reported for a question about vibrator use within marriage, to which 87.9 percent of respondents reported that it is "not at all wrong" when a woman uses a vibrator on a man, and 90.2 percent reported that it is "not at all wrong" when a man uses a vibrator on a woman. These data suggest that there is a clear gender gap *outside* of marriage (men have more sexual partners than women). *Within* marriage, however, CSIS respondents' sexual attitudes and practices appear to support a gender egalitarian framework.

By focusing on the sexual pleasure of both men and women within marriage, the logic of godly sex eases tension between traditional religious beliefs and salient values of modern culture. Godly sex, at least on the surface, is available equally to Christian men and women. Because good sex requires the satisfied participation of both husband and wife, the logic of godly sex validates women's choices, tastes, and interests within the marriage relationship. Yet, as I go on to describe in chapters four and five, women's entitlement to sexual pleasure does not dismantle Christianity's uneven gender regime.

GODLY SEX GOES ONLINE

Christian sex advice—both online and offline—is of a self-help genre, in which, as sociologist Robert Wuthnow describes, "the individual is the measure of all things."[50] The users of Christian sex advice websites draw from salient cultural ideas that emphasize personal choice and unique tastes to make claims about what is sexually possible. This logic allows a wide range of sexual acts to be practiced and encouraged within conservative Christian marriages. At the same time, these Christians draw from religious beliefs that maintain that the Bible is the literal word of God and that instructions for how to live a Christian life are straightforward and black and white, with no exceptions. This sets the boundaries for who is allowed to be sexual—only married, heterosexual, monogamous couples.

The logic of godly sex upholds the major tenets of conservative Christian faith but also keeps up with contemporary attitudes about sex. Yet it does more than improve individual sex lives. Christians who write about sexual pleasure tell believers what they should experience sexually and how to interpret these experiences.[51] As such, evangelical sex advice is an example of sex "put into discourse." As Michel Foucault writes, discourse "permeates [. . .], penetrates and controls everyday pleasure."[52] Discourse, as conceived by

Foucault and scholars following in his tradition, refers to the language that produces the categories through which we come to know ourselves and others. As Eve Sedgwick puts it, discursive power grants us "material and rhetorical leverage" to define who we are.[53] Those who set the terms of godly sexuality define *what sex is according to religious beliefs.* These Christians hold "leverage" over who should be allowed to engage in sexual acts and what those sexual acts should be. Talk about the utterly private and intimate act of sex reveals that sex is not removed from the social world but is rather reflective of it. Yet Christian sex advice, especially that given online, suggests that this relationship between social rules and sexual practices is not one-way. Sexual desires influence what people are able to talk about and how they are able to talk about it.

A key theme of this book is that online dialogue grants certain leverage to the conclusions ordinary believers make about sexual possibilities. Throughout this chapter, I have interwoven passages from published evangelical sex advice books, stories from Christian conferences, and online discussions among users of Christian sexuality websites. In some ways, online discussion exists seamlessly alongside prescriptive evangelical advice. Yet website users also take up the new opportunities offered by the Internet to radically alter how they understand their sexual lives within the context of their faith. Christian sexuality websites are places of *emergence,* or as sociologist David Snow describes, "departures from, challenges to, and clarifications or transformations of everyday routines, practices, or perspectives."[54] Online dialogue allows ordinary believers to collectively work to present sexuality in ways evangelical authors or preachers likely did not anticipate. These Christians use the logic of godly sex to integrate their sexual desires, practices, and identities into their moral framework. In doing so, website creators and users expand and simultaneously maintain the boundaries of religion and heterosexuality.

TWO

Overcoming the Obscene

USING RELIGION TO TALK ABOUT SEX

The Internet seems like an evangelist's dream when it comes to spreading the gospel. Take, for example, one of America's most famous evangelical leaders, Billy Graham. He spoke to his largest crowd in 1991 in New York City, an estimated audience of 250,000. That number is only a fraction of the millions of people around the world who listened to his radio program, the *Hour of Decision,* at its peak in the 1970s.[1] Today, the Billy Graham Evangelistic Association (BGEA) uses a number of websites to spread its message, including an organizational homepage, other sites hosted by BGEA (like PeaceWithGod.Jesus.Net), and social media accounts on Facebook, Twitter, and Instagram. One BGEA Facebook post shares a link to a familiar Christian tract, a step-by-step guide to eternal salvation: accept that God loves you, that man is sinful, and that Jesus died for your sins, and then pray a simple but sincere prayer to accept Christ as your savior. Over 25,000 of BGEA's Facebook followers "shared" this message with their own networks of Facebook friends. If each of these followers had 338 Facebook friends (the estimated average number for members in 2013), roughly 8.5 million Facebook users saw this BGEA post.[2] Compared to speaking appearances in front of large crowds or the production of radio and TV programs, Graham's ministry's online presence seems remarkably efficient and powerful. Anyone with a computer and an Internet connection can share a message that has the potential to reach millions nearly instantly. With the Internet counting over three billion users across the globe, online proselytizing is the perfect tool to achieve the goal of the BGEA—"to proclaim the Gospel of Jesus Christ by every effective means and to equip others to do the same."

Mediated religion offers believers a sense of religious community and fellowship without a congregation or physical church. Long before the Internet, evangelicals challenged traditional ideas about what makes a church, establishing "churches" in people's homes and in strip malls, for example. Mediated religion, whether on the Internet, the radio, or television, offers believers an alternative way of feeling like they are connecting with others while receiving religious messages. Yet unlike television or radio, where believers do not participate in the production of religious messages, the Internet can be interactive. Jeffrey Hadden and Douglas Cowan distinguish between "religion online," which resembles other forms of noninteractive media in that individuals learn about religion from formal institutions and recognized leaders, and "online religion," which allows individual website users to construct religious faith through online practices.[3] From leaders to laypeople, evangelicals can make use of digital media to understand their religious lives.

Creators of Christian sexuality websites share with the BGEA the goal of proclaiming the Gospel of Jesus Christ by every effective means. Yet beyond theological alignment, they have little in common with Graham, the evangelical celebrity. Ordinary people create the vast majority of Christian sexuality websites; they are rarely ordained pastors, distinguished speakers, published authors, or trained therapists.[4] Only five of the thirty-six sites in this study are affiliated with a formal organization or an author whose work has been published by a press. The creators are not web designers or computer programmers (though some do enlist the help of people with formal training in these areas), and their websites run the gamut when it comes to aesthetics, ranging from clunky and amateur to slick and professional. Formal credentials are not what creators use to establish themselves as authentically Christian. Indeed, these are largely missing from Christian sexuality websites. The information given on these sites will typically not divulge whether the creators have college degrees, if they are members of a specific Christian denomination, or even if they attend church. This chapter examines the various ways that website creators construct authority on the sites.

Spreading the message of godly sex is not an easy task. Even though the majority of Americans use the Internet—more than half of all American adults are members of Facebook, for example—it comes with perceived dangers, many of which have to do with sexuality. Media stories about pornography, perverts, cyber-stalking, and cyber-bullying give the impression that virtual reality is one where innocence is lost, "family values" have declined, and risk is paramount. It is no wonder that 50 percent of parents of American teens with Internet access use parental controls to block or monitor online activity.[5] On her blog, WeddingNights.com, Lisa writes candidly about the risky relationship between cyberspace and sex: "Typing 'sex' online quickly lures some of the most appalling junk you can imagine." She describes blogging about Christian sexuality as a struggle: "There is so much out there trying to impair marriage. We who blog about this face outrageous obstacles online." Lisa, like many others, considers the Internet to be a space of perversion. Those who want to use it to blend messages about sexuality *with* Christian values have much work to do.

All Christian sexuality website creators I interviewed expressed some amount of Internet ambivalence, acknowledging that, when used to tackle topics related to sexuality, virtual communication brings with it vast possibilities (take, for example, the single BGEA Facebook post that was seen by millions) but also inherent risks. Holly illuminates this ambivalence in how she justified the need for a sex-toy store like hers, StoreOfSolomon.com, within the Christian community. "The reason we [Christians] stay away from some things," she explained to me, "is not the product or the activity but the places you have to go to be a part of them. Sex toys are great, but if we have to look at twenty-three people having sex on posters to get the products we want, we won't do it. The commandment to have sex with only your spouse includes your fantasies." In other words, Christians should not shop at online stores that expose their customers to pornographic images because to do so would violate God's commandment that forbids adultery. The commandment that Holly is referring to is Matthew 5:28: "But I tell you that anyone who looks at a woman lustfully has already committed adultery with her in his heart" (NIV). Most evangelicals interpret this to mean that looking at pornography or even imagining sex involving someone other than a spouse is a clear violation of God's word. For Christians who believe God wants for them to optimize their sexual pleasure, this sets up a need for pornography-free Christian spaces that discuss sexuality and even sell sex toys.

Yet the catch-22 for Holly is that *she* must be exposed to pornography in order to create and maintain her business. As someone who does not personally manufacture sex toys (and this is the case for all Christian sex toy stores in my study), she must work with secular mass-distributors to choose and buy products to then resell on her site. She therefore encounters porn on a day-to-day basis, while shielding her customers from it. How does she reconcile this seeming contradiction? On the one hand, the risks of the secular Internet are too great for Christians to use it for improving their sex lives, whether through advice or purchasing sex toys. On the other hand, Holly and other website creators like her must immerse themselves in the dangerous and sinful world of the secular Internet—the Dante's inferno of cyberspace—in order to fulfill what they believe to be God's call to serve their fellow Christians. "My beliefs are not so fragile so it doesn't bother me to go where not many Christians have gone before ☺," Holly told me. But she said she was confident in her faith in God, which gives her the ability to reject the temptation of lust while viewing pornographic labels.

Instead of reasoning that an unwavering faith in God would make it possible for *all* pious Christians to be exposed to pornography without committing sin, Holly uses her beliefs to reason that she is the *right kind* of Christian to do the work she does. She sorts through products that she finds acceptable (those that do not contain any nudity in their packaging) and those she does not. What makes her the right Christian for this job is both her personal relationship with God and her beliefs about gender differences. She explained, for example, that when she went to an adult product show in Las Vegas, she decided to ask her mother to accompany her instead of her husband. "I think guys are much more visually stimulated, so I go through catalogues and attend shows." Even though Holly's husband helps with some aspects of her business, he does not view products before Holly has chosen them. Holly generalizes that women are the right kind of Christians to run sex toy stores: "Women, being less likely to be tempted by visual stimulus, have the upper hand when it comes to finding resources/products for sex lives." All online stores in my sample were, in fact, managed either by a woman or by a married couple together, something I discuss later in this chapter.

A common way Christian sexuality website creators justified running their sites was to explain that they believe they were the *right kind* of Christians to do it—either because they were women, because of their happy and secure marriages, or because of their devotion to God. This hints at the logic of godly sex presented in the previous chapter, wherein some conservative Christians make sense of sexuality distinctly for *themselves*—combining religious and secular ideas to privilege their status as married, monogamous, heterosexual Christians and making their sexual lives appear to be without limits because they obediently live within God's rules about sexuality. Website creators draw from the logic of godly sex that is presented in popular evangelical literature to establish a place for themselves in the secular and sinful Internet. They use their beliefs in God to determine who is allowed to be sexual and expand the kinds of sexual dialogue that are possible online. In doing so, they extend their religious beliefs in order to legitimize the spaces they create online as authentically Christian.

Website creators justify online conversations about sex primarily by using three tenets of their faith—what I categorize as personal piety, marital exceptionalism, and God's omniscience. This trio of beliefs moves beyond the prescriptive rules about who is allowed to have sex (only married, monogamous, heterosexual couples) and further cements within the logic of godly sex all that couples can do within the boundaries of God's design for sexuality. This chapter shows how these beliefs act as *spiritual capital,* allowing website creators to legitimize their Christian identity while talking about sex online. Spiritual capital draws from Bourdieu's theory of *cultural capital,* which he uses to explain social divisions and inequalities. He contends that no cultural symbol, practice, or knowledge—from food preferences to alma maters—is value neutral. Instead, they all exist within a hierarchy in which we associate some of them with elevated and exclusive values. Having access to these desirable symbols, practices, and knowledge produces cultural capital, which secures what Bourdieu calls *symbolic power:* authority gained through distinction, legitimation, and recognition. When applied to religion, spiritual capital allows ordinary believers to draw from the cultural products of their religion—such as knowledge of scripture and familiar prayers—to give them authority within their social worlds.[6]

Displaying personal piety, marital exceptionalism, and God's omniscience reflects what Bourdieu calls *dispositions*—versus *positions.*[7] The creators of Christian sexuality websites gain traction with a Christian audience by constructing religious authority outside of formal institutions. This is in contrast to evangelicals who write sex advice books and rely largely on their *positions*—as, for example, doctors, psychologists, or pastors (credentials that are often displayed prominently on the jackets of evangelical sex advice books)—to write about sex from a Christian perspective. Online, however, website creators are uniquely situated to construct forms of religious authority in different ways than evangelical authors. They rely not on traditional forms of religious authority but rather on an online presentation of religious knowledge that validates their Christian status. Personal piety, marital exceptionalism, and God's omniscience resemble familiar and generally accepted Protestant Christian beliefs, but website creators extend them in a way that juxtaposes openings and closures within the logic of godly sex. These beliefs keep out certain *others* from participating in godly sex and legitimize the actions of those who fit within its framework.

In order to establish their work as distinctly Christian, Linda Dillow and Lorraine Pintus, authors of the evangelical sex advice book *Intimate Issues,* rely on typical forms of authority to bolster their credibility. Since the book was originally released in 1999, over 250,000 readers have purchased it, and thousands of churches have used it in small-group studies. Dillow and Pintus have also hosted over twenty Intimate Issues conferences in churches across the country, sharing their message with thousands of Christian women. To promote the conference and book, they advertise endorsements from a wide range of Christian authorities: pastors, therapists, and medical doctors. The book jacket includes praise from leaders of a well-known Baptist seminary, for example, who declare that *Intimate Issues* is a "gem to be shared" and "a powerful resource for counselors and teachers, well-documented and deserving of serious attention."[8] In the church lobby at the Intimate Issues conference I attended, volunteers were selling other books written by Dillow and Pintus. The sheer number of titles (eleven in total) gives the impression that these women are leading authorities on the topics they write about.[9] The back of the conference program includes the information that Dillow and Pintus have appeared on TV and radio programs, including the *700 Club* and *Focus on the Family,* and that *Intimate Issues* is "best selling" and "award winning." They also rely on their own physical appearances to show their audience that they have both the expertise and the care to talk about such sensitive topics. Inside the sanctuary, Dillow and Pintus spoke with confidence and poise about how they, as devoted followers of Christ and as women who are wives and mothers, have important insight on matters related to sexuality.

During the conference, Dillow and Pintus talked about sex in ways that were notably different than how it is generally approached on Christian sexuality websites. They recognize that many women attending Intimate Issues conferences are sitting next to their mothers, sisters, and friends, and this requires them to choose their language and anecdotes so that their audience will be comfortable. They rely heavily on humor and euphemisms to broach subjects that are rarely, if ever, talked about within church walls, such as sexual arousal, women's orgasms, and God's approval of oral sex. While Dillow and Pintus use the analogy of "crock pots and microwaves" to describe the differing sexual responses of women and men, websites tend to be much less euphemistic. Take, for example, names of some of the products that online Christian sex toy stores sell: the Climax EZ Bend Shaft vibrator, the

Screaming O penis ring, or the OptiMale Reversible Stroker. As with many online discussions, these toe the line between descriptive and obscene.

Websites include specific instructions and frank language that "gets to the point," providing concrete advice for couples who seek it. John, one of the creators of BetweenTheSheets.com, for example, wrote an article with instructions for women who want to perform a striptease for their husbands (for a gender analysis of these instructions, see chapter five). It is a lengthy post that describes, in excruciating detail, each step involved in his version of a striptease, from how to set up the best lighting to how to best accomplish the "grand finale" of the performance—masturbation and climax. John tells women readers:

> He likes to see you touch where he wants to touch, so rubbing and touching your breasts and crotch is good. Do this over your clothes, under your clothes, and when you get rid of your clothes. You can accentuate these things by making a face that says, "that feels good." The magic word is: tease. Tease with what you say. Play with your nipples and ask if he likes it. Touch yourself under your panties and tell him what you feel.

Despite the relatively tame language—John uses words like "breast" and "crotch" instead of more vulgar alternatives—these instructions clearly convey a sexual scenario and do so quite explicitly. Although stripping is most often depicted as a form of late-night entertainment for men *without* their wives, John reclaims it as part of a Christian marriage, to be enjoyed by husbands *with* their wives. He unapologetically reclaims the lust, fun, and flirtation that reside so comfortably within sexualized secular culture and places them within a Christian setting. He gives stripping a godly virtue.

In my interviews with members of BetweenTheSheets.com (BTS) and readers of LusyChristianLadies.com (LCL), respondents frequently mentioned their appreciation for the "step-by-step" approach that is taken by many Christian sexuality websites. LCL, for example, includes a link near the top of its homepage called "The LCL Positions." When I first clicked on it, I expected to find a list of rules that the LCL bloggers support—that is to say, their *theological* positions. Instead, I found a list of ninety-nine *sexual* positions and links to instructions for how to perform each. Next to the name of every position is a label indicating whether the position is graded "easy," "advanced," or "master." A small red heart indicates a position that allows for face-to-face kissing.

LCL Position number forty-four is called "Surf's Up." To perform this position, blogger Bunny instructs readers: "Ask your husband to lay down on the bed. Then climb on top of him and place your knees on either side of his face. Then start surfing. [...] Grind, move, ride against your husband's tongue and mouth as you surf to the top of the wave for climax!" LCL readers reply with enthusiastic support for Surf's Up, posting comments that explain their great success with the position. Like a review for a product purchased on Amazon, one reader, Jen29, writes, "This is an amazing position, you will not be disappointed!!!!" Another reader, CC, confirms, "Ditto Jen's experience. I too have very aggressive orgasms in this position. My husband was so taken with this position that his oral ferociousness caused me to ejaculate for the first time. Our lovemaking has become sooo spiritual that we're like kids in a candy shop." CC's use of the word "spiritual" to describe the Surf's Up position undoubtedly points to her feeling that the sex she has is "out of this world." But it also illustrates the seamlessness with which Christian sexuality website creators and users merge talk of religion with explicit talk of sex. Taking her cue from the detailed descriptions the LCL bloggers use when writing about sex, CC confidently shares that she ejaculates as she climaxes. This detail might seem decidedly out of place in a religious space and only considered to be appropriate in pornos or crude jokes, but CC proves otherwise, writing frankly about female ejaculation as a spiritual practice within her Godly marriage.

Is CC's comment more explicit than descriptions published in sex advice books? Certainly, the vast majority of books included in this study do not address female ejaculation, nor do they describe the sex position known as Surf's Up. Yet the description of this position and CC's response to it mirror the general tone used online and in books. Both book authors and website creators use similar strategies to desexualize the language and images they use to talk about sex so that they are not pornographic. Both prefer anatomically specific, seemingly neutral, and noninflammatory terms when describing bodies, using words like *clitoris, vulva, penis,* and *testicles.* BetweenTheSheets.com's administrators give explicit instructions to the site's members, for example, to "limit sexual language to medical or mild slang terms." Terms such as *cock, dick,* and *pussy* are automatically deleted if a member tries to include them in a post.

Both websites and books are also careful when it comes to incorporating images as instructional tools. A picture paints a thousand words, so the saying goes, and authors and website creators do use images to explain the practicalities of sexuality: how bodies work and fit together. They often rely on anatomical drawings that depict men's and women's reproductive organs

FIGURE 10. "The clitoris with labia," a drawing from *A Celebration of Sex,* by Dr. Douglas Rosenau. Rosenau notes, "There is no perfect size but each unique shape will become intensely erotic to the woman's husband" (31). (Illustration by Douglas Rosenau, © 2002; used by permission of Thomas Nelson, www.thomasnelson.com)

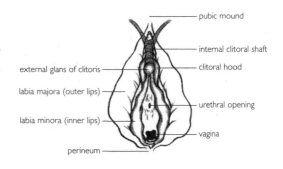

FIGURE 11. "Positioning for premature ejaculation training session using squeeze control," a drawing from Ed and Gaye Wheat's book, *Intended for Pleasure.* Appearing in a chapter called "Solutions to Common Problems," this illustration shows how a wife can help delay a husband's ejaculation. (Illustration by Dale Ellen Beals, adapted from a drawing in *Female Pelvic and Obstetrical Anatomy and Male Genitalia,* a Schering Clinoptikons booklet, 1958)

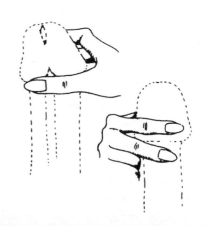

FIGURE 12. "Having a ball. . . . The ball can put a twist on an old position that you may have previously not liked!" (Photograph by Cameron Stefanowski, adapted from an illustration on LovingGroom.com)

(like figure 10). These drawings mirror the ways in which seemingly un-sexual and respectable institutions like schools or hospitals educate an audience about sexuality. Similarly, both websites and books rely on faceless line drawings or photographs (like figures 11 and 12) to help instruct couples how to engage in various sexual positions. These images, according to those who use them, do not count as pornography because they do not depict images of actual nude bodies.

All Christian discussions about sexual pleasure—whether in print or online—skirt the line between sound religious teaching and what may be considered obscene. Like U.S. courts that have struggled to regulate obscenity, the Christians who write and talk about sex cannot objectively define what counts as obscene. As Supreme Court justice Potter Stewart famously declared about pornography, "I know it when I see it." Because website creators do not automatically have religious authority based on formal positions as clergy or other appointed church leaders, they use other strategies to legitimize their ability to talk about sex without appearing obscene. These Christians use some of the core beliefs of their religious faith as forms of spiritual capital to host frank discussions about explicit sex acts. Their beliefs about personal piety, marital exceptionalism, and God's omniscience help legitimize Christian sexuality websites as Christian spaces.

PERSONAL PIETY

Lisa started her blog, WeddingNights.com, to share her story with other Christian women. Her first marriage ended because of problems related to sexuality. While she was struggling in that relationship, she turned to women in her church for advice. These women were like family to her; they saw each other several times a week at church and in small group Bible studies. They were sympathetic, having suffered themselves from many of the problems Lisa described—such as miscommunication about sex and difficulty prioritizing it in their daily lives—but they offered few helpful remedies. After she divorced, Lisa spent time in prayer and read Christian books about marriage and relationships. This prompted the revelation that her marriage had ended in part because she hadn't been sexually available to her husband. When she remarried a few years later, she made a commitment to herself, to her marriage, and to other women: "I vowed that I wouldn't let sex just fall by the wayside in my marriage. And I vowed to encourage other women and make the church a safe place to talk and be heard."

Before focusing her efforts online, Lisa designed a ten-week Bible study on sexual intimacy for a small group of women in her church. In many evangelical churches, lay members are able to lead small group studies that take a democratic approach to religious practice. They may focus on a wide range of topics of interest to contemporary believers, from personal finance to politics.[10] With the help of the Holy Spirit to guide them, ordinary believers insist that they have access to insight and godly knowledge, just as ordained ministers do. And so although Lisa *led* a Bible study group, she does not consider herself a *leader*. She credits the group's success to her humble approach in writing and teaching that focused on personal stories of struggle and growth rather than packaged and prescriptive advice:

> I really think that people want to know that I am a real person. That resonates with people more . . . They don't want lofty theories. They want someone who hears them. Even if I cannot completely relate, I have found that the more I speak/write out of my own journey, that gives people freedom to speak about their journey. The truth is that sex was a mess in my first marriage . . . That's a big reason why I'm so passionate speaking hope into other people's situations.

Lisa describes herself as a wife, mom, Midwesterner, and writer, but first and foremost a "follower of Christ." She does not call herself as a leader, teacher, or counselor but instead points to a passion she has for "speaking hope" to others by sharing her own experiences and beliefs. After her Bible study ended, she felt called by God to continue to share her message, and so she decided to start a blog. In describing this decision, she gives credit to a higher power rather than to her own abilities or credentials: "I know that I have a heart to encourage, so I think God wanted to use me in this particular way." Lisa describes *encouragement,* not leadership, as her calling from God.

In her blog, Lisa draws from personal experience to weave messages about morality into discussions about sexuality. This is a common strategy for book authors, too, but blogging allows Lisa, as she described above, to use her stories to connect immediately and directly with her audience. Lisa begins one blog post by reminiscing about a conversation she had with her mother on the differences between men and women. Lisa was feeling exhausted from the never-ending tasks of being a homemaker, and she asked her own mother why it seems that husbands don't feel the same way. Her mother replied that "women just *see* more that needs to be done." Lisa agreed with that, and in the post, she gives her readers some examples: "As wives and mothers, we do see so much that needs to be done. Dishes to wash. Stained clothes to soak. Toy cars to pick up. Etc. Etc. Etc." And then comes the punch line: "I'm sorry, but I've got to call you on these excuses. If you are trying to do it *all* before you have sex, you are lying to yourself. That's the way it is. You are finding ways to avoid being intimate with your husband. That will ground its way into your marriage, and you do not want it to." Lisa passes judgment on those who make excuses to avoid sex, but she does it in the way a friend might. She writes informally, couching her judgment in language that is both apologetic and full of conviction. The remainder of the post centers around the theme of sympathizing with women who feel daunted by their to-do lists (Lisa admits that she also often feels this way) but reprimanding women who use this "lie" to avoid sex.

Less than twenty-four hours after she added this post to her blog, one of her readers, Don, posted a comment and plea: "THANK YOU! This is so true (from a man's perspective at least). I wish I could get my wife to read this. How will she change? Her priorities have been wrong for years. PLEASE HELP!" Two hours later, Lisa replies. She thanks Don for his comment and offers some general tips on how he and his wife might communicate better. She closes by humbly acknowledging, "these are just some ideas," and then offers an opportunity for Don's wife to contact her directly: "If she wants to email me to have another woman to talk with, I'm open to this. Sometimes that can help in working through obstacles and embracing a new outlook." Lisa, who positions herself as just "another woman" offering "some ideas," opens up dialogue between her and her readers in a way that casts her as one of them. Over the next two days, comments poured in from readers sharing their thoughts about Lisa's post and also about Don's dilemma. These readers offered their own advice to Don, always situating it within their own experiences. One reader, RK, commented, "Don, I really admire your commitment to your wife and marriage. I would suggest don't make evening activities about sex every night. Speaking as a wife, if I feel like my husband is using something as a ploy to get sex, I'm resistant even when I don't want to be." Lisa, RK, and Don all related to each other: Lisa started by speaking of her own history; Don agrees with Lisa but has a wife who doesn't; and RK is a wife who can relate to both Lisa and Don's wife and attempted to find a middle ground to offer Don realistic advice about his circumstances.

Website creators are uniquely accessible when offering Christian sex advice. Don could find advice similar to Lisa's or RK's in any number of sex advice books. For example, in his book *Sheet Music,* Kevin Leman makes a point similar to RK's comment, instructing men to "Show emotional interest in your wife. Curb your appetites long enough to get emotionally involved with your wife."[11] But if Don read this advice in the book, he would not have been able to retort, "I've tried that, and it's not working!" like he was able to do in the comments section of Lisa's blog. Creators of Christian sexuality websites are different from the popular evangelical authors who write sex advice books, and they emphasize that fact.

As the example from Lisa's blog suggests, Christian sexuality websites also differ from popular evangelical literature by giving a distinct voice to women. Men almost always author evangelical sex advice books, if not as single authors then as husband and wife teams in which they usually take the lead. Shannon Ethridge, Linda Dillow, and Lorraine Pintus, although frequently mentioned in this book and on Christian sexuality websites, are outnumbered by their male counterparts.[12] Yet the gender distribution of people who create Christian sexuality websites is quite different. Women appear to have much control of the web; they make up a disproportionate number of bloggers and online sex toy store owners. Of the blogs in my study, eight are run by women, four are run by men, and four are run by husband-and-wife teams. Of the sex toy stores, twelve are operated by husband-and-wife teams and five are operated by women.[13] None of the online stores in my study were solely operated by men, probably due to what Holly described at the beginning of the chapter about men's perceived weaknesses when it comes to pornography.

The significant number of women running these sites supports the gender-equal language that is a hallmark of the logic of godly sex, but it does not offer substantial authority to women over men. Women who start up their own blogs or sex toy stores do so as a service to God, not because they feel they have specific expertise on the subject of sex. Blogger Maribel explained to me that she started her website to "share" what she's learned from her own marriage. A couple of years after she began blogging, she started to feel overwhelmed by the amount of emails she received asking her for advice. She decided to set up an online payment system so that she could be compensated for the time she spent writing to her readers. In describing this decision, however, Maribel repeatedly emphasized that she does not consider herself a professional authority on sex:

> I was spending several days in a row working on one person's issue and emailing back and forth with them, and I'm not a licensed marriage counselor or

anything like this or a therapist, but I just needed to be compensated for my time a little bit to move people up the line who specifically needed more help. Generally, I refer people to a counselor. I say, "You should go talk to a therapist, but I'm happy to give you my input." So it [the compensation] was kind of a little supplement to help me get the people who really wanted desperately somebody to talk to. I think a lot of times women need to hash it out with somebody.

Maribel, like other bloggers, emphasized the value of sharing and listening and stressed the fact that this required no expertise. And like Holly and Samantha, other store owners I interviewed, Maribel framed what she sells (her time and attention) as a "supplement" to help in Christians' marriages, something extra that could help couples along. If professional advice is the cake, Maribel's support is the icing.

Website creators reinforce a piety that is personal rather than prescriptive, ordinary rather than expert. All of the creators I interviewed emphasized the importance of sharing pieces of their individual stories with website users. Maribel, for example, says very little about herself on her "About Me" page—only that she is a married Christian woman who loves God and her husband. Yet her posts reveal tidbits about her life: she is a mom; she leads a women's group at her church; she and her husband are relatively newly married. We also learn mundane details about her life: she is a horrible dancer, likes to cook, and doesn't like her downstairs neighbors. This information gives readers a sense that they are reading the stories and advice of a real person—someone who is who she says she is and with whom they can relate. The creators of BTS, John and Barbara, told me that website users "want to know there is a real person there," and that's why they reveal certain facts about their lives that are unrelated to their faith or sexuality, such as where they live, their political leanings, their hobbies, and their reading interests. Maribel, John, and Barbara do not cast themselves as authority figures over website users; instead, they portray themselves one of them, sharing in all of life's joys and tedium.

Many website creators choose not to disclose any identifying information (such as their names or photographs of themselves) on their sites. Of the eight website creators I interviewed, only half gave their names on their websites, and only about 30 percent of all sites in my study (eleven out of thirty-six) included their creators' first and last names. Some creators I spoke with said that protecting their real-life relationships was their motivation for keeping their online activity private. Holly, the owner of StoreOfSolomon.com, is open with many of her friends and family members about how she makes a living, but she doesn't disclose her identity on the site. She explained to me that even though she is not ashamed of her business, she realizes that some people might make assumptions about her character based on what she does. "I need time to explain what I do. If I don't have time to explain what I do, I don't broadcast it. It isn't the same at a PTA meeting as saying you sell Mary Kay [cosmetics]." Holly feels that others in her community (like fellow members of a Parent Teacher Association) might pass judgment on her based on how she makes a living, which is very different from a seemingly innocuous and uncontroversial career of selling cosmetics. Kitty, the pen name of a blogger on LustyChristianLadies.com, told me that she and her fellow bloggers intentionally keep their identities private: "We feel that it is enough for the readers to know our love for God and our message through our writing without needing to show them pictures of ourselves or tell everyone our names." Instead of using photographs of themselves and their real names, these bloggers use cartoon avatars as their profile pictures and make up pseudonyms for themselves, such as Kitty, Bunny, and Chariot. Some website creators do not identify themselves on their sites because, in their minds, it is their Christian message that is important, not their identities.

By de-emphasizing the importance of their identities, website creators frame the work they do on their sites as undeserving of high praise or personal glory. Instead, they justify their sites by stating that they were simply driven to answer God's call. They believe that God uses the Internet to reach Christians who need to receive important information about sexuality. The owners of one online store, Corinthians.com, share on their homepage that they created their business to "help the body of Christ through education and provision of written, audio, or video material and also more literal means of help through marital aids." They go on to say that married coupes who "become more intimate with each other" will also become more intimate with Christ. These kinds of declarations insist that Christian sexuality websites serve the ultimate evangelical project—helping others become closer to Jesus—vis-à-vis helping couples have good sex in their marriage. Bloggers and owners of online stores refer to the work they do in creating and managing their sites as forms of *ministry* and *service,* not unlike missionary work in a foreign country or a soup kitchen run by a church. WeddingNights.com's creator, Lisa, explained why she decided to start her blog by stating, simply, "God wanted to use me in this particular way."

All of the website creators I interviewed talked about their relationships with God and, more specifically, the *conversations* they had with God about creating their sites. Ann, who created Corinthians.com with her husband, described God literally stirring her from sleep to start her on the path to establishing her online sex toy store:

> After the birth of our first child, I had a hard time feeling intimate with my husband. I went online to try to find something to kind of jump-start things and was disgusted by what I was filtering through just to add some spice to my marriage bed. A year later, I was lying in bed thinking and praying about the same topic when the Lord put it on my heart to do something about it. I woke my husband and told him, and we ended up staying awake for hours discussing ways to offer intimacy products for married couples like ourselves.

Ann insisted that the idea to start her online business was not her own, rather it was God who put the idea "on her heart." She explained that she relies on God's will, rather than her own, when contemplating the future of her business: "I do not care if the business is gone tomorrow; it is actually a lot of work some days. I just lay it down before Jesus each day for Him to direct it as He may, and He continues to bring people to us for help." By detaching herself from the outcome of her business and emphasizing that God controls her life, Ann frames her store as a reflection of her Christian values and distances herself from critiques of her business.

Calling their sites a ministry is more than a metaphor for some website creators, even if they are not ordained ministers. John and Barbara, for example, accept donations to maintain BetweenTheSheets.com and have added the site to a division of a national evangelical organization so that it is a tax-exempt ministry. In order to create Samantha's, the online sex toy store, founder Samantha was awarded a custom website design by a company that builds a complementary website for a different ministry each year. She explained how owners of the company followed her journey on the BTS message boards and responded to her interest in starting her business: "I got a private message from these people that said, 'We have a website-building company and once a year we do a pro bono site for a ministry. If you could offer the full range of these kinds of products [sex toys] but in a non-pornographic way, we would really think that's a ministry, so we would like to offer our web-development services.' And I said, 'Well, my gosh, I accept, yes.'" The owners of the company who created Samantha's website believed her work to be a ministry, albeit an unconventional one.

The piety that Christian sexuality website creators construct on their sites is utterly *personal*—whether they create it through sharing anecdotes from their lives and relationships; emphasizing their "ordinariness"; or describing their intimate conversations with God about His call to create the sites. Protestant Christian beliefs demand a personal relationship with Jesus that is up to the individual, and the logic of godly sex applies similar spiritual reasoning to matters of sexual ministries. Website creators see themselves as called and inspired by God, and this way of thinking enables them to rationalize and validate their websites and businesses. The logic of godly sex appears when these website creators justify explicit discussions about sex by citing their piety and faith in God. This excludes online discussions led by those without this piety.

I will now examine another form of exclusivity: how the marriage relationship uniquely situates Christian couples to discuss sexuality online.

MARITAL EXCEPTIONALISM

Though a money-making business, MarriageLoveToys.com boldly and unapologetically turns away some potential customers. Visitors to the site find this message clearly displayed on the homepage: "This site should NOT be viewed if you are unmarried! Only married couples should view these products as they are intended to be used for sex as God intentionally designed it: for husband and wife." The owners of the site feel that limiting their customer base to align their business model with their religious beliefs is more important than potential profit. Similarly, creators of other sites usually offer guidelines for how they envision their sites to be used, and these often state explicitly that their sites are intended exclusively for married couples (both husbands and wives). Before becoming a member of BetweenTheSheets.com, users must agree to the site's terms of use, which include confirming that they are married or soon-to-be married. John and Barbara informally encourage both husbands and wives to join the site, and they advise users who look at the message boards alone to disclose their online activity to their spouses. Couples who are engaged (with a "ring and a date") but not yet married are restricted to posting in the "Engaged" section of the site. Attempting to restrict an online audience is similar to the efforts of some popular evangelical authors to control who reads their books. For example, in his book *Sheet Music,* Kevin Leman offers reading guidelines that differ for single and married readers, instructing his single audience to read only the first half of the book.[14]

Website creators use marriage, which they consider to be a spiritually exceptional relationship, to justify the sexual content on their sites. Their logic goes like this: since God allows married couples, and married couples only, to *have* sex, God also allows married couples, and married couples only, to *think* and *talk* about sex. *Doing, thinking,* and *talking* are inevitably linked *within* a marriage relationship, as website creators emphasize that couples must communicate and contemplate in order to have good sex. But thinking and talking about sex also extends *beyond* a marriage relationship to include others within the Christian community. Website creators treat the marriage relationship as a holy and exceptional form of religious devotion, constructing a form of spiritual capital I call *marital exceptionalism*. This means that website users can participate on Christian sexuality sites while remaining faithful to their spouses because their marriages are the reference points they use to frame all thoughts, discussions, and actions related to sexuality.

Although website creators rely on personal stories and experiences to establish their personal piety, they take care to avoid what they deem to be overly personal details about their own sexual practices and interests. Creators reason that providing fewer details about their sex lives will make it less likely that website users will imagine their sexual activity. John and Barbara share their real names, personal photos, and an autobiography on their site, BetweenTheSheets.com, yet they are intentional about what they disclose and what they do not. They explained to me why they do not give many details about their intimate relationship: "We don't want people to use us as a standard. We want people to take the word of God and look at themselves against that standard, so we try to be as helpful as we can with some information about ourselves. People know that we're happily married and that we enjoy each other in the bedroom, but what we do specifically, we don't talk about." John and Barbara feel comfortable revealing some personal information about themselves, but they consider their specific sexual interests and activities to be off limits. They also instruct BTS members to take caution in choosing what to share on the site, suggesting a few questions for them to consider before posting: "Does this post invite people to imagine my spouse and/or myself naked and/or being sexual? Is what I'm posting offering information that is helpful to others?" John and Barbara use these questions to attempt to regulate what information is available to website users and to preemptively obstruct any sexual fantasies that could stem from discussions on BTS.

Individuals' imaginations are a double-edged sword for these conservative Christians. Despite attempts by website creators like John and Barbara, who censor the details of their sex life from viewers of their site, website users do inevitably confront sexual material outside of their actual sexual lives. On the one hand, evangelicals believe that imagination can lure an individual to sin if one has thoughts and fantasies that involve lusting after someone other than one's spouse. On the other hand, imagination is also what makes Christian sexuality websites useful, according to many website creators. Even if website users confront sexual details that exist beyond their physical realities, they are then able to apply those details to the activities within the reality of their own sex lives, and this can help enrich a couple's intimate relationship. For instance, Steel, an administrator of BTS, began a message board thread titled "Share Your Story," which was for couples to share how they came to find sexual satisfaction and pleasure in their marriage. He described the purpose of the thread as "edification"—meaning that couples could learn from and improve their own lives by reading the stories. This intention is evident in one member's reaction to another's story about designing a "sex room," a room used exclusively for marital intimacy: "I am lusting after this. In a good way. Really thinking hard how we could get this to work in our house . . ." Learning about a "sex room" gave this user ideas to enhance his own marital relationship. The concept of this "good kind" of lust reinforces the logic of godly sex, which allows for couples to talk explicitly about sex so long as it is firmly within the context of their marital relationships.

Website creators who write about sex believe that imagination helps within the context of marital exceptionalism but hurts in any other situation. Reinforcing the conviction that godly sex applies only to the *right kind* of relationships, imagination is appropriate and encouraged only when it is focused on sexually enticing and pleasing one's spouse. It is fundamentally inappropriate in all other sexual situations. This is why Chariot, a blogger for LustyChristianLadies.com, encourages women readers to take boudoir-style photographs of themselves to share with husbands. Boudoir photography, referencing the French term for a woman's private dressing room, allows women to pose in sexually suggestive ways, wearing little to no clothing. On LCL, Chariot invokes the imagination when describing her favorite setup for a photograph: "My favorite pose is seriously sensual. Lay on your back wearing bra and panties. Have the photographer straddle you and point the lens down so that the photograph looks as if your husband is on top of you. HOT! HOT! HOT!" Chariot says that the image is effective because of its positioning, which allows the recipient of the photo, her husband, to imagine that he is on top of her, his wife. This makes the image "seriously sensual" while remaining appropriate within the guidelines of Chariot's faith.

Another blogger, Mae, who writes the blog FaithfulFantasticFun.com, approaches boudoir photographs with slightly more reservations than Chariot but ultimately believes they can be a part of a Christian marriage. She writes, "I don't think it's wrong if someone else sees you naked. Think about it—we show off as much to the bikini waxer and the spray tan attendant, but I'd be really careful about choosing someone [as a photographer] and make a plan so that no one else gets a hold of those photos." Mae doesn't question the morality of posing nude when it is necessary to the process of maintaining cultural standards for personal grooming, so she doesn't make boudoir photography off limits either. However, Mae encourages women to remember that these photographs are *representations* of sensuality and that they shouldn't replace sex in marriages: "Yes, it's fun, but it's not intimacy. You don't want your husband lusting after a picture of you. You want him lusting after YOU. The picture can be an appetizer. It's a preview of the main course." As Mae puts it, photographs (and, by extension, other forms of sexual fantasy) can do important work within a couple's marriage by "previewing" a real sexual encounter. Erotic images within a marriage relationship become one possibility available to the sexual repertoires of Christian couples in the quest for godly sex.

The imaginative possibilities when it comes to marital sexuality are what fuel one online business, GodOfLove.com, which sells customized erotic stories for married couples. The owners noted the popularity of erotica and explained why people find it appealing: "Some *non-Christian* therapists suggest that erotica can help get couples eager for intimacy. They may suggest sexually explicit fiction or even films." These Christians understand the appeal of erotica, which can add excitement to the tedium of everyday life and help individuals get turned on. They even suggest that trained authorities, such as therapists, would recommend the practice. Yet GodOfLove.com cautions Christians against using secularly produced erotica: "Nearly every Christian pastor would firmly disagree with this approach. There are too many risks and disadvantages of [secular] sexual books or videos." These risks stem from the fact that consuming erotica typically means that one imagines the people in the story, people other than one's spouse. GodOfLove.com notes, "while the emotions can be there, the intimacy with your spouse is not. These can pull people onto a possibly destructive path of unrealistic illusion." Here, GodOfLove.com has constructed a dilemma for conservative

Christians: erotica can help add excitement and arousal but is ultimately off-limits in its commonly found, secular form. This is where GodOfLove.com provides a Christian solution, offering personalized erotic stories for married couples.

Like Christian proponents of boudoir photography, GodOfLove.com distinguishes between godly and sinful fantasies. Those that involve just husband and wife as leading characters are okay, while those that involve anyone other than a husband and wife are not. "At GodOfLove, we believe that fantasies are not sin if they involve just the married couple reading the story. Sexual imagination in this context can improve desire and prompt the great sex that God wants for Christian marriages." Far from committing sin, they contend, fantasizing about one's spouse actually improves a marriage relationship in a way that receives God's approval. The products the site offers provide a way for married Christians to fantasize about their spouses without relying solely on their own creativity. GodOfLove.com has created a series of templates for erotic stories that the owners personalize for their customers. Couples can purchase these stories for ten dollars a piece. They choose their story's "flame rating" (the higher the rating, the more explicit the story) and its theme (such as "vacation fun"). Customers fill out an extensive profile about themselves and their spouses, noting details such as their names, heights, and eye colors, as well as hobbies and favorite foods. The owners of the site, in the style of a Mad Lib, use this profile to fill in the details of the stories so that they include only characters that resemble the customers. The stories they present allow couples to have sexual fantasies in which they and their spouse are directly and specifically involved. The owners of GodOf Love.com frame their site as a service for fellow Christians that pleases God because it directs and enhances the Christian imagination within marriage, which enhances a couple's intimacy.

The creators of Christian sexuality websites believe that married Christians are given special permission by God to be sexual and experience pleasure, which gives them access to thoughts and deeds that they believe to be off limits to anyone else. Bunny, an LCL blogger, writes that "sex is a gift from God and something to be shared in fidelity between a husband and wife." Therefore, she believes that GodOfLove.com provides erotic stories "with a twist that we fully support." She explains that "in all of these stories, the man and woman are Christian and married." Much like the "innovators" sociologist Robert Merton describes in his theory of social deviance, creators of Christian sexuality websites have created an exceptional case in which they can achieve what they want—sex that is good *and* godly—through a range of means that remain deviant and unacceptable for all others.[15] So long as they remain within the confines of their own monogamous, heterosexual marriages, these Christians insist that they are free to consume and produce erotica, purchase sex toys, and even read about the sex lives of others on message boards. This marital exceptionalism establishes Christian sexuality websites as spaces that uphold religious values rather than undermine them. Website creators use this belief as a form of spiritual capital to make a place for themselves in the secular and sexualized spaces of the Internet, optimizing both the sexual pleasure and the sense of religious devotion of their users.

GOD'S OMNISCIENCE

Despite their best efforts to regulate who views Christian sexuality websites and to what ends, the creators of these sites cannot prevent their online content from being used for sinful purposes. This is true, of course, for evangelical sex advice books, as well, but online spaces exacerbate the problem of an unknowable audience. Anyone may stumble upon these sites—perhaps a friend shared a link to one of them on Facebook, or a Google search for "married sexuality" returned one of the sites as a top result. This is part of what makes the Internet seem risky. Advice given on Christian sexuality sites or sex toys purchased from online Christian stores may be used for sexual relationships not supported by the creators of these sites. Even Christian users of these sites may fall to temptation while reading posts and fantasize about someone other than their spouses. Language and images that seem utterly un-sexual (like a photograph of a car with its trunk open to accompany instructions for the sexual position "Doggy Style") can still connote sexual scenarios. Christian sexuality website creators cannot deny that their sites may—however unintentionally—provoke sinful thoughts.

Website creators must reconcile themselves with the unknowable uses of sexual content associated with their sites. How they do this has to do with the basic Christian belief that God is omniscient. This belief becomes a unique source of spiritual capital for believers who create Christian sexuality websites. Followers of God lack knowledge that God naturally possesses about other people's thoughts and intentions. Focusing on God's judgment, they assert their fundamental inability to control how others use their sites. They draw from biblical scripture—for example, 1 Samuel 2:3 (KJV), "For the

Lord is a God of knowledge, and by Him actions are weighed." Having established a sense of religious positioning through personal piety and marital exceptionalism, the creators of the sites reason that it is God's job, not their own, to do the regulatory work of monitoring and possibly punishing those who use Christian sexuality websites in ways other than they are intended.

Holly, owner of StoreOfSolomon.com, explained her relationship with her mostly unknown customer base: "What they choose to do with what they order is ultimately between them and God." When I commented that she didn't seem too concerned about not being able to monitor them, she responded, "I have a link [on my site] called 'Better Than Sex' that explains what it means to be a Christian and follow Christ. If someone comes to my site who isn't a Christian, my hope is that they would be exposed to a little bit of God's love."

Even though Holly excuses herself from accountability, she does take an opportunity to proselytize to any customers who are not Christians. Clicking on the site's "Better Than Sex" link produces a webpage that explains that visitors will be "saved" if they sincerely pray the following sinner's prayer: "Lord, Jesus, I need You. Thank you for dying on the cross for my sins. I open the door of my life and receive You as my Savior and Lord. Thank You for forgiving my sins and giving me eternal life. Take control of the throne of my life. Make me the kind of person You want me to be."

Then comes the question, "Did you pray this prayer?" Clicking "yes" opens a new webpage with the message: "Congratulations on your decision to accept Christ!" Messages about accepting Jesus Christ as savior make the appeal of evangelicalism all the greater to users of these sites. The sites promise not only that their users can have good sex like God designed but also that they will be guaranteed a spot in Heaven for all eternity. Cleverly masking a message about Christian salvation behind the enticing title "Better Than Sex," Holly shares her beliefs about being born again and exposes her customers to, as she puts it, "a little bit of God's love."

Like Holly, other website creators use their sites as a platform to share the gospel of Jesus Christ as they believe it, alongside their messages about godly sex. Samantha, for example, hopes that non-Christians who use her site will learn a Christian approach to marriage and intimacy: "I believe the offer of the gospel—life and health and healing—is an invitation to everyone. I don't want anyone to feel disqualified [from shopping at Samantha's], and if they happen to grow in their faith and take the next step, then that's cool, but I'm not an evangelist. I'm more like offering a positive alternative."

Samantha insists that she is "not an evangelist," yet her actions reflect an evangelical effort to work for the salvation of others. She endeavors to show the "positive alternative" that is available to non-believers and prays that they will "take the next step" and develop a relationship with Jesus. Just as evangelical churches routinely offer an "altar call" at the end of Sunday service providing an opportunity for any visitor or member to commit or renew his or her life to Jesus Christ, website creators give visitors what they need to embark on or continue their spiritual journeys.

Ultimately, though, website creators cannot know the relationships their users have with God, which means that they cannot control how users interact with their sites. They emphasize, in particular, that they cannot know or be in charge of when others sin. Individuals, website creators insist, are accountable only to God. A comment written by Bunny, a blogger for LustyChristianLadies.com, exemplifies this attitude: "For the man who can't handle how a woman modestly dresses up, who is so weak he will commit the sin of lust, I do not hold accountability for him. It is not my job to manage a man's sin. It is not my job to wear dowdy and drab clothes so that he can keep it together. His problem is not my problem." Like website creators who believe they use "proper" terms and images to discuss sexuality, Bunny believes that the way she chooses to dress falls within some undefined conception of modesty. She is not responsible for anyone who may be tempted to sin by what she deems to be modest, just as Christian sexuality website creators reject accountability for anyone who uses their sites in ways they deem inappropriate or sinful. Such users have "a problem with lust" that website creators "cannot control."

Website creators use the familiar evangelical Protestant belief that individuals are accountable only to an all-knowing God to excuse themselves from the responsibility of monitoring how their sites are used. This means their sites may be complicit in sins committed by users without reducing the creators' confidence that their sites are authentically Christian. As an effective form of spiritual capital, God's omniscience creates a division among those who use Christian sexuality websites. It legitimizes the actions of website creators as good and holy and delegitimizes the actions of those who use the sites for sin, considering their actions beyond the control of creators of the sites.

The combination of personal piety, marital exceptionalism, and God's omniscience supports the foundations of godly sex and God's approval of Christian sexuality websites. To illustrate the way these beliefs are simultaneously cited by the creators of these websites in justifying their work, I conclude this chapter by examining how Samantha, owner of the eponymous online sex toy store, overcomes the obscenity involved in selling sex toys. Because many sex products contain labels that include nude models simulating intercourse, some owners of Christian sex toy stores remove the instructions or simply do not offer those products. Samantha, however, works directly with companies to alter these images. One product, for example, required an instruction manual that included pornographic images: "We took the photos and traced them and rendered them as line art so that the product is still in color but the model or couple are a black and white line drawing. It's educational, but it's certainly not titillating. Nobody's going to 'get off' on our line art! But they can certainly now see what's available and what's possible." Samantha transformed a secular and sexually explicit product into one that she could confidently sell in a Christian setting, simply by replacing real photographs with line drawings. Like the instructional images in sex advice books, these illustrations of sexual acts bypass being labeled pornography because they are not realistic depictions of people.

I pushed Samantha on this conclusion: How does she reconcile having to look at the pornographic images in order to make the line art? Can she really claim that the image does not titillate simply because the photographs were removed? After all, the images still depict a couple having sex. Samantha paused for a moment before responding,

> I knew there were people from BTS that really indicated a desire to purchase these products, but they didn't want to purchase them from a porn-supporting place. And it was our desire to offer this product to people, and for me personally, I don't feel triggered by these images. I don't have a problem with sexual addiction, and this was a way that we could serve people. People can get these products from me or a porn store. I'm glad they can get them from me in a non-porn, classy place. As for the line drawings, these are representations of people. We made them *not* real people. They could be you and your husband. Or, if you're not married, they could be you with your future husband on a really awesome honeymoon. If you think differently, well, it is not my job to be the Holy Spirit and convict people. My job is to love

people and to help them and let God do the work to convince them and change them. I completely reject that as my role.

Her response is representative of how evangelical website creators as a whole justify their online presence, cementing the new logic of godly sex within their evangelical framework.

Samantha's reasoning can be divided into three parts. First: "It was our desire to offer this product to people, and for me personally, I don't feel triggered by these images. This was a way that we could serve people." Samantha points to a higher calling—a higher good—that justifies exposing herself and her assistant to pornographic images. She deploys personal piety as spiritual capital. She believes that she has been called by God to do this service and is therefore protected by Him in her actions (she claims that she does "not feel triggered" by the erotic images she sees). Ultimately, she describes her work as selfless, explaining that she does it for the good of others rather than for personal gain.

Second: "These are representations of people. We made them not real people. They could be you and your husband. Or, if you're not married, they could be you with your future husband on a really awesome honeymoon." Samantha points to an imaginative potential that is protected by God so long as it remains in the context of an individual's own marriage—or even of a future marriage. Using marital exceptionalism as spiritual capital, she argues that there is a qualitative difference between the line art used on her site and actual photographs. The institution of marriage has an exceptional power when it comes to thinking about and writing about sex. By framing online images within this framework, Samantha is able to find religious support for the work she does.

Third: "It is not my job to be the Holy Spirit and convict people. My job is to love people and to help them and let God do the work to convince them and change them. I completely reject that as my role." Samantha excuses herself from being responsible for those people and thoughts she cannot control, who may use the images she provides to conjure up fantasies about someone other than their spouses. In this instance, she uses God's omniscience as spiritual capital. Using a familiar Christian belief—that God is the ultimate judge of individual action and intention—she distances herself from the potential consequences of selling sexual products to anonymous customers.

Ultimately, Samantha said that her business strategy is simple: "A lot of prayer. A lot of prayer." Yet website creators like Samantha must actually do much more than pray to validate their identities as sex-loving Christians. They justify their sites using familiar religious knowledge: (1) God protects and guides the actions of those who are faithful (personal piety); (2) God grants married couples special privileges when it comes to sex (marital exceptionalism); and (3) God holds individuals accountable for their sins (God's omniscience). As we have seen, the logic of godly sex allows the evangelicals who run Christian sexuality websites to position themselves in ways that align with secular, sexualized culture rather than simply opposing it. While they will never have religious authority akin to that of Billy Graham, they ultimately don't need it—instead, they engage in new media, using subtle markers to demonstrate their status, simultaneously upholding major evangelical tenets and extending what is considered possible within a conservative Christian worldview.

Religious persons who create virtual communities have unique opportunities to shape the meaning of religious expression. In this way, their online communities display similar beliefs to those of evangelical churchgoers, which cultural anthropologist Omri Elisha describes as reflecting "varying degrees of *plasticity* as well as constancy."[16] Individuals who prescribe to Christianity are at least somewhat limited in the kinds of spiritual capital (religious knowledge and dispositions) they express, since the religion has well-established beliefs and customs that have been developed over two thousand years. Yet *lived religion,* online or otherwise, confronts, as Elisha writes, "a host of quotidian dilemmas, aspirations, innovations, and frustrations that are not always easily explained (or dismissed) by a single, cohesive, uniformly authorized system of doctrine."[17] Online religion in particular allows website creators to construct new forms of participatory religious expression; they are able to shape what religion looks like, how it is practiced, and how their beliefs affect daily life.[18] It is this balance between tradition and innovation that makes the logic of godly sex so compelling: it reinforces believers' religious beliefs while extending the possibilities of their sexual lives. In the following chapters, I shift my focus from the creators of Christian sexuality websites to the users of these sites to show how they, too, draw from religious beliefs to talk about sex online.

THREE

Virtual and Virtuous

FORMING ONLINE RELIGIOUS COMMUNITIES

Wyoming, a forty-eight-year-old teacher living in New England, had never visited an online message board before he started reading BetweenThe Sheets.com (BTS) in search of advice that would help his marriage. He got married later in life than most of his friends, when he was forty-one. After being married for a couple of years, he began to experience difficulties becoming erect for sexual encounters, which strained his relationship with his wife. In addition to the doctors and pastor he consulted, Wyoming started searching online for insight from other people like him. "I wanted to see if there were suggestions and answers that came from a religious perspective," he told me. "You can find all sorts of ideas about sex on the Internet, but many are not respectful of faith."

After finding BTS, Wyoming lurked for some time. Skeptical of a website with anonymous users claiming to be a Christian place to discuss sexuality, he checked the message boards almost daily and followed several discussion threads that interested him, about other men who experienced erectile dysfunction and had difficulties reaching orgasm. Gradually, he accepted that BTS was what it claimed to be—a site for people who were devoted to God and who openly discussed their sexual problems—and he became a member. When I asked him why, he replied, "I guess I felt like, 'Now I have a sense of the way that people talk here, the limits of conversation,' and felt comfortable that the environment was safe to discuss things." He paused momentarily before continuing, "I think I just started wanting to be a part of that community."

Wyoming pointed to what have long been recognized by scholars as key markers of community: how people talk, and what they choose to talk about and not talk about. He recognized that *community* is more than a descriptor of people in groups; rather, it is a construction of shared meaning and expectations for how to live.[1] When I asked him to elaborate on what he meant by "community," Wyoming explained, "Well, I felt like people there respect each other and really care. It was just obvious from some of the prayer requests and the kind things people said to each other. And I wanted to feel some of that." *Feelings* are central to the community Wyoming describes; he *felt* like he knew the intentions of BTS members (they "respect each other and really care"), and he wanted to *feel* like BTS members respected and cared about him. To become a member of the site, Wyoming completed the online registration form. He chose "Wyoming" as a username, decided on a password, and filled out a brief profile about himself. Before he could finalize his registration, he was asked to confirm that he was married and a Christian. And then, with the click of a mouse, he became an active member of BetweenTheSheets.com, able to contribute to the online discussion.

BetweenTheSheets.com—a site that today boasts over 30,000 registered members and over 250,000 posts—had humble beginnings. In the late 1990s, its founders, John and Barbara, created an amateur webpage associated with an email Listserv that they moderated for Christians who wanted to discuss sexuality. Soon after, they transitioned the site to a small message board hosted by America Online (now AOL). Barbara explained why they made the switch: "We had some non-Christians come on and trash the original website, and we found that we were busy defending our faith rather than talking about marriage and sexuality, so part of the motivation for creating the boards was to create a safe space for Christians to talk about marriage. When it moved to the message board, I would say the sense of community really grew." John and Barbara now lead a team of other administrators that manages BetweenTheSheets.com, a message board that, in its current iteration, is heavily moderated and only allows members to post comments. The result, as Barbara, Wyoming, and other members described, is an online religious community, where Christians can feel comfortable discussing what they consider to be the most intimate matters—their sexual relationships and their relationships with God. As discussed in the previous chapter, John and Barbara use religious knowledge, what I describe as *spiritual capital,* to establish their site as authentically Christian. Website users, like the creators discussed in the last chapter, also use religious knowledge to perform their online identities.

Becoming a part of BetweenTheSheets.com takes more than simply registering as a member of the site. Wyoming and other users must prove that they are a part of the evangelical Christian community—*us* rather than *them*. Erving Goffman calls this "impression management"—when individuals attempt to "incorporate and exemplify" the values of society in any given situation, even if they exhibit contradictory behaviors in private.[2] He offers the example of an aristocratic woman who keeps prestigious magazines on her coffee table but reads romance novels in bed. Similarly, website users showcase the aspects of themselves that are most desirable in these online communities. The stories they tell, the language they use, and the people with whom they engage online all work to construct an online identity that is legitimately Christian. Rather than justifying the sites as *spaces* that are authentically Christian, website users draw from their beliefs to assert *themselves* as authentically Christian. Establishing an "authentic self" is a highly charged undertaking in online settings, where website users must interact virtually in ways that will prove they are "real."

Although online communities lack the spatial demarcations that typically define "real-life" communities, both establish and attempt to preserve boundaries between insiders and outsiders. Although some scholars have argued that the Internet provides equal access to users and therefore promotes diversity in unprecedented ways, others have shown how the Internet can be used to bolster exclusive communities made up of members who share strict sets of beliefs. Sociologist Robert Glenn Howard calls a group of fundamentalist Christian websites that he studied "self-regulated enclaves of like-minded believers."[3] He found that, rather than facilitating difference, these online religious communities actually reinforce what their users already believe. The fact that most members share the same beliefs makes it difficult for those with differing beliefs to join, even though practically speaking they may have access to the sites. This boundary making, what Paul Lichterman calls "group-building customs," relies on implicit assumptions that distinguish insiders from outsiders.[4] Establishing a sense of belonging within the communities formed on these sites allows them to construct boundaries between those who belong and those who don't.

As I outlined in chapter one, the logic of godly sex operates by suggesting that "anything goes" within straight Christian marriages. This creates a sense of openness and possibility for those who participate in Christian sexuality websites while drawing attention away from the boundaries that this online community affirms and perpetuates. One LustyChristianLadies.com (LCL) blogger, for example, explained to me that readers of the site include "a vast demographic—from men to women, liberal to conservative, feminist to submissive, Catholic to Protestant, young to old." It may be true that regular readers of LCL are a diverse group, but my survey and interview data do not support this claim. Of LCL readers who completed the CSIS, 84 percent were evangelical Protestant and 87 percent report that it is "always wrong" for two adults of the same sex to have sex. The authoritative voices on the site—the bloggers who post and the vast majority of readers who comment—support a very narrow definition of godly sex. The dominant perspective on this site and other Christian sexuality websites presents unambiguous and unanimous support of the defining traits of this sexual logic: heterosexuality, monogamy, and marriage.

The online performance of website users relies on these and other typical evangelical Protestant tropes to establish users as pious followers of God. These performances then reinforce the websites users are a part of, strengthening their status as Christian spaces, where online dialogue serves to make meaning of religion through the collective and exclusive interpretation of users. This chapter examines this trajectory: how users find Christian sexuality websites, become a part of them, and ultimately create new realities for religion through their online participation. I find that their contributions to these sites offer more than self-help and personal advice.[5] Through collaborative online discussions about their sexual problems and possibilities, users create a religious community that extends the logic of godly sex to affirm their sexual desires and interests.

FROM GOOGLING TO GATHERING

One can search the Internet to find responses to any of life's questions. Most of the website users I interviewed found Christian sexuality websites through online searches for information related to their sexual desires, practices, and problems. Often, they included they keyword "religion" in their searches, but no one I spoke with found the sites by looking for websites focused solely on religion. In other words, the most pressing questions of these individuals were about sex, not God. These users of BetweenTheSheets.com and LustyChristianLadies.com are similar to the majority of Americans who have searched the Internet for information regarding personal health, and their quests reveal a distinctly individualist use of the Internet.[6] Many respondents told stories similar to Sunshine, a member of BTS: "I did a Google search for orgasm difficulties, and [...] the main BetweenTheSheets website was near the top. I read through many articles on the site and then noticed a link to the forum, so I joined to get some Christian feedback on some difficult areas that my marriage bed was facing." Sunshine found BTS after searching for information related to a specific problem—orgasm difficulties—but later decided to participate more broadly in the site. Skeptical of Sunshine's claim that such a generic search that did not include any words related to religion would return BTS as a top result, I performed the Google search myself and indeed found the site near the top of the results page. Another respondent, Ella, told me that she found LCL after searching the Internet "to do research to spice things up in our marriage bed." Both Ella and Sunshine felt that information about sexuality was something they needed to retrieve from external sources. Their upbringing and experiences were inadequate in providing advice that would help them solve their sexual problems or make their sex lives more exciting.

The website users I interviewed expressed distrust of nearly all forms of non-Christian sex advice. Even websites that appeared decent but were moderated and used by non-Christians were considered to be potentially dangerous, as they could contain unwholesome advice or links to an "unsafe" website (one that includes pornography). One reader of LCL commented after finding the site, "I didn't think in this age of porn and filth that I would ever find a site like this. God bless each and everyone of you!" Samwise, a BTS member, explained to me that he specifically searched for "Christian sex advice" because most generic sex advice "borders on pornography." "I find it offensive," Samwise told me. "I don't want to be exposed to pornography but rather to wholesome advice that will strengthen my marriage." For him, the site's Christian identity ensures that its users will offer advice reflecting his own values.

When I asked BTS and LCL users why they didn't stick to offline resources, such as Christian books or trusted friends, for information about sexuality, many suggested that alternative resources hadn't crossed their minds. They cited reasons anyone might use to explain why they browse Facebook's newsfeed while enjoying a morning cup of coffee instead of reading the newspaper. The Internet is immediately accessible, culturally salient, and can easily be personally tailored to people's lives. One BTS member, who fittingly called himself PCSage, described himself as a "tech geek," who finds it "easy" to use the Internet to get "all sorts of information." It makes sense that individuals who are already online—checking email, participating in social media sites, and reading virtual newspapers and magazines—would search the Web for answers to pressing questions about sexuality. Mr_Jones, on the other hand, a forty-nine-year-old man with a full-time job and four children, reports that he doesn't have very much free time to surf the Internet. Yet, when I asked him why he decided to Google "Christian marriage," he responded, "I'm not sure. I guess I was just wondering about things that I was not discussing with anyone 'live,' and why not Google it? I found good wisdom there with anonymity." For Mr_Jones, the accessibility and ease of Internet searches and the anonymity online made it an obvious place for looking for Christian sex advice.

The possibility of anonymous but interactive exchanges gives the Internet advantages that other forms of Christian sex advice lack. Christian books can help readers in the privacy of their own homes, but they are prescriptive rather than collaborative. Conversations with Christian friends, family members, or religious leaders are interactive but often not well suited for honest disclosure about topics as sensitive as sexuality. BernardG, a long-time member of BTS, first heard the idea that God wants Christian couples to have satisfying sex when he and his wife were given two classic evangelical sex manuals as a wedding present. He describes *The Act of Marriage* and *Intended for Pleasure* as a "good starting point" but "not all that helpful," since the authors appeared out-of-touch with some of the realities of today's Christian couples. As an example, BernardG notes that they do not support oral sex, a practice he considers to be commonplace and acceptable within a Christian marital context.

BernardG has close real-life relationships with many other Christians, but he does not feel comfortable talking about sex with them. He and his family—a wife and five children—live in South America, where they work closely alongside other families as Christian missionaries. Although he would like to openly talk about sexuality with some of his friends, he doesn't:

> There are some aspects of sexuality that I think we can and should be able to talk about with IRL [in real life] friends. Unfortunately, not too many Christians are willing to talk about things like that, mainly because of squeamishness or the sense that sexuality is somehow sinful or tainted. Also, I think people are unwilling because they want to be private, which I understand. BTS allows for me to ask questions I would never ask anyone else. I quickly saw that it was a great community of people who loved God and also wanted to have great sex within marriage. You could talk about sex and you could do it anonymously and talk about things that you probably couldn't share with most IRL friends.

Reflecting the inhibition paradox I described in chapter one, BernardG laments that many Christians have the sense that sexuality is "tainted." To his surprise and delight, he found that BTS offered an anonymous way to interact with fellow Christians to openly and positively discuss their sexual lives. Using Christian sexuality websites does not replace users' real-life religious communities (website users who completed the CSIS attend church more frequently than evangelicals nationally, in fact).[7] Instead, Christian sexuality websites coexist with real-life religious communities, providing Christians with support for topics often not talked about in offline Christian settings.

The possibilities for interactive advice are also what drew Kylee2000 to the BTS site. Before finding it, she described herself as "desperate for help" to improve her sex life with her husband. Kylee2000 was forty-two and had been married for twenty-one years when I interviewed her. Throughout her marriage, she had struggled with having a higher sexual drive than her husband. She hadn't found helpful information in Christian sex advice books, since they tend to discuss men with high sexual drives and women with low libidos. "I had read *Sheet Music* and didn't find any help in that. It just perpetuated stereotypes," she explained. The book, which is frequently discussed on BTS, describes sexual encounters based almost entirely on generalized gender differences, with separate chapters for husbands and wives.[8] Kylee2000 joined BTS to try to find advice for her specific and seemingly unique situation.

Initially, Kylee2000 encountered the same stereotypes she had found in books on BTS. Shortly after she started posting to the site, another BTS member, a man whose wife had a low sex drive, accused her of being a man disguising himself as a woman. At first, she felt extremely discouraged about this encounter. "It was very disheartening," she told me. "I had just been very honest, but he really didn't believe my story. I don't think he was able to see past his own situation." Immediately following this exchange, however, several other BTS members came to Kylee2000's defense and offered her encouragement and support. They were wives who also wanted to have sex more frequently than their husbands and husbands who wanted sex less than their wives.[9] Kylee2000 began to have a private-message conversation with another woman who could relate to her. So after a contentious beginning on the site, she found herself engaging in meaningful discussions with members who offered advice and support. "This was the first time where people could relate to me and I could share in my frustration," she explained. Unlike books,

Christian sexuality websites allow their users to interact and glean advice that attends to their specific lives and relationships.

The BTS users I interviewed often continued to visit the site long after finding answers to the questions that had brought them there. Some of them had additional questions that they sought answers to within these online communities, but more often, they grew attached to the online networks and learned to contribute to them in ways that were personally fulfilling, like by sharing their personal experiences and advice with newer members. ThisIsMe, for example, found herself drawn to BTS because, as she explained, "the fact that these people were willing to talk about sex and be frank about everything and yet still show the love of Christ was intriguing." This intrigue gradually led her to become an active and long-term member of the site. Like many other long-time members I interviewed, ThisIsMe continued to check the site at least once every day, even though she had been a member of BTS for eight years: "There have been days I've spent many, many hours of the day on the boards just looking for different stuff. Now I check at least once a day, but if there is something I'm thinking about I will spend more time." Among those BTS and LCL users I interviewed, reading frequency did not drop for long-time website users. Rather, long-term members and readers continue to actively follow the sites, and in the case of many respondents, the longer they had followed the websites, the more frequently they viewed them.[10]

As BTS users grow increasingly committed to the site, some of them form relationships with members in other online settings or even in real life. Table 4 provides details about the online and real-life relationships related to BTS membership of those members I interviewed. The shading on the table indicates that members have more than one relationship with other BTS members; the darkest shading shows members with the most relationships. Although all interview respondents reported that they disclosed their Internet activity to their spouses, not all had partners who shared their interest in discussing sex in online Christian settings. Of the married BTS members I interviewed, half (twelve of twenty-four) reported that their spouses were also BTS members. The vast majority of BTS interview respondents (twenty-one of twenty-five) had used private messages on the site, engaging in one-on-one correspondence with another member. Some members (nine of twenty-five) had online relationships with other BTS members beyond the site—the most frequent example of this was Facebook friendships—and these members were also likely to have offline contact, like phone conversations or face-to-face meetups, with other members. Most interview respondents, however, had no

TABLE 4 Online and real-life relationships among BTS members, interview sample

BTS username	Spouse is a BTS member	Has messaged privately with other members	Has online relationships with BTS members outside the website	Has met members in real life
1999pq		X	X	X
4Christ	X	X	X	
Azaria		X		
BernardG	X	X	X	X
BoyNextDoor	X	X	X	X
Chloe	X			
ChristopherB		X		
Cody		X		
Colonel_Mustard		X		
ExodusGuy		X	X	X
Kylee2000		X		
Leia		X		
LoneStar		X		
Mr_Jones		X		
PCSage	X	X		X
PhoenixGirl	X	X		
Popeye		X	X	
Rebecca	X			X
Samwise	X			
Staccato	X	X	X	X
Steel	X	X	X	X
Sunshine	X	X		
ThisIsMe	X	X	X	
Wagner				
Y2K		X	X	X
Totals	48%	84	40	36
	(*n* = 12)	(21)	(10)	(9)

NOTE: The shading on the table indicates that members have more than one relationship with other BTS members; the darkest shading shows members with the most relationships.

contact with other BTS members beyond the site itself. Although online and real-life realities sometimes merge, the communities forged on Christian sexuality websites exist almost exclusively online.

While most of the off-site relationships I heard about between BTS members were the result of individual efforts, one long-time member and moderator of the site, David (who calls himself Steel online), decided to organize the first-ever face-to-face conference for BTS members to meet and discuss marital intimacy in person. David, a pastor, hosted the conference at his church and charged a small registration fee to cover lunch and dinner for attendees and travel costs for John and Barbara, the creators of BTS. In the months leading up to the conference, the message boards buzzed with excitement about the possibilities for this real-life exchange among members. While some members expressed reservations about encountering people in real-life with whom they had shared such intimate conversations online, most offered enthusiastic support for David's idea. Even if they couldn't attend the conference due to work schedules or location, many encouraged those who could to attend and asked for reports following the event.

In the end, there were only nine couples that traveled to the weekend-long conference, eighteen participants in total. I also attended. I arrived at David's church on a warm fall afternoon and soon realized that everyone looked as nervous and bewildered as I felt. The small size of the group made it impossible to get lost in the crowd, and couples stood around awkwardly in the church lobby before the first session began. Their online connections meant that, in a sense, the participants both knew and didn't know one another, and this made small talk seem just as out of place as more personal conversations. All participants included their "real names" on their name tags, and they introduced themselves as strangers would. "Hi. I'm Blake, and I'm from Euclid, Ohio, a suburb of Cleveland," I heard one man say to another. They talked about trivial things like the amount of time it had taken them to get to the event and what interstates they had used. It was after attendees started sharing their BTS member names that they began to warm to one another. "Oh!" one man exclaimed when he learned that Amy, the boisterous woman he had been talking to, was actually Butterfly from the boards. "You're not like I imagined you. I always thought that you would be someone soft spoken," he laughed to himself.

There was a stark contrast between the BTS meetup and the other face-to-face events I attended, like the Intimate Issues conference, where it seemed like many participants were hearing Christian speakers talk about sexual pleasure for the first time. At many times while sitting in on BTS conference sessions, I felt like speakers were "preaching to the choir," so to speak, because attendees seemed like they already knew and accepted what was being said. There was no debate, for example, when one speaker read aloud a passage from the Song of Solomon and then declared God's support of oral sex within marriage. Everyone seemed familiar with the interpretation. They all nodded their heads in familiarity when one speaker mentioned the popular book *Stripped Down,* which discusses one couple's challenge to have sex every day for thirty days.[11] No one was surprised, except for me, when David announced that the conference attendees' names had been automatically entered into a raffle to win a vibrating massager that was prominently displayed in its packaging at the front of the church sanctuary. Participants and speakers made jokes about sex and church and the differences between men and women. At one point, David exclaimed, "I couldn't talk like this on Sunday morning!"

The BTS conference allowed each person there to affirm what they already knew, that BetweenTheSheets.com is an online community of *real* people—people like them—devoted Christians who sing the same praise and worship songs, turn to the same biblical passages for guidance, and pray for their marriages and their sex lives. Throughout the conference, attendees affirmed the strength of the online BTS community. In their introductions, every attendee mentioned how important finding BTS was to the success of their marriage. "God bless each of you," one woman proclaimed, "especially John and Barbara. You have given the world such a gift." They focused less on the conference itself than on the fact that the BTS message boards had been a marriage-saving resource in their lives.

Website users who establish themselves as insiders within BetweenThe Sheets.com and LustyChristianLadies.com do so by emphasizing their *real* value, for example, by fostering authentic relationships online and offering practical advice and spiritual guidance that helps website users in their marriage relationships. Attempting to convey what it's like to be actively involved in the BTS message boards, user ExodusGuy told me, "Imagine a long-distance pen pal friendship. I'm almost fifty-three, and when I was a kid it was popular to get a pen pal, someone you never met who lives far away (even overseas), and just start writing... You pour out your heart. VERY close friendships are forged here at BTS. It's real even though it's virtual." ExodusGuy is one of BTS's earliest members, having participated in the site since it was a rudimentary Listserv about a decade ago. He is now an administrator and usually reads and posts to the site multiple times a day. He insists that BTS is a place where "real" relationships can be formed, despite their virtual context. It is a place where members share details about their personal lives and develop friendships with others who share their values. Although users of Christian sexuality websites often find these sites by searching for specific and individual problems, their collaborative use of the sites serves a purpose greater than their questions being answered. These sites are religious communities that collectively construct a logic of godly sex that supports the desires and interests of their users.

CREATING BOUNDARIES

The sense of belonging Christian sexuality websites cultivate is maintained by efforts to censor who posts to the sites and how they do it. This selection occurs, in part, through formal rules set forth by website creators. On BTS, a post written by Barbara, "Beliefs of the Board," outlines the explicit expectations of message board members: "Members must be married (one man, one woman), and followers of Jesus Christ and His Word. Jesus, and Jesus alone, is the ONLY way to salvation, and the Bible is the ultimate authority. The basic tenets of the Christian faith are not debatable issues, but minor theological differences will be gently accommodated." Barbara and the other administrators of BTS prioritize the foundations of evangelical beliefs— salvation through Jesus Christ and biblical inerrancy. In doing so, Barbara asserts that her belief system is representative of Christianity. She makes off limits, for example, "any defense of the practice of homosexuality, so-called 'gay marriage,' or the like" even though the acceptance of gays and lesbians is becoming an increasingly legitimate and visible topic of discussion in many Christian denominations.[12] All of the bloggers I interviewed screen comments before they post them, rejecting anything they consider inappropriate (mostly spam, but sometimes posts from users who stand in opposition to what Barbara defines as "the basic tenets of the Christian faith"). Website creators have the power to monitor and manage activity on their sites, which allows them to remove content that overtly challenges the logic of godly sex, shaping the sense of community that develops.

BTS and other Christian sexuality websites leave room for non-evangelical Christian believers to participate on the message boards to varying degrees. In the BTS forum called "The Bible and Sex," where users discuss and debate what Barbara calls "minor theological differences," members are generally accommodating of practicing Catholics, for example, whose interpretation of scripture may differ from Protestant members. The same goes for Protestants of various denominations whose beliefs have been shaped by particular religious teaching. However, administrators of BTS instruct members that the site does not support the Mormon faith. Members have referred to the religion as the "Mormon cult," and administrators remove any content that claims the Book of Mormon is inspired by God. Still, BTS administrators write that they will take members "at their word" if they claim to be Christian. This suggests that Mormons, Catholics, or any other self-identifying "Christian" can actively participate on the message board so long as they do not accentuate their theological differences and align themselves with beliefs that privilege heterosexuality, monogamy, and marriage in the context of sexuality.

As table 5 indicates, non-Protestants comprise a very small percentage of CSIS respondents from most of the websites that hosted the survey. Catholics and Latter-day Saints comprise between two and four percent of respondents from most of these websites. The notable exception is the blog MaribelsMarriage.com, where Mormons make up over half of survey respondents. Maribel identifies only as "Christian" on her site, but she explained to me that a popular Mormon blogger had recommended MaribelsMarriage.com as a resource for Mormon marriages. She was surprised to learn that, at least according to the CSIS, a majority of her readers were LDS, but she told me, "that doesn't really matter. I think, no matter what religion you are, it's just a basic belief in God and that marriage is important. All the principles are all the same. Sometimes you get caught up in, well this religion believes this and this religion believes this, but I think that all, or most human beings believe that strengthening your marriage is a positive thing. So I don't think it makes a difference on religion." Maribel describes the desire to strengthen one's marriage as an almost universal human condition, but she takes for granted that her audience will agree with her conservative definition of what marriage is. Just as users of Christian sexuality websites create a dialogue that reflects their beliefs, Maribel generalizes about religion and marriage in a way that reflects her own beliefs.

Website creators and users enforce boundaries through more than the formal guidelines presented on the sites about who should use them. John, cocreator of BTS, pointed out in his interview that "specific rules help us to corral those who are clearly out of line," but most often, moderating content requires more than making sure everyone follows the basic guidelines of the site. "Moderation is an art not so much a science. When people are walking the line, we give them the benefit of the doubt. We try to coach and teach people because a lot of people coming into the boards may or may not know reasonable etiquette—they may not know how to function well within this group. So if they're open to it, you can coach and help them through it." John explained that people deserve the "benefit of the doubt" when using the

TABLE 5 Religious affiliation of interview participants by referral website, CSIS sample

Website	Evangelical Protestant (%)	Mainline Protestant (%)	Catholic (%)	Latter-day Saint (%)	Other or none (%)
LovingBride.com	81	13	3	3	0
LustyChristianLadies.com	84	9	3	2	1
LovingGroom.com	81	11	3	4	1
MaribelsMarriage.com	22	11	4	60	2
BetweenTheSheets.com	83	14	3	0	0
StoreOfSolomon.com	81	12	5	2	0
WeddingNights.com	78	17	2	0	3

NOTE: Because of rounding, some totals do not equal 100 percent.

message boards, since the online community expects a certain type of online "etiquette." This etiquette involves implicit social norms in addition to the explicit rules listed on the site. Website users display etiquette on the sites not only by posting content that is clearly Christian but also by conveying personalities that are credible and authentic to evangelicals and other conservative Christians. These personalities are basic criteria that users employ to prove that they are actual people sitting behind the computer screen—*real* people with interests, relationships, and struggles.

Chloe, a thirty-eight-year-old woman who had been married for nine years, found BTS a year prior to our interview after a friend referred her to BTS cocreator Barbara's personal blog, LovingBride.com. In our interview, Chloe brought up the lessons she learned in the past year about gaining acceptance to this online community:

> I think it takes a long time to actually "break into" the community [at BTS]. [. . .] I think the "long-time" BTS members are very wary of new folks; they protect the old folks like close friends [. . .] and are wary of someone coming on to stir up contentious issues. Even though I'm fairly new, I will not respond right away to a seemingly "strange" [. . .] question from a "newbie" unless a few others have responded. Especially if the question isn't very clear—like it's not coming from their real life.

Chloe explained the gatekeeping she observed and the effort it takes for a new member to become a part of the BTS community. Regular users of

Christian sexuality websites must work to make themselves known and accepted in these anonymous online settings. This process helps them feel like they are a part of these online communities and inadvertently forms boundaries between insiders and outsiders. Users who have participated in the site since its inception over a decade ago feel "like close friends." New users have to learn to recognize which questions are "strange" or "contentious."

Long-time BTS members generally expect new posters to share a certain amount of personal or background information in their first few posts. New posters who do not do this breach online etiquette and encounter significant scrutiny. Chloe told me about one post where a new user created a poll asking about frequency of oral sex: "They [the original poster] asked their question but left no information about themselves, didn't answer their own question. [. . .] Almost too much anonymity. Like two fifteen-year-old boys got on, thought it would be cute to get all these married people to post about [oral sex]. [. . .] Things like that give one pause on a new post."

Chloe was wary of a thread started for ambiguous purposes, where the motives of the original poster were unclear. Had the question been posed in a different context—if, for example, a married man who stated to the group that he would like to have oral sex more frequently had posted it with the clear intention of gauging how often the practice takes place in others' marriages—the outcome may have differed. On this particular thread, however, other members refused to engage with the original poster. Another similar thread started by a new member asked bluntly: "Men, what's the worst thing you've done and been forgiven by your wife?" One long-time member answered the question and then immediately added a follow-up post: "Sorry, I didn't notice that this was your first post. Welcome to the boards. Interesting first topic. Why are you curious about what we've done?" The original poster never returned to better introduce himself, and the exchange served as an example to other new or potential members of what *not* to do in a first post. No other member posted to the thread.

ESTABLISHING INSIDERS

Even though they do not all identify as evangelicals, BTS members must find ways to integrate tropes of evangelical Protestantism into their online presentations in order to gain credibility on the site. In this context, personal piety serves as a form of spiritual capital that reinforces an implicit hierarchy among BTS members, just as it does for website creators. Some users have more of a sense of belonging than others. Becoming a respected member of BTS doesn't require formal training in divinity. Rather, reflecting a broader trend within evangelicalism that gives unique authority to the laity, users of Christian sexuality websites gain respect by drawing upon their individual convictions regarding their beliefs about sexuality. Common phrases on blogs and message boards like, "after prayerful consideration, I've decided that..." or, "my personal conviction of that scripture is that..." suggest that individual believers need only their individual faith to make important decisions regarding their beliefs about sex and how to act on them. The online personas that website users create are grounded in personal piety that shows that God is an active participant in their lives. They prove that their individual histories "add up" to authentic Christian identities, that their questions are sincere efforts to strengthen their marriages, and that they are qualified—through their faith alone—to offer advice and feedback to fellow members. All members of the site whom I interviewed used references to their personal spiritual journeys to position themselves within the online community.

If we think about online posts as stories, website users choose characters and plot lines that resonate with an evangelical worldview. God, Jesus Christ, and Satan have leading roles, and narrative arcs often involve overcoming sin and accepting salvation. One of the first ways that website users establish themselves as insiders is by talking casually and intimately about God, which is typical of contemporary evangelical discourse.[13] They often write about "conversations" they have with God or, in reference to their prayer lives, times when they "talked" with God. For evangelicals, prayers are not simply messages they send out to a distant deity; rather, God responds to prayers in ways that believers can recognize. One reader on LCL responded to another reader's question about her low sex drive: "Make time to talk to Him [God], and see what He has to say about it." By talking about God in this way, website users show others that they hold particular religious beliefs and that they are personally devoted to Jesus Christ.

In addition to users encouraging one another to pray, the websites themselves become places of prayer for their Christian users. On one message board thread started by Gwendolyn about her husband, who she says watches pornography and has not been saved, member SallyH comments with a prayer: "Father, you came to bring us life. You came to bring Gwendolyn life.

You came to bring her husband life. And freedom and healing. Out of darkness. Please comfort our sister. Speak to her. Remind her that you know what's going on, and you want freedom for both of them." Her punctuation creates the cadence of a prayer. Her words make it seem as though everyone who reads the post is praying for Gwendolyn alongside SallyH. Instead of addressing Gwendolyn in the post, she addresses a higher power. In doing so, she reveals her belief that God is an active participant in Christian marriages. She also makes it clear that she believes there are possibilities for prayer beyond the bedside or church walls.

A second way that users can confirm a place within Christian sexuality websites is to mention Satan and the hold he has over the secular world. This message reflects evangelicals' broad emphasis on the spiritual battle between Christians and the devil, which they believe is fought in daily life, even—and especially—in a couple's bedroom. Indeed, Satan is considered an active threat to Christians' sex lives. "Satan" is mentioned on the BTS message boards over one thousand times. One LCL reader expressed her belief that Satan actively attempted to ruin her (sex) life: "My husband and I have both discovered how our past sinfulness got in the way of what God wants for us. We love each other deeply but Satan is crafty. We couldn't know what we were missing by not letting God be a part of our sexuality." This reader reveals her evangelical beliefs through the ways in which she framed her sexual experiences: the problems she and her husband faced were caused by a "crafty Satan," and the solution to these problems was to incorporate God into their intimate relationship. Referencing Satan is a reminder that, for evangelicals, all of life's events culminate in a path of eternal salvation or damnation.

A third way website users can establish a sense of belonging is by telling salvation stories. For evangelicals, these conversion narratives are quite commonplace and highly formulaic, describing the teller's transformative journey from sin to salvation.[14] Website creators and users do not claim to have perfect records when it comes to sexual morality. In fact, disclosing former sexual sins, followed by redemption through Jesus Christ, can help create a believable online persona. Message board threads are frequently started by a member who is struggling with (or whose spouse is struggling with) a sexual problem, often involving sinful behavior. Responses almost always start with an expression of sympathy, other members telling the original poster that they, too, were once in their shoes. In a thread where a member asks the group how to overcome an addiction to pornography, the first respondent comments: "You can win, Jesus can heal and overcome this. I spent twenty-two years as a Christian still in chains. It's God's grace that rescues us." Posts combining sympathy with a tale of salvation allow website users to connect with one another while revealing their religious commitments.

Evangelicals using Christian sexuality websites believe that being saved is directly related to one's sexual and marital relationship. On one BTS thread, a member consoles the original poster, DBalle, who fears that his wife, who isn't a Christian, is having an emotional affair: "Most of all (as if it isn't obvious), I'll be praying for your wife's salvation." This poster almost seems to suggest that all of the problems that DBalle faces are inconsequential given that his wife is not a Christian. One long-time BTS member, AngelBoy, responded in a similar way to the thread created by Gwendolyn about her non-believing husband who refuses to quit watching pornography:

> If your husband isn't a Christian, that should be your FIRST priority. [. . .] Right now, he's on his way to hell. Yes, his watching porn is cheating on you. Yes, I know it hurts. But, to a non-believer whose moral compass is questionable at best, he probably doesn't see the problem with his watching porn. Heck, I'm a Christian and it took me sixteen years to understand why it's wrong. I believe this kind of addiction cannot be conquered absent of Christ.

AngelBoy blended his own salvation narrative into his response, sharing that he, too, once watched pornography. With the help of Jesus Christ, though, he was able to overcome his "addiction." He implies that the morality of non-believers is "questionable at best" and insists that the only way for Gwendolyn to save her marriage is by her husband's salvation. Gwendolyn's question about sex posed on the Christian site BetweenTheSheets.com must also be a question about faith. AngelBoy ended his post with a statement about what he believes represents reality rather than optimism: "At this point, all you can do is continue to pray for his salvation."

How website users incorporate the various dimensions of personal piety—especially prayer, salvation, and God—is evident in one discussion thread that merges spiritual and practical advice to help Girl_Of_God communicate with her husband. Girl_Of_God was a BTS member for nearly eight months before finally posting to the site to ask for advice from other members about the struggles in her marriage. Her original post suggests that she had been reading other discussions on the site and therefore understood how to craft her question in a way that would solicit feedback and support from other members. She titled the thread, "HELP! Planning The Talk," and she begins her post by apologizing for its length: "Please forgive me. I don't know that this post can be condensed and still include everything I need it to." She goes on to describe the first four months of her marriage and the sexual encounters between her and her husband. "I think what irritates me about it is that he really doesn't seem to notice AT ALL that I'm not orgasming, even when I tell him I am frustrated. I can't count how many times I cry after sex while he showers or else touch myself feeling sad. I can't share my pleasure with him because he could care less." She then lists a host of problems: her husband is unwilling to stimulate her beyond having intercourse with her; he never initiates sex; he seems turned off by the tastes and smells of her body. She admits doubting her faith: "I've frequently prayed and cried to God that the command to wait for marriage for sex is extremely unfair. There was no way for me to know my husband would be so selfish in this area." She writes that she wants to confront her husband with these concerns and solicits advice from other BTS members about how to proceed: "I just don't know if there is even a solution to all this. Any advice on how to package this conversation would be GREATLY appreciated."

The post would eventually become a fifty-comment discussion among twenty-seven members, with comments going back and forth between offering practical suggestions and giving spiritual advice. First to respond is Mo, with words of general encouragement: "Good advice soon will come. For now, though, I will pray for you today. As far as God's command being 'extremely unfair,' goes, well I beg to differ and I pray that you will, too. Blessings to you, sister." Not ten minutes later come additional responses, each echoing and elaborating on the general sentiment put forward by Mo. Mr. T lists a few of the reasons why some people dislike the sensations associated with sex and mentions some ways that Girl_Of_God could thoughtfully communicate her concerns with her husband. He concludes his post: "I'll pray this goes well." Next comes a comment from Steel, a site administrator, who wonders if Girl_Of_God's husband is a survivor of child sexual abuse and if that could perhaps be the root cause of his sexual problems. Before Girl_Of_God answers Steel's question, another member, Phrixus, chimes in to suggest that, regardless of whether there had been past sexual abuse, she thinks the issues Girl_Of_God describes require therapy to overcome: "Sister, your marriage requires more than BTS can give in the form of words of support. I'll pray for you. Others here will pray for you. But you need some Biblically based counseling. Are you both full-time, committed Christians? Christ is our rock, and only He can change hearts." Although Phrixus mentions Christian therapy, she then shifts her suggestion to focus on the importance of salvation, intimating that Girl_Of_God and her husband will only be able to improve their marriage if they are "full-time" Christians.

As the discussion continues, Girl_Of_God thanks the other members for their comments, confirms that she and her husband are committed Christians, and shares the information that her husband is, in fact, a survivor of child sexual abuse. In light of this, members emphasize the need for Girl_Of_God to be sensitive to her husband's past and encourage counseling. Girl_Of_God then asks a question to those who suggest seeing a therapist: "I see a therapist about once a week for my history with body issues. The downside is that she is not saved. Is it appropriate to talk to her about all this sex stuff?" Phrixus responds to this, blending her support for counseling with statements reaffirming her belief that God is ultimately in charge of any change that happens during therapy: "That's great that you already have a counselor. Mine is not saved either. Dear husband and I would prefer to have someone we can pray with but she is helping us so much right now that we're just thankful God is working through her." Phrixius admits that, although she and her husband would prefer a Christian therapist, they believe that God is working through the therapist's services, despite the fact that she is a non-believer. This story asserts that Girl_Of_God should believe the current support she has in her life—even that of a non-Christian therapist—is a sign of God's work.

As the conversation carries on, the focus on past abuse wanes, and members discuss alternative solutions. Some focus on medical solutions, suggesting that Girl_Of_God's husband see a doctor to check his testosterone levels. Boynextdoor writes: "I agree that he needs to get a medical checkup and have his hormones tested." Gwendolyn confirms: "Make an appointment to see the doc about having your husband's testosterone checked. Like others have stated, his lack of sexual interest *is not normal.*" Although some members encourage the help of professionals such as therapists and doctors, members mention the power of prayer more than any other advice. Many affirm their prayerful support of Girl_Of_God and remind her to look to God for the answer to her marital problems.

Wed 11:25am   User: ForHIM927   Posts: 5264

> I would suggest praying together before you have your conversation. Thank God for each other and your marriage and the love he has blessed you with, and pray that God would continue to bless your marriage and your

discussion, that he would draw you closer to each other and to him, and that you each could learn how to please the other sexually and to experience the joy and fulfillment that God intends for the both of you. Nothing is impossible with God.

Wed 4:22pm   User: ConstantComment   Posts: 7409

Praying for tomorrow. The following scripture was a guide for me: Ephesians 4:25–32.

Wed 4:53pm   User: Anani   Posts: 620

I am praying for you, and I would like to give you a big hug right now.

Thur 6:05am   User: GoBears   Posts: 363

You need to both approach this as loving, committed, no mater what, partners . . . who will find a way with God's help, build trust, and enjoy the joy of marriage.

Thur 8:32am   User: ExodusGuy   Posts: 6648

Be bold. Be strong. The Lord your God is with you.

Thur 9:04pm   User: Staccato   Posts: 198

I'm praying for you two. Hang in there!

Thur 10:10pm   User: Graceful78   Posts: 1237

I'll be sending one upstairs for you guys.

Excerpts from BetweenTheSheets.com thread topic
"HELP! Planning The Talk" in the message board forum "Sexual Attitudes"

Rather than following up on advice to seek medical and therapeutic solutions, Girl_Of_God eventually shares an update explaining that God has changed her situation: "Well the talk did not occur, but some of you must have been praying cause something else DID happen. Dear husband gave me MS [manual stimulation] out of the blue, without my asking for it or even expecting it. And then WE ACTUALLY HAD SEX IN THE MORNING (twice!)!!! And he said it needed to be a priority! Wow, praise God!"

Girl_Of_God attributes the recent spontaneous sexual encounters and successful communication with her husband to the online religious community that prayed for her marriage. Although fellow BTS members offered much thoughtful and sincere advice that involved the couple seeking help from a therapist or doctor, Girl_Of_God focused on the spiritual support offered by the online community of believers. In fact, Girl_Of_God does not spend much time lamenting the initial conundrum that brought her to the site. While she admits that she and her husband "still have some work to do," she writes that she believes the power of prayer transformed her husband, giving her hope for an improved marriage. A member who found the thread four days after Girl_Of_God's final update made one of the final comments posted to the thread, summing up members' beliefs in the power of God and *the power of BTS:* "When I read this post, I immediately began praising God for the great wisdom and insight he'd given members of this site."

BTS members foster their identities as Christians within the site through the content and style of their posts. Evidence of personal piety is scattered through the message boards as members write about their prayer lives and conversations with God; their stories of sin, redemption, and salvation; and their personal convictions about matters related to marriage and sexuality. In using BTS, they reaffirm their quest to find sex advice that reflects their own Christian values.

WHAT GOD KNOWS

Establishing personal piety opens up additional possibilities for online exchanges for Christian sexuality website users. First, it allows them to frame anonymity on the sites as a benefit rather than a detraction. Website creators monitor their sites so that what people say online adheres to the logic of godly sex. Yet it is impossible for website creators or users to know if what people say reflects "who they really are." When asked about this, some of my interview respondents expressed concern, but most indicated that they don't worry much about deception. Pointing out that only God has the power to "really know" who anyone is (indicating their belief in God's omniscience, discussed in the previous chapter), these website users suggested that they don't worry about duplicity online any more than they worry about it in their real lives. One BTS member, Azaria, told me that she doesn't really worry about this because "we all have our 'public selves' and 'actual selves' IRL [in real life] anyways." She recognizes that the way she is perceived in public may be different from her "actual self," which God knows about, but others may not.

Like Erving Goffman, who analyzes social interactions as series of performances for different audiences, website users recognize that online interactions attempt to hide undesirable traits and instead put forth one's "best self."[15] BTS member Boynextdoor put it this way:

> I don't see it much differently than IRL [in real life] situations where people are putting on masks and act differently around you in a social setting than they would at home to those who know them intimately. If I meet a person at a restaurant I don't really know them; they might be acting totally different than they would when not working there or when going there for a meal if they don't work there. So it's the same type of thing on BTS. These people are real people, they may or may not be representing themselves honestly, but it's the same risk IRL.

Boynextdoor was among several interview respondents to mention the "masks" that we all wear in social interactions. Evangelicals believe that only God has the power to see past these front stage performances, the "masks" that we put on for the benefit of a particular social setting. It is therefore a futile task to attempt to uncover the "true" identities of fellow users of BTS.

The second advantage website users gain by establishing personal piety is the ability to navigate the secular World Wide Web while maintaining Christian sexuality websites as their "home base." LCL reader Lizzy99 explained that she takes secular sex advice "with a grain of salt" but doesn't necessarily avoid it entirely. Some website users said they use secular sites for what they described as "objective" information regarding sexuality. However, users who do look at secular sites tread cautiously. One LCL reader, Junebug, told me that she might hypothetically search a secular site for ideas about sexual positions as long as "it wasn't all smutty and stuff." Tara, a long-time reader of LCL, told me that some information about sex can be "scientific" and therefore doesn't need to be faith-based: "You know, I think it is certainly good to learn about the function of the G-spot and things like that, and I don't necessarily need to know if that researcher believes in the Nicene Creed or not."

Tara presents some information about sex, like the physiology of sexual arousal, as value neutral. She reasons that this information would be presented in exactly the same way regardless of whether the person presenting it declared a faith in God and Jesus Christ or a faith in Swiss cheese. Yet when I asked her for specific examples of secular sources that she trusts for this kind of information, she was at a loss: "You know, I guess a lot of the scientific information I read has been directed from BTS. John, the creator, is really good at summarizing scientific research." Tara, like other website users,

TABLE 6 Sex toy purchases made by married respondents in the past twelve months, CSIS sample

	Number of respondents	Percentage of total sample
Made at least one purchase	366	51.8
100% at Christian store(s)	75	10.6
About 75% at Christian store(s)	25	3.5
About 50% at Christian store(s)	23	3.3
About 25% at Christian store(s)	20	2.8
100% at secular store(s)	221	31.3
Made no purchase	341	48.2
Totals	707	100

NOTE: Because some respondents answered the survey question about whether they purchased sex toys but did not answer the subsequent question about where they purchased them, the total of the figures in the shaded area does not match that of the overall number of respondents who purchased sex toys. Respondents were included in analyzed data if they completed at least 90 percent of the survey.

described secular sites as sometimes useful in a hypothetical or theoretical way but did not regularly visit them.

How users of Christian sexuality websites interact with non-Christian sexuality sites are most evident in where they go to shop online for sex toys. According to the CSIS, the majority of Christian sexuality website users purchased sex toys, and most did so exclusively at secular online sites (see table 6). Of the CSIS respondents who purchased sex toys in the past year, only 21 percent (75 respondents) made all of their purchases at Christian-owned stores. More than half of those who purchased sex toys (61 percent, or 221 respondents) felt comfortable shopping at secular sites and didn't shop at all at Christian-owned ones.

Sunshine, for example, shopped exclusively at secular stores, explaining to me that she makes decisions on where to shop based on best prices and convenience: "I like to shop at Drugstore.com, since the site is clean. I have also gone to my local sex shop, which is not so clean but easy to get to." When I asked her if she had thought about shopping at Christian-owned online sex toy stores, she responded, "I have looked at one or two, but if I can find what I am looking for [for] cheaper, I tend to go that route." She also confirmed that she was usually the purchaser of toys for her and her husband, explaining, "I don't feel tempted. And since I'm the one who needs a vibrator to orgasm, I will go ahead and find what appeals to me."

Sunshine makes her adult-product purchases based almost entirely on matters of practicality: convenience and price. She prioritizes these factors over making her purchases at a Christian-owned site because she claims that she doesn't "feel tempted" by lustful thoughts when visiting secular sites. Her confidence in her relationship with God and knowing what tempts her allows her to use Drugstore.com to purchase adult products. Yet she continues to actively participate in BTS rather than secular alternatives. Secular sites are able to give her some of the literal tools for sexual pleasure, but BTS provides important context for that pleasure.

Personal piety offers website users the best of both worlds—secular and religious—as it allows website users to justify all the ways that they use the Internet. Christian sexuality sites provide users with opportunities to practice their faith, as described by users who understand anonymity not as a risk but as a test of one's devotion to God. Paradoxically though, personal piety does not allow for substantial difference to infiltrate Christian sexuality websites. Rather than using personal piety or "what God knows" to confidently engage with the Others of godly sex—for example, unmarried or gay or lesbian couples—website users rely on personal piety to keep them out. Website users distinguish their beliefs in God and sex as exclusive and right. By piously participating in sites like BTS—through prayer, sharing stories about their faith, and looking for markers of similar beliefs in others—website users create and define an online community.

INTERACTIVE PREDESTINATION

Christian sexuality websites offer one way for religious conservatives to make sense of their sexual lives. Jess35, a frequent reader of LustyChristian Ladies.com, described the church in which she grew up as "schizophrenic" when it came to sex: "Sex is bad, bad, bad, then good, good, good. There was a LOT of fear of 'lust' but also everybody knowing that sex in marriage is what you're supposed to do." To reconcile the tension between her Christian faith and her sexual desires, she looked to multiple Christian sources—books, friends, and finally the Internet. A question that remained unanswered for Jess before finding LCL was whether or not God permitted masturbation. "It seemed to me that most people around me probably didn't approve, but I thought I might be okay with it, and I wondered if I was just crazy."

She explained that she started masturbating and at first felt as if it aligned with her faith. She gradually began to question whether or not others considered masturbation to be sinful or not.

> I felt very conflicted about it. I grew up touching myself above my clothes but not really knowing what I was doing. Shockingly, I was really ignorant about sex to the extent of not even knowing what a clitoris was until college. So when I started knowingly masturbating in college, at first it was just a private thing, and I didn't feel weird about it at all. I was just excited to be exploring my body, and I actually felt like God would approve. But over time I started to wonder about what other Christians would think about it.

Jess tried reading Christian sex advice books, but she received conflicting advice from various authors—most advised against masturbation, but Jess wasn't satisfied with their reasons. "They just seemed out of touch," she explained to me. "Any 'reason' was either a vague sense that masturbating would be lusting and lust was bad." She tried to talk to a close Christian friend about it: "My girlfriend said she masturbated, too, but she thought she probably shouldn't be, but it was hard and confusing." Jess agreed that it was difficult to understand where masturbation fell on the spectrum of godly sexuality—it seemed to her that it was muddled between what was clearly allowed (sex between a husband and wife) and what clearly wasn't (sex between an unmarried or same-sex couple). She decided to search the Internet to see if she could find any Christian perspectives that were sympathetic to her hunch that masturbation "might be okay."

When she first found LustyChristianLadies.com, she spent hours pouring over past posts. She read about various techniques and practical advice about achieving sexual pleasure and also posts about the bloggers' positions on a variety of sexual practices:

> They are remarkably free sexually—like many of them have tried anal, which I just think is gross. They had posts about women using strap-ons with their husbands and stuff like that, which my husband thought was a combination of gross, sketchy, and maybe even morally questionable . . . But I admire them for stepping out of the Christian stereotype in so many ways. And I have found comfort in the fact that I'm not alone in doing that, at least in the realm of sexuality.

Jess doesn't share all of the same interests as LustyChristianLadies.com bloggers, but she values the site for challenging assumptions about Christians being anti-sex and offering perspectives that are similar to her own. She wrote simply about the impact LCL had on her sexual life: "It led to a sense of freedom." She then elaborated, "It made masturbation more normative. It helped me to feel more confident about being sexual and not feeling like I needed to apologize for that." Jess both reflects and personalizes the logic of godly sex as she describes her evolving understanding of sexual identity. Within the framework of godly sex, a scenario in which Jess came to believe that masturbation was *not* appropriate for *her* life would be equally plausible: "I decided that masturbating is fine and normal for me. It doesn't mean nobody ever does anything wrong in conjunction with masturbation, but I see that as a separate issue." Jess compartmentalizes masturbation in order to make sense of it. For her, it is permissible. For others, she resists casting judgment.

Although this chapter has focused on how users of Christian sexuality websites engage in dialogue to help construct a sense of community, the relationship between the websites and their users is reciprocal. Finding LustyChristianLadies.com confirmed what Jess already believed about masturbation by providing her with credible religious opinions from an online community of believers. Before finding the site, Jess feared that her beliefs about sex and her beliefs about God were oppositional. Finding the site made her beliefs about sex compatible with her beliefs about God. Online communities influence website users' sense of themselves as religious and sexual persons. David Snow calls this *interactive determination,* a process through which our identities are shaped and influenced (indeed, *determined*) by interacting with others.[16] Given their users' belief in the power of God, these websites are perhaps best understood as places of *interactive predestination.* Website users believe they are led by a divine, all-knowing God, with whom they have a personal relationship. Yet they use these sites as collaborative conduits of religious values when it comes to sex. Interactive predestination emphasizes the need for others in order to make sense of what conservative Christians describe as spiritual, personal, and private. On the surface, godly sex is malleable because it depends upon individual tastes and choices. Its logic is situational rather than universal, evolving rather than static. Yet it is a social and utterly human process that legitimizes godly sex for website users and maintains boundaries between others not like them.[17]

FOUR

Sexual Awakening

DEFINING WOMEN'S PLEASURES

CarrieForChrist firmly believed that, as a married woman, God allowed—even required—her to enjoy sex with her husband. But starting on her wedding night, sexual intercourse was "extremely painful." She knew it wasn't *supposed* to be, but she did not know how to enjoy it, having only learned of the perils of sex from her evangelical Christian family, friends, and church. "The way I grew up, you didn't talk about sex," she told me. "You know, the old 'sex is bad' or taboo. I never got 'The Talk.'" Carrie didn't pursue information about sex for fear that what she found would offer ungodly advice; if it didn't come "from a faith-based perspective, it'd lead to confusion." And so she entered her marriage knowing very little about her sexuality. She confided to me, "I didn't know zilch about how my body worked down there before I got married—well, not counting the cycle every month ☺." The playful smiley face emoticon transfers the candid and intimate nature of women's conversations on Christian sexuality websites to our interview—women on these sites are, Carrie told me, honest, unpretentious, and friendly.

CarrieForChrist learned about LustyChristianLadies.com from her younger sister, whom Carrie describes as more "in touch" with her body, even though she's not yet married or sexually active. Carrie spent weeks carefully exploring the interactive blog site after first discovering it. She began to follow the routine daily posts. On Mondays, the website posts a weekly poll to LCL readers with a question like, "What's your favorite time of day to have sex?" On Tuesdays, there is a "task" for readers to accomplish that week, such as, "Leave a series of notes for him to find, all starting with 'I love your . . .' Make some of them serious and some of them steamy!" On Thursdays, one of the LCL bloggers publishes a commentary about some topic related to sexuality, often prompted by a reader's question to the blog team. On Fridays, the site publishes various sentences related to sexuality and marriage, such as "The smell of___ is a turn on for me!" and readers are asked to fill in the blank. They reply with comments like "Men's cologne," "His beautiful man parts!" and "Jasmine vanilla massage oil."

From this online dialogue, CarrieForChrist learned from other Christian women who loved sex and loved to talk about it. She read about practical tips to ease the pain she experienced during intercourse and got advice about ways to increase her pleasure, like by touching herself during sex with her husband. LCL bloggers and readers also convinced her that she shouldn't feel ashamed or embarrassed about giving or receiving oral sex, activities that appealed to CarrieForChrist but also gave her anxiety. "I remember one of the Tuesday tasks was something along the lines of 'surprise your hubby with something,' and I timidly put in a comment that I wanted to have the courage to give my husband a BJ [blow job]. Some of the comments were like, 'You can do it, girl!' And after I did it and LOVED it, I went back to that post and commented, 'it was WILD!'"

LustyChristianLadies.com helped CarrieForChrist realize her sexual potential and understand that she could be confident sexually and enjoy having sex with her husband. "It was encouraging to know that I wasn't the only one having difficulty," she told me. Carrie learned to overcome physical obstacles related to the pain she felt during intercourse, to overcome emotional hurdles of shame and embarrassment that she felt about sex, and to amend her belief system to incorporate religious values that encourage sexual pleasure. In short, Carrie learned that God wants her to like sex, to "just have fun in the marriage bed." Carrie credited this transformation to both LCL and her own spiritual devotion: "I would say it was 30 percent LCL and 70 percent doing [spiritual] battle and praying."

CarrieForChrist called her story a sexual awakening. Sexual awakening stories are well established in the vernacular of Christian sexuality websites. Like evangelical salvation narratives or testimonies, they follow a distinct formula: the narrator lives through a time of sin and suffering that he or she then overcomes by believing in God, who has the power to transform believers' sexual lives. LustyChristianLadies.com has even provided its readers an instructional blog post on the topic, "How to Have a Sexual Awakening." The post describes the experience as "a sudden revelation of God's intention to have a richer sexual relationship with [one's] husband." Blogger Kitty describes the early years of her marriage, when she had only a "minor interest in sex" and didn't communicate about it with her husband. Then, "quite all of a sudden and surprisingly," she experienced a sexual awakening. She credits God with her transformation, and tells her readers that faithfulness is key to achieving sexual fulfillment: "The most practical thing you can do to change is to pray continually for God to change you. He is on your side. He wants your spouse to be free even more than you do. Ask Him to make you who you need to be in order to be a blessing to your spouse. Do all that He leads you to do." Although she places change and transformation ultimately in the hands of a divine creator, Kitty also tells her readers to actively pray and urges them to *do* all that God leads them to do. Sexual awakening stories, like salvation stories, deftly combine a sense of human agency with submission to God's will. As Virginia Brereton argues about salvation narratives, conversion requires an *actor,* someone who "accepts Christ" rather than "is accepted by Christ." This centralizes the responsibility of individuals when it comes to their own eternal fate.[1]

How believers imagine themselves as actors, rather than acted upon, depends on how they tell their religious stories. In this chapter, I analyze how some Christian women interpret their sexual experiences by describing them according to a particular narrative form. Like creators of Christian sexuality websites, who emphasize how their actions align with their faith to justify the sexual content on their sites, women tell sexual awakening stories that align their sexuality with their evangelical Protestant beliefs. They make their unique experiences conform to the particular narrative components of obstacles and redemption that make up the before and after of the awakening experience. This points to the importance of personal piety, the marriage relationship, and Christian sexuality websites themselves in shaping what is sexually possible and permissible in a Christian setting. In telling sexual awakening stories, women prioritize their choices and desires, although they do so in a way that fits an evangelical mold.[2]

Though both men and women tell stories that they call sexual awakenings, these narratives are uniquely positioned to give voice to women's experiences. I do not analyze men's stories in this chapter for two reasons. First, the vast majority of sexual awakening stories are told by women, and I have only limited data on men's stories. Men make references to their "awakenings," but there are few detailed narratives.[3] Second, and more important than the *quantitative* differences in the number of stories told by men versus by women, men's stories are *qualitatively* different than women's. Despite gender-equal language that permeates the logic of godly sex, men and women who use Christian sexuality websites present their stories on different and imbalanced trajectories. Secular and religious talk about sexuality recognizes men as sexual and encourages men's heterosexual desire for (and access to) women. Christian men are not removed from their sexual identities in the same way as Christian women, making it more difficult for men to tell stories that contain the narrative components important to a sexual awakening story. In other words, men are already sexually "awake" when they become sexually active within marriage.

Women's stories suggest that women's bodies and the pleasure they experience are deeply connected to others—God and their husbands—and that they must balance their own needs with selfless acts that prioritize their marital relationships and family. This maintains gender imbalances between men and women and restricts women's sexual expressions. Contradictory messages of sexual entitlement and selflessness within women's sexual awakening stories serve to situate them within a conservative Christian culture that continues to perpetuate gender hegemony. Reflecting a postfeminist sentiment that combines anti- and pro-feminist messages, Christian sexuality websites are places where women make sense of sexual pleasure in multiple ways without challenging male privilege within their sexual relationships. Sexual awakening stories show how women both theologize and sexualize their bodies to make sense of the pleasure they believe should be a part of Christian marital intimacy.[4] Their stories are as much about the relationship between the body and religion as they are about the body and sex.

WOMEN'S PLEASURE

In contemporary America, women's sexuality shows up in all kinds of unlikely places. It appears in expected red-light spaces—through pornography, erotic dancing, and sex work—but also in spaces that are quite ordinary, even "wholesome." There are at-home sex toy parties organized by suburban housewives; fitness centers that offer pole dancing exercise classes; and vibrators sold at chain pharmacies like Walgreens. Talk of empowerment often exists alongside these depictions of women's sexuality. Popular media depicts secular, white women as in control of their sexuality and free from gender inequality. Feminism—at least the kind that equates sexual autonomy and pleasure with women's freedom—has gone mainstream.[5]

Women's entitlement to sexual pleasure was central to second-wave feminism; if bad sex (forced or obligatory) signaled women's oppression, good sex on women's terms was a part of their liberation.[6] Yet contemporary representations of women's sexual pleasure have largely lost their political and radical edge. This is indicative of what some scholars call *postfeminism,* a cultural trend that merges anti- and pro-feminist ideas that give women a sense that they control their sexuality while at the same time encouraging a sexuality that acquiesces to men's interests. Women who boast sexual confidence do so within a social structure that permits ongoing sexual violence and maintains gender imbalances in education, at the workplace, and at home.[7] Despite what often appears to be gender-equal language, popular discourse supports and expects gender difference that tends to privilege men, especially when it comes to sexual desires and expressions.

When this "common cultural script" meets evangelical Christianity, it becomes, in the words of sociologist Michelle Wolkomir, a "divine mandate."[8] Christian sexuality website users construct a godly sexuality for women akin to what Rosalind Gill calls "compulsory (sexual) agency"—the contradictory notion that women feel social pressure to *choose* to improve their sex lives.[9] Although these users emphasize the mutuality of sexual pleasure (see chapter one), for Christian women, being "sexually awakened" means experiencing pleasure within a very specific, male-dominated context. Nonetheless, Christian sex advice uses religious beliefs to justify women's pleasure. Authors Ed and Gaye Wheat, for example, write that the ability to orgasm is what "God designed for every wife." Shannon Ethridge tells women that "sexual confidence isn't just for the supermodel or porn star. It is the birthright of every woman." In fact, Ethridge would say that sexual confidence, as envisioned by God, is *not* for supermodels and porn stars at all but *only* for Christian wives.[10]

Evangelicals write about women's pleasure—describing it as "mysterious," "elusive," and "just out of reach"—to demystify it. Christian sexuality websites and sex advice books offer women and their husbands the tools to help women achieve physical pleasure: step-by-step instructions on how to arouse a woman, anatomical drawings identifying the clitoris, advice on lubricants, suggestions about what time of day to have sex, lists of romantic gestures, and descriptions of sexual positioning—all intended to optimize women's pleasure. Just as authors did during the feminist movement of the 1970s, Ethridge, in *The Sexually Confident Wife,* writes candidly about clitoral orgasms. She tells women to "delightfully indulge in the pleasure of the moment" and instructs wives to allow their husbands to focus on making them aroused before having sexual intercourse: "Let him manually, visually, and orally explore your private playground, showing him how you'd like to be touched if necessary. Don't feel rushed to reciprocate yet. Just enjoy the pleasure signals your body is sending your brain right now. Let this pleasure nourish your spirit and draw the two of you closer emotionally." Ethridge prioritizes women's bodies and pleasure within the sexual relationship. She gives them permission to be selfish—even if just for a moment. Yet unlike women's liberationists, Ethridge carefully contextualizes pleasure as being good for women's spiritual and marital lives, making both God and women's husbands key to women's experiences.[11]

Women's stories discuss sexual pleasure in ways that parallel a feminist sensibility about women's entitlement to pleasure and their bodies while reflecting a conservative Christian sensibility about the role of marriage and God in women's lives. Ethridge writes positively about female pleasure, even going so far as to suggest women's natural potential for pleasure exceeds that of men. *The Sexually Confident Wife* includes information like, "Did you know the female clitoris has eight thousand nerve fibers? That's almost twice as many as the male penis!" Ethridge quotes secular science writer, Natalie Angier, who writes, "[Some women] never bought Freud's idea of penis envy; who would want a shotgun when you can have a semiautomatic?" Women's sex organs—the semiautomatics—hold the potential for intense and long-lasting pleasure. Yet at the same time, Ethridge frames what she describes as exceptional female pleasure potential as only possible within the pleasure of the marriage relationship:

> Women have the luxury of a much shorter refractory period, which means she can be an orgasmic Energizer bunny and keep going and going if she wants to. A woman's body is capable of experiencing these intense waves of pleasure over and over for several minutes [. . .]. Usually, it's an overwhelming desire for intercourse with her husband that brings these orgasmic waves to an end, as she demands he replaces his fingers with his penis.

In explaining G-spot orgasms and the potential for multiple orgasms, Ethridge first focuses only on women's bodies and the pleasure women can experience. Ultimately, though, she describes a woman's pleasure—however powerful and long lasting—as inevitably leading to an equally intense desire to be penetrated by her husband. Ethridge gives women agency in this scenario—a woman "demands" that her husband penetrate her with his penis—but limits women's choices to this quintessential act of male sexual dominance. As she states clearly in the subtitle of the book, Ethridge defines sexual confidence as "connecting with your husband—mind, body, heart, spirit."[12]

Sheet Music author Kevin Leman writes extensively about women's orgasms but also prioritizes women's pleasure vis-à-vis men's. In the chapter "The Big 'O,'" he writes admiringly about women's bodies and the pleasure they experience: "Many women are surprised when I tell them that a large percentage of men are jealous of their orgasms." He goes on to describe women's orgasms magnanimously: a woman having an orgasm feels like "the world is exploding" and she is "riding the waves of ecstasy." Yet he describes women's pleasure as ultimately benefiting the self-image of men:

> Women, this might surprise you, but even more than your husband wants to have sex with you for his own sexual relief, the truth is, he wants to please you even more than he wants to be pleasured. It might seem like it's all about him, but what he really wants, emotionally, is to see how much you enjoy the pleasure he can give you. If he fails to do that, for any reason, he'll end up feeling inadequate, lonely, unloved.

Leman frames women's pleasure as a way for men to prove their sexual prowess—to show "the pleasure he can give you." Although he prioritizes women's pleasure within the marriage relationship, it is not for women themselves but rather for the benefit of men, so they do not feel "inadequate, lonely, unloved." Leman's repeated comment that he might "surprise" women with his information suggests that they do not already know much about their bodies.[13] Instead, Christian women need male experts to inform them.

As much attention as popular Christian authors give women and their orgasms, women appear to have trouble applying this prescriptive advice to their lives. Women who use Christian sexuality websites often join these sites because they suspect they should enjoy sex but don't know how. Stories of sexual awakening trace the process by which this cognitive knowledge about God's design for sexuality becomes *embodied* knowledge. As one woman who shared her sexual awakening story on BetweenTheSheets.com described, "I knew when I got married that sex wasn't dirty or sinful. At least I knew this in my head, but it just never worked its way through my subconscious." Sexual awakening stories explain how the body transforms to reflect what these website users already believe in their minds. Whereas prescriptive Christian sex advice gives women permission and guidelines to experience pleasure, online discussions go further to help women to overcome their unique obstacles and circumstances.

Because sexual awakening stories are always told after women have experienced an awakening, hindsight allows women to make meaning of the obstacles that prevented them from experiencing sexual pleasure. Whether these obstacles are the result of past sexual sins or physical ailments, sexual awakening stories consistently present women's bodies as their source. In chapter one, I described what I call an inhibition paradox, which simultaneously encourages and condemns Christians' sexual pleasure. This is especially true for women, who hear a constant refrain of messages that downplay or vilify their sexuality. Sexual awakening stories show how women *inhabit* the inhibition paradox. They internalize and individualize it, describing distinct physical, emotional, and spiritual barriers to their sexual pleasure. The body—which is the catalyst for sexual pleasure and marital wholeness—is also the barrier that prevents women from achieving sexual pleasure.

Even though conservative Christian messages condemn sexual activity outside of marriage unequivocally, both for men and women, these messages frame men's sexual desires as natural and expected but are relatively silent when it comes to women having desires of their own. This compounds the inhibition paradox for women; they may experience sexual desire but feel guilty or self-conscious about it, even in the "proper" confines of marriage. Samantha, owner of the online sex-toy store, describes this pointedly:

> When sex is talked about in church, it's talked about like this: men have sexual needs and women have emotional needs. And nobody talks about the fact that someone with ovaries may indeed have a sexual need EVER. And I want to raise my hand and go, 'excuse me!' It's just so not talked about. And if it's only talked about from the pulpit that men only have sexual needs, then that means that women's needs (a) don't exist or (b) aren't important to God.

Christian men are not removed from their sexual identities in the same way that Christian women are. Even men who have never engaged in sexual acts, Samantha points out, are more likely to have been exposed to positive sexual talk geared toward them. Sexual awakening stories reveal how men and women set out on different and uneven sexual trajectories.

Christian women do not receive positive messages about their sexuality from church, and they don't receive it from secular culture, either. Evangelical women who are "in the world" but not "of the world" must make sense of secular messages that they are exposed to but that shouldn't apply to them. One LustyChristianLadies.com reader, XYZ, called this the world's "worship of sex," explaining, "For much of the unsaved world, sex has become a 'God.' They worship the creation of sex rather than the *creator* of sex." Many women website users are particularly critical of secular depictions of women's sexuality, calling them ungodly. Blogger Maribel told me that she created her blog, MaribelsMarriage.com, because she believes that secular messages that sexualize women inadvertently make Christian women feel like they shouldn't be sexual: "I think a lot of Christian women have a lot of guilt with sex. It's often referred to as the 'good girl syndrome,' where they don't think they're a good girl if they're enjoying sex because they've been told their whole life 'no, no, no, no you shouldn't be doing this. Good girls don't have sex.'" What Maribel describes as "good girl syndrome" adds a gendered critique to the inhibition paradox: women's unique inability or hesitance to enjoy sex in marriage.

Before experiencing a sexual awakening, Christian women describe many contrary sources of inhibitions. A religious upbringing may lead women who try to experience sexual pleasure in marriage to feel guilt, insecurity, and a lack of knowledge, but an upbringing without religion can skew women's sense of their own sexuality and what is godly. A past of sexual sins can get in the way of a woman's current sexual relationship just as much as a past of abstinence may prevent a woman from optimizing her sexual pleasure by stunting her as a "good girl." These inhibitions affect who women are and who they think they should be. Tara, a LCL reader, put it this way: "Christian women know they don't want to be Carrie Bradshaw [the promiscuous New Yorker from the hit TV show *Sex and the City*], but they don't want to be prudes either." Finding space in between—to be sexual in the way that God approves—is difficult for women who experience disconnect between their religious beliefs and sexual desires.

Dinah, a member of BetweenTheSheets.com, entered her marriage with what she described as "a lot of baggage." As she shared in a post on the site, she did not have a relationship with God before she met her husband. Instead, she had been sexually promiscuous, suffered sexual abuse, participated in sex work, and had low self-esteem. After she married, she became born again and attempted to follow God's plan for marital sexuality. Yet her sex life suffered: "My poor husband was lucky if we had sex once every three months. I believe this was because when I was with my husband, I was plagued with memories I didn't want. I felt that if I ever felt sexual, my husband would lose respect for me. I knew God created sex for enjoyment between husband and wife, but I couldn't apply it to my life." Dinah's story describes her emotional trauma, sparked by past abuse and sexual sinfulness, as an obstacle to her marital relationship. Even when her spiritual body was made whole by her commitment to Christ, her physical body was unable to experience the sexual pleasure she believed God created for marriage.

Women sharing sexual awakening stories treat the physical body as an objective reality—not something they have chosen themselves but the hand they have been dealt in life. Many of these women describe being prevented from experiencing an awakening by physical ailments and conditions, such as hormone deficiencies, stress that causes the body to shut down, complications from medical procedures, painful intercourse, obesity, and medications that decrease sexual desire. One reader of LustyChristianLadies.com explained that her sexual difficulties were entirely a result of physical conditions beyond her control: "I saved myself for marriage and was shocked to discover on my honeymoon that it was too painful for me to have sex! I got very upset and became very depressed. I had a successful hymenectomy, but that didn't solve our problems, so I went on Prozac and it has ruined my libido and ability to orgasm." She attributed the barriers to her pleasure to the body.

Women often describe their bodies as distinct from the rest of themselves. Highlighting the inhibition paradox, many women experience cognitive and physical dissonance, in which the mind believes one thing, but the body does not behave accordingly. LustyChristianLadies.com reader Tara explained to me how "fixing" her body led her to feel sexual desire:

> I had severe medical hormone deficiencies that had been previously undiagnosed. [. . .] Once I started working with a really good endocrinologist and got my hormones balanced, I realized, holy smokes, I've got a libido! And it was really quite something, you know, because I was already a mother and everything. [. . .] I mean, I had enjoyed the closeness of sex and had experienced some level of desire, but I had no idea that you could just want it like that. It's amazing when your blood levels are normal; life is very different.

Medical intervention transformed Tara's physical body. Yet this alone wasn't enough to cause her awakening, as her newly kindled desire did not automatically lead to pleasure. I asked Tara to elaborate on how her normal blood levels helped to improve her sex life. She continued, "This was kind of a blessing but still an odd situation because here I am years into a marriage, and all of a sudden my entire sexual needs and erotic fingerprint changes. My body was more functional, but I didn't know what to do with it." Tara talks about her body as an object that is hers but *not the same as her.* Her body became functional, but she didn't know what to do with "it." She explained that she had to rediscover her body following its physical transformation. This is what prompted the online searching that led her to the LustyChristianLadies.com blog.

Even though women telling sexual awakening stories may describe the physicality of the body and its conditions as separate from their emotional or spiritual lives, they also theologize the physical body to make sense of their sexuality and religious beliefs. These women explain their body's *past* as an external force that gets in the way of their body's *present.* Many women disclose past sexual abuse on Christian sexuality websites and discuss with other users about how to deal with the repercussions of the abuse on their current relationships. Grace Driscoll, coauthor of *Real Marriage,* writes about her experience being abused in a way that mirrors many online discussions. The abuse profoundly affected her intimacy with her husband: "I was shaped by what others had done to me and what I had done, rather than who God created me in His image to be."[14] Her words signal how the abuse she suffered transformed her sense of self and personhood.

How Grace makes sense of her abuse allows her to also understand why she struggled in her relationships with God and her husband. She concludes that her body was stuck in the abuse and was therefore unable to be what God intended for marriage.

> When someone other than the Holy Spirit controls where you go, whom you see, what you wear, and what you do, it's emotional abuse, and it affects your life deeply. When someone stalks you, is obsessed with you, and threatens you, it's psychological abuse and it changes you drastically. When someone makes you have sex, and you continually say no verbally or through body language [...], it's sexual abuse and it affects you spiritually. All this had been a part of my past, but it was bringing death to my present and future life.[15]

Grace uses her own experiences to help her readers understand the consequences of abuse. The different types of abuse she describes—emotional, psychological, and sexual—have profound effects. Despite firmly believing in complementarianism—men's headship and women's submission—she grants control over her life to no one except the Holy Spirit.

Like Grace Driscoll, website users rely on familiar evangelical cues to interpret emotional and physical problems. As described in the previous chapter, this establishes them as insiders in the online communities hosted on Christian sexuality websites. This also allows women telling sexual awakening stories to use their spiritual beliefs to make sense of their imperfect physical bodies. For example, Chariot, a blogger on LustyChristianLadies.com, wrote that she believes that using birth control pills was Satan's way of keeping physical intimacy out of her marriage with her husband, since they lowered her libido. So she quit taking the pills and began using natural family planning methods, until she missed her period one month. It turned out that she wasn't pregnant, but she wrote that she considered returning to artificial birth control because her irregular cycle made it difficult to successfully use natural methods: "Satan threw me for a loop: here I was, no menstrual cycle, wondering, did I skip my period? How do I know if I've ovulated or not? What are my options? I've only decided one thing: I won't go back on artificial birth control ever again. I will not let Satan get a foothold in my marriage bed." Chariot believes that there is a force beyond her physical body influencing her decision to take the pills: Satan, who wants to disrupt God's plan for marital intimacy.

Evangelical women's physical bodies are never entirely separate from their spiritual ones. Evangelicals believe that Satan tries to keep individuals from accepting the salvation of Jesus Christ, and Christian sexuality website users say that the devil tries to prevent their sexual awakenings. They describe this as a spiritual battle that continuously takes place between believers and Satan. They speak of a crafty Satan who tries to thwart God's plan for sexuality in any way he can, from enticing unmarried couples to have sex to convincing a married woman to use birth control to ruin her sex drive. As one BTS user explains, "There are many tools in Satan's tool bag. Every one of them is intended to distort something good." Overcoming physical obstacles allows evangelicals to achieve victory in the battle between Christians and the devil. By focusing on external forces (like Satan or past actions) that influence the body, women set up their sexual awakenings to be dependent on faith in God.

A sexual awakening is a story in two acts: a time before and a time after. The pain, confusion, and loss that storytellers describe before they experience an awakening are overcome by faith in God. As in salvation stories, the bad times in these awakening stories are important narrative tools that illustrate the magnitude of the good—how accepting Jesus Christ has the power to transform believers' lives. Women who tell sexual awakening stories describe the time before their awakening as bad not only for their sex lives but also for their physical health, their marriages, and their relationships with God. By connecting their sexual obstacles with other obstacles in their lives, believers turn sexual awakenings into spiritual stories.

THE BODY REDEEMED: SEXUAL AWAKENING

Psalm143, a member of BetweenTheSheets.com, described her body before her sexual awakening as the obstacle to achieving sexual pleasure: "For the longest time I thought something was wrong with my body. I tried multiple times to get my body to orgasm, but it just wouldn't do it. I thought that there was something wrong with me." Like many women who tell sexual awakening stories, Psalm143 references her body as something separate from herself. Yet her body's inability to experience pleasure impacted her overall self-worth. How did she overcome these obstacles? She turned to God.

> I started to pray. I don't know why I didn't do this before. I guess I felt a little strange praying to orgasm, but I felt like God was telling me, "Stop worrying and hand it over to ME!" I realized he did care about me having sex with my husband. Eventually, God helped me to unwind and think about good feelings and what was pleasing me, and I got to the point where I was enjoying just learning. I wasn't even thinking about having an orgasm, and I really didn't care if I had one or not because I was having so much enjoyment letting dear husband explore and pleasuring him in return. Soon enough, God helped me to orgasm. It happened without warning. I wasn't thinking about it at all, it just came all on its own . . . naturally! I believe that God will allow you to release—just give it over to him.

Psalm143 describes her body's redemption: with the help of God, she was able to realize her sexual potential, connect with her spouse, and ultimately strengthen her relationship with God. She "awakens" to experience the pleasure that God designed for her marriage.

Psalm143's story reveals how women website users talk about their awakenings as deeply emotional and spiritual experiences, thereby reinforcing a holistic depiction of women's bodies. Although she mentions physical climax as part of her story, it is on the periphery: "I really didn't care if I had one [an orgasm] or not." Instead of focusing on the ability to orgasm, she centralizes the pleasure she gets from being intimate with her husband and from listening to God's plan. God told her to "stop worrying about it" and let Him take care if it. And eventually, God did help Psalm143 have an orgasm. By prioritizing her most important relationships—with God and with her husband—Psalm143 was rewarded with physical pleasure. God has the power to reconcile a woman's sexual, spiritual, and relational selves.

Achieving Pleasure

As Psalm143's story depicts, the typical sexual awakening story culminates in a woman who is able, often for the first time, to experience the ultimate physical sexual pleasure: an orgasm. Evangelical sex advice universally promotes the idea that women should be able to physically climax as part of the sexual encounter. Nearly all evangelical sex manuals of the past four decades include specific instructions on how a woman can achieve an orgasm.[16] There are dozens of blog posts and hundreds of discussion board posts about women's orgasms on Christian sexuality websites. One instructional post on BetweenTheSheets.com on how to use a vibrator to orgasm, for example, has more views than any other on the site (over 47,000). One BTS member who was praying for his wife's sexual awakening shared on the site that he would like to learn how to help her orgasm: "I really think that *this* is what it is going to take to help her have an awakening."

Women who read Christian sex advice hear messages about their entitlement to sexual pleasure and then use Christian sexuality websites to learn how to achieve it. As blogger Maribel shared with me, "The biggest topic that I receive emails about is the physics, you know, the actual how do I have an orgasm." She described an orgasm as symbolically meaningful in women's lives. Drawing from both feminist and religious language, she claims that it is simultaneously *powerful* and *binding*:

> I personally went a lot of years in my marriage not even knowing what an orgasm felt like [...]. I just felt a need to change women's attitudes. That it's not dirty or wrong if they're enjoying this with their husband. [...] I think if women would just have a little more knowledge about it, that would give them a little bit more power to realize that it can be amazing, and it can be binding and beneficial to you and your husband.

Learning to orgasm, according to Maribel, is empowering for Christian women. She validates women's sexual pleasure, challenging dominant stereotypes that may make women feel ashamed for enjoying sex. "It's not dirty or wrong," she writes, although she then goes on to qualify, "if they're enjoying this with their husbands." Maribel believes that women should feel entitled to orgasm, but she makes sure to frame the "power" of sexual climax within the context of marital closeness and improvement.

Evangelicals who write about sex online and in print idealize a woman's orgasm as an experience that occurs with her husband. Yet they also offer practical advice and frequently recommend that women masturbate and engage in solo explorations of their bodies. Orgasm through masturbation is often the moment of sexual awakening for women. One BTS member, QueenEsther, offered advice to other Christian women on how to orgasm for the first time using a vibrator. Her instructions merge practical tips with praise for God:

> First, tell yourself that this is just you time. Commit to pamper yourself . . . I recommend using a small mirror to give you a visible exploration of your genitals . . . open your legs wide and look and touch . . . God wants you to know how to use the body He gave you—He wants you to be in awe of it, amazed by it, and grateful to Him for how it works. Look at how exquisitely God put you together . . . as beautiful as a snowflake. Thank Him audibly if you can for how He designed you, and ask Him to bless this time of self-exploration and discovery.

QueenEsther sets the scene for sexual entitlement. "This is your own special time," she tells readers. "Give yourself permission to indulge yourself." Her instructions even resemble feminist consciousness-raising groups that urge women to get to know their bodies using a hand mirror. Yet QueenEsther carefully incorporates God into women's sexual pleasure, instructing women to thank God for creating their sexual bodies. She encourages women to ask for God's blessings as they embark on this sexual journey. With the husband notably absent, God becomes the male figure in this sexual scenario that QueenEsther describes.

Evangelical women justify masturbation by emphasizing how it improves their marital relationships. One member of BTS, LadyAloha, commented on why she believes God approves of masturbation for women: "The more orgasms women have, the more they desire sex. Plus, the hormonal release into a woman's body during sex with her husband does not release during masturbation." She writes that masturbation is not only acceptable but also very beneficial because it may lead to a greater number of sexual encounters with one's husband. Importantly, she reserves marital intimacy as an exceptional sexual practice—claiming that masturbation is different from (and inferior to) sexual intercourse between partners because it lacks the "hormonal release" that happens during intercourse. Ella, a reader of LustyChristianLadies.com, also justifies masturbation because she believes it makes sex better with her husband. As she explained to me, "It's important to 'think sex' during the day. [. . .] I find quiet moments to touch myself and think of my husband and look forward to seeing him again." She was happy to find examples on LCL of other women who also masturbated. She shared her "think sex" strategy in a comment on a blog post about "masturbation quickies."

Authors of Christian sex advice books and creators of Christian sexuality websites agree that sexual pleasure shouldn't be relegated exclusively to solo pursuits. This is reflected in mixed attitudes about masturbation reported in the CSIS. Only 25 percent of respondents reported that masturbation in marriage is "not at all wrong," while the majority (64 percent) indicated that masturbation in marriage is either "almost always wrong" or "wrong only sometimes." Yet married CSIS respondents reported that they do masturbate, if infrequently (see figure 13), and the data show that married men masturbate much more frequently than married women. Out of those respondents who reported that they had not masturbated at all during this past year, about three out of four were women. Of those respondents who reported that they masturbated at least weekly, about three out of four were men. This may seem surprising given how much attention Christian sexuality websites devote to encouraging women to use self-stimulation to achieve orgasm. Yet the obsession with the female orgasm in print and online is always accompanied by an important caveat: once women learn to orgasm on their own, they should apply their knowledge to their marriage relationships. Ethridge writes that "the goal for the sexually confident wife is to learn how to experience orgasmic pleasure in the presence of her husband rather than in solitary confinement."[17] Even if women initially use masturbation and self-pleasure as a way to understand how their bodies experience pleasure, it should be considered a means to the end goal of marital intimacy, not the end in and of itself.

The reported masturbation frequency of men compared to women may suggest that Christian sexuality websites promote a double standard that permits men, but not women, to masturbate. Yet findings from the CSIS suggest that women who do masturbate do not feel guilty about it. In fact, the survey suggests that they feel slightly less guilt than men. Even though men reported that they masturbate more frequently, women and men who

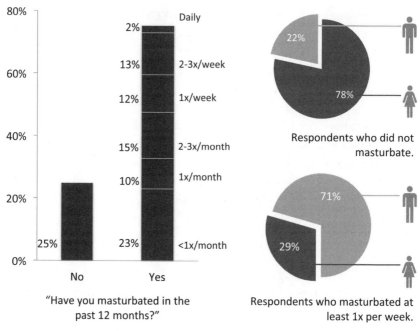

do masturbate reported comparably low levels of guilt (see figure 14): 67 percent of women reported that they never or rarely feel guilt after they masturbate, compared to 58 percent of men. This supports the logic of godly sex, outlined in chapter one, which permits a wide range of sexual activities within heterosexual, monogamous Christian marriages. Users of Christian sexuality websites emphasize that masturbation should be incorporated only if it improves the marital relationship, and so women who tell sexual awakening stories describe self-pleasure according to these guidelines. The CSIS implies that some of these users believe that masturbation aligns with their religious beliefs. Those who decide masturbation does not damage their spiritual or marital relationships masturbate without guilt.

Sexual awakening stories often describe women who literally take their sexual pleasure into their own hands in order to achieve physical climax. However, as much as evangelicals writing about sex encourage women's orgasms, the ubiquitous but vague sense of spiritual and relational intimacy at times trumps physical pleasure. Ethridge, for example, refers to more than an orgasm when she writes about what she calls "the big Oh." She uses the term to indicate insight, those revelatory moments that women experience that enhance their physical,

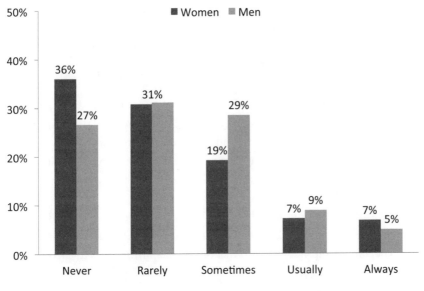

FIGURE 14. Level of masturbation guilt by gender, CSIS married sample.

spiritual, and emotional pleasure. As the next section describes, women who tell sexual awakening stories use these ideas to transform feelings of sexual inadequacy into sexual fulfillment, telling stories of sexually awakening that do not actually involve physical climax. They still call their stories "awakenings" and remain committed to their own pleasure within their sex lives.

Redefining Pleasure

Sexual awakenings make women's bodies whole, connecting them fully sexually, spiritually, and emotionally to both God and their husbands. One BTS member explained that her awakening began when her adult children began getting engaged and married: "I started to get nostalgic for what I'd had with dear husband at first." She went on to describe a transformation prompted by her obedience to God:

> I began to pray, 'God, bring back my lust for my husband. [. . .] God, awaken me!' Then, one day [. . .], quite spontaneously, God told me very clearly that I was to express desire for dear husband, even though I didn't feel it. What God asked of me asked me to take a leap of faith, but I followed His

command out of my comfort zone. Following His plan, I was suddenly over-whelmed with physical, mental, and emotional desire for my husband. It was so strong that I practically threw myself at him! From nothing to consuming desire in a matter of moments! Praise God!

This story positions the narrator's spirituality—her prayers—as the factor that altered her physical and emotional body, leaving her "suddenly over-whelmed with physical, mental, and emotional desire." Sexual awakening stories merge religious and sexual experiences. Women who tell these stories detail how God appears in the most intimate of spaces to those who are open to receiving His instructions.

Website users credit sexual awakenings with improving not only their sexual pleasure—the physical sensations associated with sex—but also their spiritual and emotional lives. Connecting their spiritual lives to their sexual experiences, women who tell stories of sexual awakening describe their sexual transformations as a way to praise God. Blogger Lisa praises God for creating the female orgasm: "Thank you, God. Kudos to you for a job well done in the area of creative design." Sexual pleasure and intimacy, according to website users, requires a strong relationship with God. As one BTS member wrote, of her sexual awakening, "It [the awakening] was indeed a work of God, though he used these circumstances in my life to do a work of freedom in me. He knew my heart was open to His work in my life, and so He saw to it that these things were used to wake me up." Christian women must accept God's transformation in their lives. Women who tell these stories credit God with leading them to experience sexual pleasure and also suggest that their sexual pleasure actually enhances their spiritual lives.

God's role in sexual awakening stories is central. God guides the events and circumstances that lead website users to experience godly sexuality. Many stories describe how God directs women to the resources necessary to improve their marriages. One LustyChristianLadies.com reader I inter-viewed, Ros, expressed gratitude to God for finding the site: "I felt like God was giving me a birthday gift, since it was my birthday when I found LCL." Similarly, a member of BTS explained that it was God working through Christian resources that prompted her awakening: "God proceeded to use the [BTS message] boards and [a Christian book,] *Intimacy Ignited*, [. . .] to begin to heal me. [. . .] He proceeded to remove the thorns in my heart that represented my wounds." Although women who experience sexual awaken-ings often say that they were helped by outside resources—like Christian sexuality websites or books—they credit God with leading them to the information.

In their sexual awakening stories, some women, rather than describing actual physical pleasure, portray giving and receiving pleasure as acts of selflessness and faithfulness that serve as examples of God's transformative power. These women define pleasure differently than those who emphasize the orgasm as part of their awakening narratives. One BTS member explained that her sexual awakening saved her marriage, but she did not mention her personal satisfaction as the motivator for an improvement in her sex life: "God stirred something in my heart. I began to realize that I had been neglecting my dear husband terribly. The more I read on Christian sexuality websites, the more I desired to have this wonderful relationship with my dear husband." Similarly, Ros, the LustyChristianLadies.com reader who described her awakening as a "birthday present" from God, said that her awakening "truly enhanced our [her and her husband's] intimacy." She did not mention any personal pleasure that resulted from her awakening. Prioritizing pleasure for the good of the marriage relationship sometimes results in women emphasizing emotional and spiritual benefits of a sexual awakening rather than physical pleasure.

One interview respondent, Solomon'sBride, told me her awakening story, but she later admitted that she had never experienced an orgasm: "I can get close, but I am still working toward that." I asked if she meant that she was trying to have an orgasm during sex with her husband or through self-stimulation. She clarified that she was referring to having an orgasm during intercourse with her husband and then went on to explain: "I never have tried it myself manually [. . .]. I really am not sure about even trying that on my own. It seems odd to do that to myself. I don't object but really don't know how either." She continued to tell me about an article she found on LustyChristianLadies.com about techniques for husbands to manually stimulate their wives: "I suppose I could probably do the same thing [. . .]. Not quite sure how that would work though, I am not sure [if] reading printed information or on the computer would be awkward during that time." Even though Solomon'sBride isn't eager to masturbate, she does believe that God wants her to prioritize her sexual pleasure. "The information on LustyChristianLadies was helpful in that I learned that this [enjoying sex] is what God wants. There was information on positions and things that may help, so I have used some of that [. . .]. I'm not giving up." Women who tell stories of sexual awakening express sexual entitlement, but many do so by prioritizing God over their own physical pleasure.

As sexual awakening stories reveal, many women website users believe that acts of selflessness can be acts of pleasure. For Heidi85, a LCL reader I interviewed, awakening happened as the result of changing sexual circumstances, specifically marrying her second husband. She explained that in her first marriage, she had not enjoyed or desired sex, and when she and her fiancé entered premarital counseling before her second marriage, she discussed her concern about having a low sex drive: "We stated our sexual expectations, and he and I were both worried that he would want sex more than I would. Once we were married, though, that was not the case. I have so much enjoyed the intimacy and closeness and fun of our sexual encounters. I usually want it more than he does." Although Heidi85 reported having a high sex drive, she confided in me that she rarely achieves orgasm during sex. She told me that she read some advice on LustyChristianLadies.com that recommended masturbating to get to know what kind of stimulation makes you climax: "I read that you can't be easily pleased if you don't know how to please yourself through masturbation. I have definitely given it a try, and occasionally I achieve orgasm, but I do not enjoy it at all." When I asked her why she didn't enjoy masturbating, and she responded, "There is nothing pleasurable or exciting about laying in bed touching myself. [. . .] I get pleasure from my husband." She chooses marital intimacy over physical pleasure yet still considers herself to be "sexually awakened." Heidi85's story suggests that, for Christian women, sexual pleasure can take many forms, beyond the ability to orgasm.

Just as women's physical responses to sex are varied, women website users have differing beliefs about godly sexuality, which guide their interpretations of their sexual awakening experiences. Some of these women, reflecting broader beliefs about men's headship and women's submission, believe that their husbands should lead all of their sexual activities and ultimately be responsible for their sexual climax. Yet even these women find ways to prioritize their pleasure in their awakening stories. When a BTS member complained about her husband's inability to help her climax during intercourse, other members suggested that she take control of the situation: "bring him to BTS"; "buy a vibrator for him to use"; "guide his hand to what feels good." These suggestions uphold a gendered dynamic within this woman's relationship—they would all allow her husband to feel that he maintains control—while encouraging her husband to work to prioritize his wife's pleasure.

Demonstrating one of the ways the logic of godly sex gets personalized online, website users propose creative solutions to the sexual dilemmas presented on the sites in ways that respect the personal beliefs of fellow users. Solomon'sBride, for example, does not believe God permits masturbation, but she reads LustyChristianLadies.com, even though the bloggers encourage masturbation in many circumstances. Since the bloggers are not insisting that *she* should masturbate, she continues to enjoy and learn from the site. Tara, on the other hand, believes masturbation is an important part of her spiritual, emotional, and physical health. She divorced her husband after experiencing her own sexual awakening and considers masturbation within the boundaries of God's rules for sex, especially when it can help believers like her discover their sexuality: "I see self-pleasuring as your emergency life support [when you can't have sex but experience sexual desire]. When you're an older single, it keeps you from being promiscuous. I think imagining your future husband is worlds different than objectifying the guy you saw at the beauty salon." Tara prioritizes her sexual pleasure, but she does so in a way that stays in line with her religious beliefs about godly sexuality, which allow sexual thoughts only within the context of heterosexual marriage.

Though their stories have in common the narrative structure of overcoming obstacles to achieve sexual pleasure, women who tell sexual awakening stories define pleasure in different ways. Just as women's bodies are, as QueenEsther put it, as unique as "snowflakes," women's sexual awakening stories tell individualized interpretations of sexual pleasure. For some women, experiencing an orgasm for the first time is the moment of sexual awakening, while for others, it is learning to enjoy the sensations and process of intercourse rather than the climax itself. Although evangelical sex advice often focuses on women's orgasms, women who use Christian sexuality websites see pleasure as more complex, as relational and spiritual rather than purely physical. They incorporate a variety of circumstances into what it means to be sexually awake.

BODIES OF CHRIST: WOMEN AND PLEASURE ONLINE

Women's sexual awakening stories demonstrate that some women theologize their lives by interpreting their sexual experiences. The stories show how website users stay attached to the experiential and embodied components of both religion and sex while sharing online, as the Internet is a medium that seems to displace the body. These Christian women theologize the body to make its physical and emotional reality something that both influences and is influenced by religious beliefs. Women's bodies matter; they are both the barrier to and the conduit for experiencing sexual pleasure. Although women often talk about the body in naturalized and objective terms, this talk is influenced by the specific socioreligious culture in which evangelical women tell their stories.[18] Women are influenced by external social factors when they interpret and respond to problems they perceive as internal to their individual physical bodies. Some women's physical restrictions—namely the inability to orgasm—lead them to imagine pleasure in new ways: not just as the ability to climax but also as engaging in marital intimacy and pleasing one's husband. What bodies can and cannot do shapes how sexual awakening stories unfold.

These stories also reinforce the logic of godly sex, which draws from dual perspectives, the religious and the secular. Evangelical beliefs frame every component of sexual awakening narratives—indeed, even the form of these stories draws from the narratives of salvation and personal transformation that have come to define the evangelical experience. Yet women also make claims about their entitlement to sexual pleasure in ways that clearly reflect liberal, secular, and even feminist notions about individual choices. While women are careful to describe their sexual lives in relational terms, the stories of sexual awakenings are those of individuals. They are stories of self-improvement, undoubtedly a product of the therapeutic and women's movements of the late twentieth century. Evangelical women express gratitude, joy, and even "empowerment" upon finding Christian sexuality websites, since the sites provide faith-based, sex-positive messages geared toward them. These websites accommodate these women's religious values alongside their sexual desires and interests, insisting that, contrary to popular stereotypes, conservative religious beliefs are compatible with women's sexual pleasure. Women who tell sexual awakening stories talk about how they learned to prioritize and achieve a pleasure that is their own.

Yet in order for the sexual pleasure of these women to be legitimate, it must connect to male authorities in their lives—God and their husbands—meaning that women must continually balance their own desires with their marital and spiritual relationships. These sexual awakening stories show that the logic of godly sex is distinctly gendered, limiting women's experiences and desires. In this way, Christian sexuality websites participate in what Feona Attwood describes as efforts to "recuperate women's sexual pleasure in the service of heterosexual relationships."[19] Heterosexual marriage provides conservative Christian women with the means and the ends to women's pleasure.

These women's stories are shaped by contradictory structural and cultural forces that on the one hand allow them to feel empowered by their sexuality but on the other hand produce pressures that influence their choices.[20]

As the next chapter will show, men must also contend with religious beliefs that prioritize the relationship between believer, spouse, and God. Yet for men, this relational "holy trinity" makes possible a wide range of sexual acts, even, at times, ones that are on the margins of what is considered acceptable. The relationship between women, God, and their husbands, however, seems to temper women's sexual possibilities. Though women express a firm commitment to their own sexual pleasure, their desires tend not to deviate far beyond what Stevi Jackson and Sue Scott describe as the typical "sexual sentence," penile-vaginal intercourse.[21] Men, on the other hand, find ways to go off script.

FIVE

What Makes a Man

MAKING "BAD" SEX "GOOD"

Wed 9:03pm   User: PrinceCharming   Posts: 104

The act of pegging is very much appealing to me. Anal penetration is quite pleasurable to me, and I am hoping to get my wife to agree to some strap-on sex very soon. In anticipation, I have a few questions. What positions do you find most comfortable? Can a guy reach orgasm through pegging without any other stimulation? Lastly, what does the wife get out of this whole thing?

Wed 11:45pm   User: AngelBoy   Posts: 1222

You may want to consider a strap-on/harness combo that has a built in vibrator that can give dear wife pleasure during the process.

Thur 9:35am   User: PrinceCharming   Posts: 105

AngelBoy, which one do you have? I'm currently looking at the Nexus Maximus but am waiting on the wife.

Thur 11:00am   User: Timid   Posts: 12

My dear husband and I have just started trying this. As for what the woman gets out of it, I REALLY enjoy seeing the look on my husband's face and knowing I am able to give him that much pleasure. I also recommend the combo—that's what we got, and I can O [orgasm] with it as well.

Thur 11:05am   User: nola   Posts: 74

Here's a site that has a lot of good reviews. I recommend the Nexus Maximus. It's big but the least phallic looking, if you care about that. We prefer doggie style—it's just "sexier" to us.

Thur 2:56pm   User: TheDude   Posts 1496

My wife and I haven't done strap-on, but I think it would be totally TJ$@#%S hot. Would love to try it soon. We have used a vibrator on me several times that produces the most mind-blowing orgasms I've ever had.

Thur 10:25pm   User: AmericanEagle   Posts: 2

I am so glad I found this site. We have wanted to do this for a while but don't know where to start. And frankly it's not your everyday sex thing, so most people act taboo about it. They don't know what they're missing!

Excerpt from BetweenTheSheets.com thread topic "Interested in Pegging"
in the message board forum "Anal Delights"

As BetweenTheSheets.com user AmericanEagle points out, anal sex—and especially anal sex in which a man is the receiving partner—is "not your everyday sex thing." Scandal can erupt when straight people reveal even slightly crooked sexual interests. Congressman and New York City mayoral candidate Anthony Weiner, for example, was declared a "sex addict" by media pundits after it was uncovered that he had shared sexually explicit photographs with women over the Internet, leading to the end of his political career.[1] Yet around the same time as this news erupted, AmericanEagle found himself participating in an online discussion thread on a Christian sexuality website that treated male anal play as mundane and normal.

The questions PrinceCharming posed about pegging (the anal penetration of a man by a woman) deal with matters of practicality: What positions are best? How can both partners experience pleasure? What dildos do you recommend? User nola recommends the Nexus Maximus, casually mentioning that it is the one that least resembles a phallus—"if you care about that." Despite evangelicals who speak out against anal sex between gay men, some Christian men interested in pegging do not mind if the dildos they use resemble penises. These men bypass what may seem obvious questions about their sexual preferences (for example, does this interest signal closeted homosexuality?) and instead normalize conversation about what seem to be far-from-normal sexual interests.

Website users on this discussion board did not debate whether God approves of anal sex or whether dildos represent a phallus. Still, BTS members cannot take their masculinity for granted. As queer theorist Guy Hocquenghem quips, "Seen from behind we are all women."[2] In contemporary Western culture, the prevailing and predictable sexual narrative depends upon the man having the role of a penetrator, dominating women.[3] Although what counts as good and normal sex includes a broader range of acts today than in decades past, sexual acts that challenge what men and women are "supposed" to do in bed are consistently labeled as deviant by religious, medical, and legal authorities. The organization Focus on the Family summarizes the pervasive conservative Christian understanding of heterosexual sex: "her parts and his parts each have their own order and function."[4] Evangelical men who desire to shift the order and function these "parts" during sex, therefore, must find ways to reconcile their sexual interests with their status as Christian patriarchs.

Focusing on two gender-subversive acts—pegging and cross-dressing—this chapter examines how some conservative Christians, men in particular, use the logic of godly sex to justify kinky sex. Website users' definitions of pegging are varied—some refer to any form of male anal penetration as pegging, whereas others only use the term to refer to sex where a female partner wears a strap-on device to anally penetrate her male partner.[5] Christian users of these sites give more uniform definitions of cross-dressing, which is understood by most as men who wear women's intimate items (like lingerie) during sexual play. In total, I analyzed about fifty blog posts or discussion threads that mentioned male anal play or cross-dressing.[6] Not surprisingly, conversations about so-called kinky sex take place much less often than conversations about vanilla sex practices. Still, website users and administrators do not treat those who discuss these practices as marginalized freaks or provocateurs trying to incite disagreement or upset among members. Instead, online discussions about these kinds of non-normative practices take place among well-respected and frequent users of BetweenTheSheets.com and LustyChristianLadies.com.

When engaging in sex that removes them from their roles as active penetrators, Christian men must find other ways to construct their masculine identities. These men affirm their masculinity while supporting gender-deviant sex by relying on a definition of gender that is based on their relationships with their wives and with God. This construction of gender, what I call *gender omniscience,* depends on the presence of a spouse and on God's unique ability to know a man's "true" gender. Gender omniscience can render even non-normative sex quintessentially heterosexual and gender normal. Like website creators who use a belief in God's omniscience to justify the sexual content on their sites (see chapter two), website users interested in kinky sex incorporate established evangelical beliefs into their understanding of sexuality in order to normalize non-normative sexual practices. Illuminating the malleability of godly sex, website users frame gender as relational and spiritual, thereby extending their beliefs to encompass the sex acts in which they engage.

GENDER HEGEMONY

Shifts in the conception of evangelical masculinity in recent decades have made possible new conversations among men about intimate issues, including sex. The evangelical men's movement known as Promise Keepers emphasizes traits like compassion, expressing emotions, and developing close friendships with other men. Founded in 1990 by a university football coach, Promise Keepers offer an outlet for masculine Christian men to be emotional, vulnerable, and intimate. This movement, along with evangelical self-help literature and other organizations, like the ex-gay group Exodus International, encourages men to share their sexual struggles with each other, whether these struggles are related to promiscuity, pornography, or same-sex attraction. Yet the saliency of what W. Bradford Wilcox calls "soft patriarchy" within contemporary evangelicalism means that evangelicals remain committed to heterosexuality and gender distinctions between men and women, even when men are committed to relationships and family life.[7]

Christian sexuality websites present language that appears gender equal: rules about who is allowed to have sex are the same for men and women, and God created sexual pleasure to be enjoyed fully by both husband and wife. Yet the results of the CSIS offer persistent indications of men's privilege, or gender hegemony, when it comes to sexual knowledge and experience. For example, men who completed the CSIS were more likely than women both to have had multiple sexual partners (see figure 8) and to masturbate (see figure 13). This is partly why the previous chapter focused on *women's* sexual awakening stories—typically, men enter their marriages already sexually "awake," while women struggle to achieve sexual pleasure. The CSIS data highlight the general opinion I observed in online discussions: men's sexual desires and experiences tend to be more expansive than women's.

When it comes to online content, evidence of gender hegemony can be subtle. For instance, website users often describe women's sex appeal as something that women must *do,* whereas men's sex appeal is described as something that men *are.* The instructions BetweenTheSheets.com creator John posted for women on how to give a striptease, presented in chapter two, is one example of this. Through a striptease, women literally *perform* in order to make themselves sexually desirable to their husbands. Similarly, LustyChristianLadies.com bloggers frame women's sex appeal as something they can accomplish through choosing the right clothes and accessories. This is illustrated by the site's "Fill In the Blank" questions, for example: "I feel really sexy whenever I put on___." This is in contrast to the types of questions LCL asks about men's sex appeal: "My husband doesn't realize how sexy I find his___." Readers respond to these statements differently, according to the prompts. Women's sexiness, for example, comes from stiletto heels and mini skirts, whereas men are sexy because of their broad shoulders, biceps, butts, and chests. Men's bodies, by default, are what women describe as appealing, whereas women describe having to "put on" what makes them sexy.

Gender hegemony does not mean that men present themselves overwhelmingly as sexually dominant, self-assured, or arrogant. Some do, but most don't. Many website users—men and women alike—struggle with sexual confidence. Women and men, for example, describe attempts at weight loss and insecurities about their bodies (though women do this much more frequently than men). Men, just like women, find Christian sexuality websites to ask questions and seek advice about their personal sexual problems. The problems that men write about having—like struggles with marital communication, addiction to pornography, or trouble maintaining an erection—reveal that men's lives often do not neatly reflect the stereotypes presented in prescriptive literature. Nonetheless, men protect and maintain their masculine identities while exposing the ways in which they do not meet the standards of hegemonic masculinity.[8] This chapter is one example of how this occurs.

The simultaneous stronghold and slipperiness of male privilege persist not only in evangelicalism but also in society at large. Hegemonic masculinity operates by subordinating both femininity *and* other forms of masculinity. Yet even men who do not perfectly embody hegemonic masculinity benefit from what R. W. Connell calls the "patriarchal dividend." Gay men and men of color, for example, may find ways to exert masculinity through a variety of "manhood acts," even when they cannot embody distinctly heterosexual and white hegemonic masculinity. In her study of straight-identified white men who have sex with other men (and often refer to themselves as "str8"), Jane Ward reveals the complex relationship between race and sexuality, demonstrating that these men are still able to use archetypes of white masculinity to associate themselves with heterosexual culture. In a study on ex-gay Christian men and their wives, Michelle Wolkomir shows how her respondents rely on norms related to heterosexual culture (love and monogamy) in order to justify their "mixed-orientation marriages" as normal and good. Similarly, some Christian men find space to write guiltlessly about their interest in pegging or cross-dressing by emphasizing their socially acceptable traits in order to mitigate their deviant ones.[9]

WHAT MAKES A MAN?

Within published evangelical sex advice, there is near universal support for gender complementarianism—the idea that God created men and women to fulfill distinct and balancing roles. This applies equally to intimate and non-intimate aspects of a married relationship. For intimate encounters, beliefs about gender translate to *sexual complementarianism*—the idea that God created men and women to fulfill different roles when it comes to erotic behavior. As an example of what Gayle Rubin calls the "domino theory of sexual peril," sex acts may be scrutinized if they can "'lead' to something ostensibly worse."[10] This is why, perhaps, Tim and Beverly LaHaye's *The Act of Marriage* does not discuss non-normative sex but instead firmly supports a traditional understanding of gender, naming "feminine dominance" as a possible cause of men's erectile dysfunction and instructing women to strive for "submissive grace."[11] While website users do not uniformly support men's headship and women's submission, it appears that virtually all of them believe in a gender binary and that most believe that sex acts that violate gender norms are forbidden by God. As one member of BTS argued on a thread about pegging, "It would seem a potential danger for a man to take on a receptive role [. . .] and one which would be contrary to the parameters [. . .] God created men to inhabit." Many evangelicals are wary of acts that challenge typical notions of femininity and masculinity.

Part of the tension that takes place on Christian sexuality websites occurs when multiple individuals attempt to apply these messages about gender and sexuality to contemporary everyday life. Website users, even those who read and agree with evangelical authors like the LaHayes, use the Internet to debate the implications of objective declarations about masculinity and femininity, and sometimes they pose alternative questions. On the BTS message board "Headship and Submission," one member, SheComesFirst, posed a question to fellow users, whom he assumed all agree that God created men and women to be naturally different: "Should church leaders be judged by cultural standards of masculinity?" More to the point, he also asked: "How do we as Christians describe masculinity or maleness without relying on cultural markers?" He described a budding leader within his congregation, a man in his early twenties who often attended church on Sundays wearing bright pink polo shirts. "Is this appropriate?" SheComesFirst wondered.

At the heart of SheComesFirst's questions is the relationship between gender expression and sexuality. Though his questions are not explicitly about sexuality, they implicitly bring up the stereotypical association between effeminate men and homosexuality and whether something superficial, like the color of a polo shirt, can represent a deviation from masculinity (and potentially a deviation from heterosexuality).

BTS member Sugar was the first to respond to SheComesFirst's post, insisting: "While some may claim that God doesn't care what you look like as He only looks to the heart, it would appear that from scripture we find that God does care how we look insofar as our dress is a reflection of our gender identity." Sugar's vague reference to scripture is supported by another user who directly quotes Deuteronomy 22:5 (NIV): "A woman must not wear men's clothing, nor a man wear women's clothing, for the Lord your God detests anyone who does this." Sugar confirms this sentiment: "If there is a cultural shift toward an androgynous society and the inherent blurring of gender lines that God has intended for His image, then that cultural shift is a repudiation of the scriptural concept that God created." She insists that a man wearing a pink shirt, superficial though it may seem, signals larger cultural values that are unwholesome—a disrespect for a clear gender binary and thereby a disrespect for heterosexuality.

Members quickly pushed back against Sugar's absolutist perspective, challenging an automatic association between effeminate appearance and homosexuality. Many state with confidence that a godly man can, of course, wear a pink shirt, since this is a superficial stereotype about masculinity. One member, ExodusGuy, explains, "I've had some really great friends who are male but have an 'artistic flair' about them that comes a bit close to 'effeminate.' But if a man is brave and strong and steps up to the plate to do his job, and he is heterosexual and faithful, I'd call him masculine." According to ExodusGuy and many other BTS users, God doesn't focus on outward appearance but rather on a way of being ("brave," "strong," "stepping up to the plate") that transcends outward appearances and defines masculinity.

And importantly, heterosexuality is a marker that a man, even one who wears a pink shirt, is doing masculinity right. Another member, KyleForChrist, focuses on how stereotypes of masculine appearance are culturally specific: "Different standards are defined for a region, setting, and time. The standard for masculine swimwear in some societies might be what we would call a pair of ladies' bikini bottoms. Is it any less masculine? Not if it's worn in a place where that is acceptable for men."

Sugar, ExodusGuy, and KyleForChrist all offer different perspectives on the same dilemma, as described by sociologist John Bartkowski: "What is the 'essence'—the defining characteristics, if any—of masculinity and femininity?"[12] These website users struggle to find the point at which a Christian man no longer lives up to his godly duty to *be* a man (i.e., to look, act, and embody manliness). The boundaries of godly manhood are hard to determine because, as discussed in chapters two and three, one core evangelical Protestant belief is that an individual's relationship to God is one that outsiders can never know. Objective claims about gender are therefore inevitably limited in describing an evangelical experience of gender as God intends it, which is always subjective. Despite the absolute assertion that all men crave respect, for example, it is up to an individual man, in his unique and idiosyncratic relationship with God, to determine what respect means for him.

BENDING OR BREAKING THE "RULES"?

The guidelines presented by most evangelicals who write or talk about sex take into account the subjective nature of sexual desire and, therefore, leave open a vast range of permissible sex within Christian marriages. Indeed, this understanding is at the heart of the logic of godly sex. As popular author Kevin Leman writes, "The Bible is amazingly free in what it allows and even encourages a married couple to do in bed."[13] Put another way, by a female LCL reader: "There are far more things that you *can* enjoy together than those you cannot." That Christians can make decisions about their sexual lives that may differ from those made by other couples draws upon an often-quoted Bible verse from the book of Hebrews: "Marriage is honorable in all, and the bed undefiled."[14] This logic allows couples to establish their own sexual interests as morally acceptable. Author Shannon Ethridge, for example, explains, "as long as no harm is done and all is kept solely between consenting spouses, just about anything and everything in the bedroom can be considered perfectly normal."[15] A female LCL reader's comment on a blog post about pegging reflects this attitude that sexual "normalness" is subjective. "I know for me, God has put a red flag on it," she writes, but then goes on to state, "what is a 'sin' for one may not be a 'sin' for all." In other words, it is the responsibility of a married couple to choose which sex acts are appropriate for them.

The BTS message board "Out of the Box" was created by the site's founders, John and Barbara, to show that they believe God loves kinky Christians, so long as they are straight, married, and monogamous. Not everyone who visits the site agrees with them. "We sometimes get pretty horrible hate emails," John told me. "Things like, 'You're going to hell. Christians don't talk like this.'" Barbara continued, "But we're really big on respecting people and their perspectives [. . .] and giving room for discussion and that sort of thing." They created board topics for Christians who have unusual sexual interests to talk with openness and mutual respect. On these boards, BTS members can discuss anal sex as well as "adult nursing, foot jobs, breast sex, facials, bondage, [and] spanking." As table 7 shows, BTS topics "Anal Delights" and "Out of the Box" make up 12 percent of threads on the site that talk about specific sex acts.[16] Though this number is small, it is not insignificant, and it includes about 5,000 comments posted by BTS members. John and Barbara have also made space for members who want to debate the godliness of unusual sexual interests. There are specific board topics on the site that are devoted to discussions of whether these activities are right or wrong.

Aside from BetweenTheSheets.com, LustyChristianLadies.com, and a few evangelical sex advice books, most conservative Christian sources that discuss having sex for pleasure—including the Bible and contemporary books, websites, and programs—do *not* talk explicitly about non-normative sex. This forces believers interested in practices like pegging or cross-dressing to figure out what God thinks about non-normative sex by reading between the lines of Christian sex advice. The website users I interviewed and observed took this advice very seriously, but at the same time they learned to apply the messages presented in books and on websites to their own unique sexual desires and experiences. One reader of LustyChristianLadies.com, HiddenTreasure, told me in an interview: "I wasn't sure what was OK biblically, but now I know. [. . .] Some things are not biblically defined and are left to us for prayer and figuring out what God would see as best in our own marriage beds." When the Bible and sex advice literature leave out discussions of activities like pegging, erotic cross-dressing, or other unusual sex

TABLE 7 Distribution of BetweenTheSheets.com threads in forums that discuss sex acts, October 2011

Forum title	Number of threads	Percentage of total sample
Tricks and Trades	727	31
How to Positions	573	25
Self-Pleasure	268	12
Oral Sex	219	10
Outside the Box	153	7
Okay, Bad Idea, Sin?	128	6
Anal Delights	108	5
Female Pleasure	55	2
Manual Stimulation	46	2
Totals	2,277	100

acts, it is up to individual couples to find what they consider to be the relevant "rules" for them.

As detailed in chapter one, although conservative Christians categorize many sex acts as wrong without exception, users of Christian sexuality websites confront a wide range of sexual experiences and desires for which boundaries of right or wrong are blurry. A large majority of CSIS respondents stated that sex is "always wrong" between an unmarried man and woman (78 percent) or between two adults of the same sex (88 percent), or if it involves pornography, even within marriage (64 percent). When it comes to anal sex, though, attitudes were much more mixed. About 20 percent reported that it is "always wrong" for a married couple to engage in anal sex, but 60 percent believed that it is "not wrong at all." When it comes to reported practices, about three out of four respondents indicated that they never engage in anal sex, yet, as figure 15 shows, many respondents, especially men, expressed interest in it.[17] Most women reported that they do not find anal sex appealing, regardless of whether they are the active or passive partner. However, half of married men who completed the CSIS (50 percent) indicated that they find anal sex in which a woman is penetrated to be at least somewhat appealing, and 38 percent of married men reported that they find passive anal sex to be at least somewhat appealing. Men were more likely to be interested in being anally penetrated than women were. Only 20 percent of women reported being at least somewhat interested in anal sex in which they are penetrated.

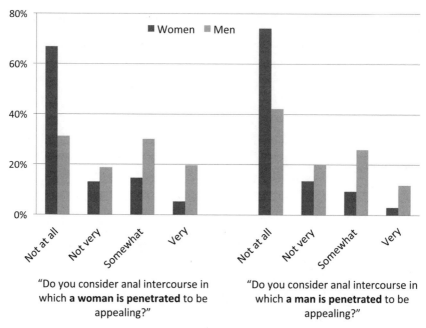

"Do you consider anal intercourse in which **a woman is penetrated** to be appealing?"

"Do you consider anal intercourse in which **a man is penetrated** to be appealing?"

FIGURE 15. Interest in anal sex by gender, CSIS married sample.

Still, pegging and cross-dressing are two sex acts that provoke mixed reactions from both male and female website users. Users are more likely to support pegging than erotic cross-dressing, perhaps because the pleasure of prostate stimulation is gaining increasing visibility in mainstream culture through media that epitomize gender and (hetero)sexuality stereotypes, such as *Playboy* and *Cosmopolitan Magazine*.[18] Erotic cross-dressing encounters more scrutiny than pegging on Christian sexuality websites, in part because website users can use supposed "facts" of physical pleasure to justify pegging, but when it comes to cross-dressing, users must rely on subjective descriptions of the pleasure to be gained. One male BTS member asserts: "The prostate is wired into our orgasms and arousal centers." Statements like this imply that the physiology of sexual pleasure clearly invites male anal play. Yet, like cross-dressing, the act of pegging undeniably violates gender expectations of sex because it removes men from their primary role as dominant penetrator.[19]

Despite the appearance of sexual permissiveness in Christian sex advice when it comes to marital sex, gender-subversive acts like pegging and cross-dressing are considered highly questionable within conservative Christian culture at large, given the wide support of gender and sexual complementarianism and the opposition to same-sex sex. One BTS member summarizes pegging in this way: "The thought of asking my wife to use a strap-on on me is repulsive. Is it wrong? Immoral? Probably not, but it is way on the edge and would not be considered normal sexual behavior to the vast majority of Christian folks." Echoing this sentiment, Lizzy99, a LCL reader, brought up pegging when I asked her if she disagreed with anything posted by the LCL bloggers. She explained: "They're okay with pegging, and although I'm not sure if it's sinful or not, I'm not comfortable with it. They also have the philosophy that 'if the bible doesn't explicitly forbid something, then its ok.' I think that works a lot of the time but don't think it's a blanket statement you can make about anything. God didn't forbid smoking pot, but I def[initely] don't think that he wants us there smoking pot." I asked her to elaborate on why she wasn't sure if pegging is sinful or not, to which she replied: "I just mean that it's such a controversial topic and I just don't know [. . .]. I'm very uncomfortable doing it personally, but I don't know that I think it would be wrong for others if it doesn't make them uncomfortable." Explaining why it made her uncomfortable, she said: "It seems too close to a homosexual act, but on the other hand, I know that oral sex is the main way that lesbians have sex, so if I use that as the judge, then oral sex should seem wrong, which it isn't. I like to be feminine, and my husband is very masculine, and pegging seems to reverse those roles. I also think it would feel very weird wearing a strap on."

Lizzy99 ultimately decided that she did not agree with LCL bloggers about pegging and expressed nervous ambivalence when describing how she felt, repeating the phrase "I don't know" and answering without punctuating her responses (unlike her other responses, where she seemed to use punctuation to reflect natural pauses and transitions in her thoughts). She opposed the act but could not pinpoint exactly why, so she tried out a few possible reasons—it could signal homosexuality, or it could reverse gender roles—until finally, she simply stated that it would "feel very weird" for her to wear a strap-on. Lizzy99, like many website users, struggled to find clear boundaries between appropriate and inappropriate sex within marriage.

Some conservative Christians use the argument that the marriage bed is "undefiled" to claim that non-normative sex is permissible within marriage.[20] On the surface, they justify non-normative sex by conflating married heterosexuality with gender normalcy. As one LCL reader put it, even when it comes to pegging, "why assume a straight man having sex with his straight wife is doing something gay?" Similarly, a blogger on AffectionateMarriage.com responded to a reader's comment that anal sex sounded "too gay" to be performed by Christians: "Well, this is just silly [. . .]. The fact that homosexuals may (or may not) do something does not make it 'gay.' Having sex with someone of the same sex makes it gay." A BTS member also made a reference to homosexuality when offering advice on whether it would be okay for a man to wear women's lingerie if his wife asked him to: "It's not okay if she has 'lesbian tendencies,' but otherwise, it's okay." In other words, some website users argue that any sex act that takes place between a man and woman is heterosexual by default.

I argue that these explanations and rationalizations oversimplify the complex strategies that website users deploy to justify their gender normalcy to other users. In fact, if it were so simple to be sure that all sex between a husband and wife is approved of by God, these users would likely not be tediously engaging with others about the details of their sex lives. Instead, they use Christian sexuality sites to prove how their gender aligns clearly with their sense of manhood or womanhood so that the sex in which they engage should be considered normative and heterosexual. They do this by repeatedly emphasizing the figures that are universally the most important in adult Christians' lives: one's spouse and God. However, the websites themselves also play an important role in confirming or challenging individuals' interpretations of these relationships. In this way, the websites are in fact God-like, giving (and permitting) users a sense of right and wrong.

GENDER OMNISCIENCE AND THE HOLY TRIANGLE OF GODLY SEX

To maintain their beliefs about gender, website users interested in non-normative sex imbue kinky acts with alternative meanings. Users construct what I call *gender omniscience,* or the privileged knowledge of one's "true" gender based on a triangulated relationship between the self, one's spouse, and God, to guiltlessly engage in pegging and cross-dressing. Instead of basing the definition of gender on nature or science, as many conservative Christians do, these users of Christian sexuality websites present the all-knowing power of their spouses and God as the ultimate authority on gender. For example, these users do not naturalize penile-vaginal intercourse as quintessential to heterosexual identity. Instead, they consider the marital intimacy that can result from a wide range of sex acts, including pegging and cross-dressing, to be of central importance. This maintains an appearance of essentialism but actually constructs gender as subjective and based on believers' different experiences and understandings of God.[21]

Using gender omniscience to justify non-normative sex upholds conservative Christian beliefs about gender and sexuality, thereby reifying heterosexuality and maintaining a power imbalance between husbands and wives. My analysis of Christian sexuality websites shows that men who use the sites are much more likely than their female counterparts to talk about their interests in non-normative sex, despite the fact that users use gender-equal language when talking about sexual pleasure. While many women engage in discussions that talk frankly and explicitly about sex, they tend not to express personal interest in pegging, cross-dressing, or other gender-subversive acts. Inherent in website users' discussions of these practices is a gender imbalance that gives voice to men's, not women's, unusual sexual desires.

The Spouse's Omniscience

In discussing interest in pegging and men's cross-dressing, website users speak about the extraordinary nature of a married relationship, mimicking the language that appears in many sex advice books. The Driscolls write in their book, *Real Marriage,* that "sex is for knowledge. [...] This sacred and experiential knowledge means that a faithfully married couple has an intimacy and connection that is not only exclusive but also unprecedented in all their other relationships." The ability of a wife to know her husband's "true" gender identity is based on something very special indeed—a "sacred and experiential knowledge" that is unique to their relationship.[22] As one administrator of BTS posted in a thread about erotic cross-dressing, "there is a difference between sharing an odd fetish with one's spouse when it is part of their sexual relationship and a man wearing women's clothing anywhere else." That is to say, a marriage is unlike other relationships. The bond between a husband and wife is considered the most intimate bond in one's life—outside of one's relationship with God. A member of BTS advised a woman questioning her husband's interest in pegging: "You know him best." One reader of LCL asserted her special knowledge about her husband when she adamantly stated, "My dear husband is 100% man throughout, but he loves when I peg him." Similarly, a BTS member emphasized the unique spousal bond he has with his wife when he shared his experience with pegging using a well-rated dildo that "looks like a penis": "My wife knows that what I wanted was my prostate massaged and that it had NOTHING to do with being homosexual." One's spouse, like God, occupies a privileged space when it comes to knowing one's sexual and gendered identity.

According to author Kevin Leman, "a fulfilling sex life is one of the most powerful marital glues a couple can have."[23] Drawing from Leman and other popular Christian authors who insist that pleasure is an integral part of a successful marriage as God created it, website users emphasize the closeness that results from men's pleasure when justifying non-normative sex. One BTS member responded to a thread questioning the practice of pegging: "My wife finally used the strap-on that I bought and all I can say was WOW!!!! I used a vibrator on her to give her pleasure, and she caressed me while I moved and it turned out to be an amazing experience. Dear wife said it was not as bad as she thought because she really enjoyed pleasing me." This BTS member's wife overcame reluctance to engage in pegging because she saw how pleasurable the practice was for her husband. Women readers of LCL express enthusiasm about pegging because of the pleasure and intimacy it leads to. For example, women have posted: pegging "has brought us closer than ever"; "our sex life is now so much more fun"; "I do not need to be ashamed of pleasing my husband the way we both desire." These website users feel that fulfilling their husbands' deepest sexual desires is part of an extraordinary intimacy awarded to married couples.

Marital closeness is also how some website users justify cross-dressing during sex. BTS member LucilleBall commented on a message board debating this practice, "My dear husband enjoys wearing my underwear from time to time [. . .]. I don't have a problem with it [. . .]. It is an intimate act, drawing us together in another way." Many other posters strongly disagreed with Lucille, one insisting that this type of practice is "a perversion of the distinction between man and woman which God made." Yet another member contended that all sex practices that involve some unusual or potentially deviant element can actually signal a strong marriage, not the opposite: "This is the sort of stuff for mature, open, other-focused relationships. I'd not see this working or being a good idea in relationships where there is a lot of stress, selfishness, fear, or legalism." His implication is that being able to successfully engage in non-normative sex indicates that a couple has a relationship that reflects marriage as God intends it—"mature, open, and other-focused."

Although website users appear to emphasize consent equally for both men and women, conservative Christians tend to value submissive qualities of wives and promote the belief that it is the responsibility of a wife to sexually fulfill her partner. As popular authors Ed Wheat and Gaye Wheat write, "the husband delights in a loving wife who is submissive and responsive."[24] This means that men who want to engage in pegging or cross-dressing already have substantial leverage over their wives. Conservative Christian culture, reflecting broader social sexual norms, pressures women to accommodate their husbands' (sexual) interests but does not place similar expectations on men. Many of the women members of BTS who engage in active anal sex with their husbands express reservations about the practice. One member wrote, "I am finally at the stage where I can willingly do this for him because I know how much he enjoys it, although I still struggle from time to time with the moral correctness of it." Another member expressed a similar sentiment, explaining that she eventually agreed to participate in pegging because it pleases her husband: "It's not my cup of tea, but over [the course of] our marriage, I've slowly opened up to a lot of things to bless [my husband]." Of course, many men who use Christian sexuality websites also make compromises in their sexual relationships and use the sites, in part, to find advice on ways to better pleasure their wives. The difference between men and women who use these sites is that women are less likely to express sexual interests that challenge normative gender roles.

Paradoxically, then, using gender omniscience to justify non-normative sex maintains men's privileged status within Christian marriages while simultaneously giving women some power over their sexual relationships. Website users question the motives of non-normative sex acts in cases in which a wife's consent has not been obtained. They are especially wary of non-normative *solo* sex play, since lack of spousal participation could signal an unhealthy attachment to these acts. When men express interest in acts that could be considered gender deviant, like pegging and cross-dressing, website users always question whether or not they have made these desires apparent to their spouses. In response to a post in which a man admitted that he had secret fantasies of wearing his wife's lingerie, BTS members responded with harsh concern, questioning his heterosexuality and gender identity, advising him to avoid acting on his impulses without talking to his wife, and suspiciously inquiring about why he wants to keep his fantasy hidden. One member instructed him, "Either talk to her [your wife] about it, or let it go. But don't indulge in secret." This indicates that a wife's approval is necessary to confirm gender normalcy and justify non-normative sex; in order for a man to guiltlessly engage in sex acts like pegging or cross-dressing, his spouse must confirm his masculine status.

Yet because gender omniscience relies on the triangulated relationship between a man, his wife, and God, website users often encourage men to turn to God rather than simply dismiss certain sex acts that their partners have refused. One BTS member explained that he was using his relationship with God to influence his marriage relationship: "One thing I've just recently started doing is praying for our sex life. I never thought it would have such an effect [. . .]. We still haven't done it [pegging] but my wife has opened up a lot." Another member offered advice to a member whose wife refuses to peg: "Just give your wife some time and pray about it. [. . .] My wife was a little hesitant, but I do believe now she enjoys pleasing me." These stories overlook that a wife often has feelings of responsibility to participate in sex acts proposed by her husband and instead assume that God alone has the power to convince a spouse to engage in these acts. A wife's role in constructing gender omniscience therefore has a dual effect: it gives her an amount of leverage over her sexual relationship but it may also pressure her to conform to a sexual relationship determined by her husband's desires.

God's Omniscience

Men who use Christian sexuality websites draw upon God's approval of sexual intimacy and pleasure within marriage relationships to make decisions about the appropriateness of non-normative sex. Authors Clifford and Joyce Penner write, "God is in the bedroom—whether you invite him there or not." They instruct their readers to acknowledge God's role in their sexual lives: "Offer a quiet inner prayer, thanking God for those pleasant, exciting, satisfying feelings. Recognize that God approves of these feelings." Devout Christians who understand God as an active participant in their sexual lives believe that God will tell them whether or not a sex act is sinful. As authors Farrell and Farrell suggest to couples that are questioning the appropriateness of any particular sex act, "If you are in doubt, pray it out. God will show you how to respond to your mate." In other words, if pious men or women have sex outside of God's design, they'll be able to sense that what they are doing is wrong. Using feelings associated with their prayer lives, website users make claims about God's gender omniscience to justify that the sex they desire is normal and good.[25]

How website users *feel,* based on their relationships with God, often determines the outcome of support or admonition of gender-deviant sex. However, as sociologist Dawne Moon writes, "feelings do not form a solid basis for moral arguments because [...] they can point to multiple truths."[26] Yet users of Christian sexuality websites consider feelings to be the valid basis of moral arguments, for they constitute how website users make sense of God's will. In threads about cross-dressing, posters set the tone by describing their relationships with God. On one BTS thread, for example, a member disclosed his urge to wear women's lingerie and then expressed his concern about having these desires: "I have prayed over this a lot, and I feel like God is working on me, showing me the ugly parts of my heart." Other members encouraged him in resisting his urges; none suggested that his desires might be acceptable. Even website users who may condone cross-dressing in some circumstances will not validate the practice if it is presented as disrupting the relationship between a believer and God. One longtime BTS member wrote in another thread about cross-dressing: "I have no clear biblical stance that irrefutably tells you that wearing your bride's underwear is considered [sin], but I will also not talk you out of feeling guilty if God is the one poking at your spirit." As this user put it, Christians should pay attention to anything "poking at the spirit," making one question the sexual acts in which he engages.

While feelings may veer some believers away from gender-deviant sex (they feel God's disapproval), feelings about God also can confirm and validate website users' unusual sexual interests. Users are much more likely to approve of non-normative sex if a poster articulates his belief that God approves of this type of sex for him. A member of BTS put it this way, writing to another member who was interested in but cautious about pursuing pegging: "God knows your heart and the real reasons that you want this." Similarly, one reader of LCL wrote that he sensed God's approval of pegging through prayer: "I was talking [to] God about it AGAIN and I really felt the Lord say to me 'I love what you and [your] wife have together.'" In another thread, a member defended his interest in cross-dressing by stating that he had read the Bible for guidance: "While it may be a bit naughty, I don't think I am violating any OT [Old Testament] passages. [...] I am not rejecting my role as a man ... and [I am] not wanting to be a woman. [...] My conscience is clear here." Website users rely on their intimate relationships with God to make decisions about appropriate or inappropriate sexual conduct.

Because evangelicals believe in a deeply personal relationship with God, some website users refrain from passing judgment about others' marginal sexual practices. In response to one reader's negative comment about pegging on LCL—"That is a complete role reversal, and I can't imagine that God would be pleased with that!"—a site contributor responded, "I would caution any of you who presumes to know what God is thinking. Just because you are uncomfortable with a particular act doesn't mean it's inherently wrong or sinful." When it comes to gender normalcy especially, these website users rely on God's omniscience to determine if a husband and wife will be able to engage in pegging or cross-dressing while maintaining their maleness and femaleness. As one member of BTS wrote, "the Bible says that man looks to outward appearance, while God looks to the heart." Online discussions that discuss cross-dressing and pegging reveal that what is at stake in gender normalcy is not proving an objective truth related to gender appearances but rather proving a piety aligned with God's authority.

The Holy Triangle

Website users assess the merits of gender-deviant sex on a case-by-case basis, by evaluating the strength and authenticity of an individual's relationships with God and his wife. These relationships work together to make up a kind of "holy triangle" of godly sex.[27] Wagner joined BTS precisely to make sense of his own self-described "kinky" interests, which exist alongside his commitment to his marriage and to God. Specifically, he described wanting to rid himself of a "nagging feeling" that he should feel guilty for being turned on by "dirty talk" and sexual role-playing. He described that he wasn't sure what to do with his feelings before joining the site: "I was attracted to this 'dirty' type of sex but was ashamed to bring that to my wife." He learned from BTS that "part of the fun of sex is the 'dirty' aspect of it, and when you experience that with someone, it builds trust." BTS served as an interactive religious authority that supported Wagner's sense that he shouldn't feel guilty about what caused him sexual pleasure within his marriage.

In the following excerpt from my interview with Wagner, I tried to understand how he makes sense of kinky sex, both for himself and in a hypothetical scenario. I have italicized statements that privilege the holy triangle as a series of relationships that are unlike any other.

> WAGNER: The general consensus among believers seems to be that there is no problem with [kinky sex] at all as long as each person involved in it feels OK about it and nobody is violating their conscience. [...] People generally see that, in the context of a godly marriage, *things that we might consider "unwholesome" outside of the marriage bed are not "unwholesome" within it.*

KELSY: You mentioned that you are interested in what Christians think about role-playing. Have you got any helpful advice on this topic from other members?

WAGNER: This seems to be an issue that you find more of a split in what people think. Some people seem to say that it is alright *as long as the characters that you role-play are married,* while others think anything is fair game.

KELSY: What do you think?

WAGNER: I think anything is OK. We never tell kids that they aren't allowed to play cops and robbers. If I were to play teacher/student with my wife, I think that is OK. *God knows that I really don't want to be seduced by a school girl,* for that would be sinful. Instead, I want to experience the thrill of my wife acting like a highly sexual person. I think that *under the umbrella of a Godly marriage, God has given us the freedom to do whatever we want* as long as we are not involving another person in thought or deed. I think sex is meant to be fun, and we are allowed to be creative in how we do it.

KELSY: I'm wondering if you can weigh in on a debate I recently followed on BTS about a man who liked to wear his wife's underwear during sex. Some people thought that form of gender-play was not okay. What do you think?

WAGNER: I think that would be a tough one that the individual would have to decide. I guess it has to come down to motive. If you are doing it because you just want to try something kinky with your spouse because it would be exciting then I really think that's OK. But if the motivation is to satisfy a secret desire for homosexual activity then there would be a problem. The former would actually *increase intimacy between a couple because it would require a lot of trust.*

KELSY: So those kinds of kinky practices may have the power to improve a marriage?

WAGNER: Absolutely. And that's what you've got to decide. One thing you see a lot of people saying [on the boards] is that something may not be necessarily sinful, but it may still cause problems. "Everything is permissible, but not everything is beneficial." So you have to decide *if for your marriage it will help or hurt.*

Wagner described that both his wife and God share a special knowledge about his essential being and his commitment to both his marriage and God. Wagner suggested that, just as a parent has faith that the child who pretends to be a robber during a game is not and will not become a robber, Christians should put faith in fellow married believers who are interested in kinky sex, claiming that—because these individuals are pious and because marriage is exceptional—non-normative sex acts should be considered godly, manly, and right. He refers to strong marriages as godly ones, suggesting that the marriage relationship and a believer's relationship with God are mutually reinforcing. If one does not have a deep and committed relationship to God, one's marriage cannot thrive. With both, however, the possibilities for sexuality appear almost endless.

THE CONTRADICTIONS OF "NORMAL"

For religious persons, beliefs about gender and sexuality rely on more than nature and biology. Faith in the divine requires individual and collective interpretations of God's will. To describe evangelicals as supporting gender essentialism fails to capture the *super*natural dimension of religious beliefs. Anthropologist T. M. Luhrmann compares recognizing God's voice to learning to taste wine—there are guidelines for how to do it, but individual experience and understanding matter greatly.[28] Likewise, the website users in this study come to understand their gender identities through sexual sampling and honing their tastes. This chapter has shown how the dynamic and personal ways in which conservative Christians relate to God influences how they make sense of their gender and sexual identities. Gender omniscience, like essentialism, perpetuates the belief that gender is natural and fixed (and by extension, so is heterosexuality), but importantly, gender omniscience reveals how this belief comes into being through the lived experiences of individuals' sexual lives. Conservative Christians use the Internet to make meaning of sex in ways that are different from those that are presented as acceptable in popular evangelical literature. Men who are interested in non-normative sex take their religious beliefs about sexuality to a logical extreme—extending religious discourse that emphasizes mutual pleasure and sexual permissiveness within marriage to justify sex acts that are seemingly inappropriate within an evangelical context. Men who are interested in pegging and cross-dressing justify these interests by relying on the gender omniscience of their spouses and God. In proving that both God and their spouses *know* that they are gender normal, these website users are able to engage in "kinky" sexual acts within their marriages while upholding standards of their faith related to gender and (hetero)sexuality and ensuring their masculine status.

I suggest that men discuss their interest in non-normative sex on Christian sexuality websites more frequently than women because there is more at stake for men to express interest in these acts. The validation of their sexual interests that they receive from other believers helps these men maintain their privileged status as straight and godly men. The very act of talking about topics that are marginalized and taboo within broader conservative Christian culture (male anal play, for example) is a way to gain hold over those subjects and instill them with alternate meanings. Like tabloid talk shows—such as *Jerry Springer* or *Ricky Lake*—Christian sexuality websites have the potential to disrupt definitions of what is normal and abnormal, decent and vulgar. Joshua Gamson writes that TV talk shows "wreak special havoc with the 'public sphere,' moving private stuff into a public spotlight, arousing all sorts of questions about what the public sphere can, does, and should look like." The result is, as Gamson describes, "normalization through freak show": putting sexual nonconformity on display legitimizes it.[29] Similarly, Christian sexuality websites host discussions that cast "private stuff" into the "public spotlight," which gives these conversations the power to challenge and transform the prevailing definitions of sexuality that surround heterosexuality and marriage.

The Internet allows users of Christian sexuality websites to interactively reconstruct what it means to be a Christian man. Users are able to collectively offer feedback and credibility that support beliefs about gender and sexuality that accommodate both their religious framework and their unique sexual interests. The logic presented in these online discussions—that justification beyond a claim of heterosexuality is required for individuals to virtuously engage in certain gender-subversive acts—shows that gender, and specifically hegemonic masculinity, are not *inevitable* products of heterosexuality. Conservative Christian men who are interested in non-normative sex must actively work to establish their gender status as separate from, but closely related to, their heterosexuality in order for the sex in which they engage to be considered "normal" and "masculine." This supports what many theorists have argued, that gender and sexuality are distinct categories of analysis, and it pushes feminist and queer thinking further by urging us to examine the multiple ways in which gender and sexuality interact to both normalize and subvert identities. The individuals in this study use asymmetrical and binary gender categories to justify sex play that may confuse these categories and level gender imbalances.

A wide range of studies show that the everyday lives of contemporary evangelicals are more gender-equal than their beliefs would suggest. Sociologist

Sally Gallagher describes these evangelicals as "symbolically traditional"—supporting the idea of men's headship and women's submission—but "pragmatically egalitarian"—negotiating men's and women's roles based on the practical necessities of modern life. Influenced by feminist rhetoric and practical demands, like the need for a two-person income, many evangelicals adjust their expectations of gender so that women can work outside of the home and men can be loving caretakers.[30] In contrast, Christian sexuality websites present beliefs that appear progressive but actually perpetuate gender hierarchies. Even though members use gender-equal language to discuss sexual pleasure, Christian men on the sites are uniquely privileged to talk about, gain support for, and fulfill their sexual interests. Justifying non-normative sex does not challenge male dominance within contemporary evangelical culture.

Conservative Christians who insist that non-normative sex can be normal exclusively *for them* illuminate how heteronormativity and male privilege are wrought with tensions and contradictions. While participating in the sexual play they desire, these Christian men do not admit to any deviance, queerness, or effeminacy; instead, they discursively restore standards of masculinity and femininity that privilege men and exclude non-heterosexuals from "good" and godly sex. Yet conservative Christians who engage in circuitous normalizing of non-normative acts inadvertently reveal the unstable ground on which their sexual logic stands. Turning to online communities to gain religious traction for their sexual interests, website users rely on subjective and collective experiences to make sense of their sexual lives. In this way, they undermine a position that is based on the supposedly objective "truth" that God detests queer desires and identities. Religious beliefs and practices both reproduce *and undermine* heteronormativity, masculinity, and other forms of "normal."

Conclusion

PATHS OF DESIRE

On Christian sexuality websites, the pleasure of religion and the pleasure of sex are considered to be two sides of the same coin. As this book demonstrates, the desire for a fulfilling and satisfying religious faith can exist alongside the desire for a fulfilling and satisfying sex life, and each of these affects the other. One way to think about the relationship between religion and sexuality on Christian sexuality websites is to imagine what urban designers call "desire paths" or "desire lines"—the trails in parks and other public spaces that have been worn by people over time, determined by where they tend to walk, as opposed to paved sidewalks or pre-marked paths.[1] If prescriptive evangelical sex advice is the carefully planned and professionally designed route, these websites are desire lines created by people seeking Christian sex advice. They are alternative paths to religious beliefs about sex, which at times travel alongside established religious traditions and at other times cut corners, extend further, or even go in a different direction.

In the same way that desire paths provide people with the most direct route to their destinations, Christian sexuality websites can offer their users an immediate and direct route to spiritual answers about sex. Like desire paths, the sites are started by individuals and then shaped and determined by collective use and agreement. As communications scholar Matthew Tiessen describes, desire lines

> often emerge to [...] efficiently cut corners; but they are also, at times, expressions of playfulness, perhaps meandering to and fro amidst flowers or trees. The desire line's creator, when s/he blazes through newly fallen snow, is, quite literally, a trail blazer in whose steps others will follow; conversely, when, as a bike messenger, s/he navigates the inscription-resistant paved surfaces so ubiquitous in urban settings, his/her desire lines are undetectable.

Lines of desire, then, can be both visible and invisible, material and immaterial, semi-permanent and transitory.[2]

Christian sexuality websites are more trajectories than fixed places. In one moment, we may find that their content runs perfectly parallel to prescriptive evangelical advice. In another, we may notice that it contain differences—obvious or subtle—from preexisting religious beliefs. They go where ordinary believers take them—where these people's sexual desires, pleasures, and knowledge propel them.

But this impression of choice is limited by a bounded sense of where one can go. The conversations on Christian sexuality websites are shaped by what appears to be the unmovable structure of conservative Christian beliefs—specifically, restrictions surrounding who is allowed to have sex. Heterosexuality, monogamy, and marriage are the sturdy oaks that no website user tries to cut down or climb over. These requirements mean that Christian sexuality websites are paths that continue to make conservative Christianity a place that excludes sexual "others" from the possibility of godly sex. Still, these sites and their users can be dangerous to the fragile features of the Christian landscape. Like desire paths, which can irrevocably alter a natural ecosystem, Christian sexuality websites transform what religion and sexuality can be in the twenty-first century.

With deft discursive maneuvering, for example, website users are able to make men who are interested in pegging seem *more* connected to God rather than feel like religious outcasts. They portray women's masturbation as an act of submission rather than an act of independence. They make Christian marriages seem steamy and sexy, while at the same time wholesome and respectable. We see a dance between the openings website users create for sexual expression within Christian marriages and the closures they reinforce by perpetuating the regulatory systems of gender, heterosexuality, and Protestant Christianity. Collective online conversations help evangelicals do what they seem to do best: use culturally salient spaces to embed contemporary dialogue with religious meaning. This keeps them in an in-between space—neither entirely separate from nor fully participating in broader culture. Website users remain attached to religious beliefs that make them the exclusive bearers of godly values while also participating in the pleasures of modern, secular life.

Direct and explicit, online talk focuses on exactly how website users can optimize their sexual pleasure while maintaining their religious faith. In this final chapter, I consider how Christian sexuality websites generate, reinforce, and potentially change the existing landscape of American religion and sexuality. I theorize about the impact this has on lived religion—how online talk about sex transforms what religion can be for Christian sexuality website users. I also look at how this new manifestation of religious faith shapes the social construction of heterosexuality and the boundaries surrounding the definition of "normal." These are lessons for a sociology of religion and sexuality to consider: how the relationship between the two is dynamic, contested, and mutually constituent. Religion and sexuality pull together and push apart, simultaneously bolstering and undermining their collective power to define normal and decent, good and godly.

EMERGING PATHS: RELIGION TRANSFORMING

Writing in the 1960s, sociologist Peter Berger famously, and incorrectly by most accounts, theorized that modern society was moving toward inevitable secularization.[3] He argued that religion alienates believers from their beliefs and others, since believing in something divine separates religion from the rest of "real" life. Berger contended that sources of alienation would not survive in an ever-evolving society that demands a sense of belonging. What Berger and other secularization theorists at the time failed to account for is that, as anthropologist T. M. Luhrmann describes, God can be *both* "vividly human" and "deeply supernatural."[4] Or in the words of Lisa, who blogs on WeddingNights.com, that God makes life simultaneously "average" and "extraordinary."

Ethnographers of religious communities offer numerous examples of how believers understand a God that is intensely involved in their everyday lives rather than removed from it. God meddles in the mundane, giving believers the power to speak up to a cruel coworker or to make a decision about what to cook for dinner. Robert Orsi calls these "everyday miracles," wherein all of life's events—from joyful ones, like overcoming an illness, to unhappy ones, like losing financial savings—are opportunities to connect a divine force to ordinary life.[5] Contemporary Christian beliefs generate the sense that God is real and has powers that are distinctly nonhuman. In her ethnography of a nondenominational Vineyard church, Luhrmann observes that evangelical beliefs are, "in effect, a third kind of epistemological commitment: not materially real like tables and chairs; not fictional, like Snow White and the Seven Dwarfs."[6] Religion offers believers a method of grasping their realities and making sense of life's circumstances. At the same time, it leaves room for awe and wonder over things that are not completely understood.

Religion that exists between the real and the tangible and the supernatural and the divine is similar to digital media and cyberspace, which Michael Ross describes as "a space between fantasy and action."[7] Indeed, the Internet bears a resemblance to Luhrmann's description of the God evangelicals believe in. It lacks a physical presence but still feels ubiquitously present in our lives. It is not reducible to our computers or smart phones, yet it is often deeply tied to our tangible lives—to our jobs, our finances, our friends and family. Virtual reality is neither quite material nor imaginary. It is *out there,* somewhere, difficult to definitively describe and impossible to capture in scope. Perhaps the parallels the Internet shares with believing in God are part of what makes online religious sites so enthralling to their users.

Christian sexuality websites are more than confessionals where users disclose their most private thoughts and desires. And they are more than a simple display of preexisting conservative Christian beliefs. Religion online is fundamentally *lived religion:* it is participatory and iterative and therefore constantly (but not infinitely) malleable.[8] These sites still reflect long-standing religious beliefs that are firmly rooted in the evangelical tradition. However, creators of Christian sexuality websites draw from these existing beliefs and practices, what I describe in chapter two as *spiritual capital,* to justify new conversations about sex as godly. They use their own personal devotion, their belief that heterosexual marriage is spiritually exceptional, and their faith that God is all knowing to present religion online in a way that accommodates discussions about sexuality rather than dismisses them. This positions users of these websites to exceed the limits of typical evangelical conversations about sex and construct something unique. Individual users of these sites build upon these fundamental beliefs by conveying their own evangelical identities through the content and style of their posts. Evidence of personal piety takes center stage on Christian message boards and blogs as users write about their prayer lives and conversations with God; their testimonies of sin, redemption, and salvation; and their reflections on scripture. They trust that God knows who users really are, rendering the potential problem of Internet anonymity insignificant, and they also rely on familiar evangelical tropes to get to know and trust others on the sites.

When I asked BTS member ThisIsMe if it was important to her to read information about sexuality that is faith-based, she responded assuredly, "ABSOLUTELY! If you really want to know about a product you read what the manufacturer says. Since God created not only our bodies a certain way but also the gift of sex, I think it's important to see what He has to say about it." Like most of the stories I encountered while researching this book, ThisIsMe told hers with the benefit of hindsight, which allowed her to frame her sexual struggles as obstacles that God helped her to overcome. She used her beliefs to describe both why sex matters to her as a Christian (because God made it) and why a Christian perspective matters when it comes to sex (because God made it). When it comes to sexuality, ThisIsMe said that she goes straight to the source: God. Curiously, though, she is not talking here about praying or reading the Bible. God does not speak directly to ThisIsMe; instead, she believes that he speaks through Steel, ExodusGuy, Kylee2000, Sunshine, and all of the other users of BTS. She credits God directly with her sexual awakening, but on a day-to-day basis, she accesses him via online discussions with other believers.

Participation in Christian sexuality websites depends on a collective representation of reality. As website users contribute to and construct these online communities, the communities in turn shape users' identities as religious and sexual persons. I refer to this process in chapter three as *interactive predestination,* placing a Protestant spin on sociologist David Snow's concept of *interactive determination* (that the self is created through social interaction).[9] While website users believe in a divine God who directs their lives, they are also greatly influenced by ordinary people who are just like themselves. The nonbeliever might liken Christian sexuality websites to the Wizard of Oz: Dorothy and her friends believe that the wizard has the power to save them, but he is not in fact a wizard at all, just a man standing behind a curtain. Christian sexuality websites, too, can be reduced to being considered the "man behind the curtain." They are nothing without the human beings who create and use them. This is a stark contrast to our ethereal images of the divine. Michelangelo's perfectly crafted God, cloaked in white and reaching out to Adam, bears little resemblance to men and women propped in front of laptops, drinking their morning coffee and still wearing pajamas.

But it is not so straightforward as describing these websites as simply the product of human imagination. Online dialogue resembles a kind of sacred text. Religion depends upon the interpretive acts of believers—not because it is *reduced* to these interpretations, but because spiritual messages and meanings depend on real-life context and commentary. Christian traditions do not elevate scriptural interpretations to the same status as scripture, but written commentary serves as a de facto spiritual authority. Throughout

Christianity's long history, believers have helped one another understand scripture that was authored in a time and place that does not resemble the believer's world. For instance, fundamentalists in the early twentieth century adamantly believed that the Bible was the only source of religious authority, yet they also embraced commentary from other believers that helped them understand their faith. The Scofield Reference Bible, for example, first published in 1909, blends God's word with Cyrus Scofield's interpretations of it, which instructed millions how to live a Christian life.[10] His annotations work together with the sacred text to construct religion as both divine and human.

What makes an ethnography of Christian sexuality websites different from ethnographies of evangelicals in the context of churches is that websites host conversations that become public utterances, artifacts of lived religion. Like the Scofield Reference Bible, they guide users on how they should make sense of their religious beliefs. But far from being carefully crafted, edited, and approved religious commentary, online dialogue is mostly off the cuff and of the moment. As this book makes evident, on the Internet, evangelicals interpret religion subjectively through their own experiences and interests. Websites are both the products and the producers of debates over religion, gender, and sexuality. Texts and commentary on Christian sexuality websites legitimize only certain religious interpretations. They also present particular representations of what gendered and sexual bodies should look like and what they should do. Together, these religious texts construct a sense of reality, of how the world should be.

As most of their content is written dialogue, Christian sexuality websites make obvious the importance of language and text in constructing gender, sexuality, and religion. But instead of masking the corporeal reality of believers, website users take the sexual body seriously as a force distinct from religious rules and doctrines. Like religious faith, the desire for and act of sex has a transformative power. It is, as feminist theorists Ann Snitow, Christine Stansell, and Sharon Thompson describe in their anthology *Powers of Desire,* "an area for play, for experimentation, a place to test what the possibilities might be for an erotic life and a social world."[11] Website users imagine the body in multiple and interconnected forms—physical, emotional, and spiritual—and each positions men and women to either fulfill or reject godly sexuality. Some describe the body as something that gets in the way of godly sexuality. Women, for example, write about obstacles that are sometimes profound (past sexual abuse) and sometimes more mundane (insecurities about body odor). Other women describe their bodies as God's greatest gift, like blogger Lisa, who gave God "kudos" for giving her the ability to orgasm. As I describe in chapter four, evangelicals use online spaces to theologize and sexualize the body.

In a religious tradition that does much to contain and control sex, Christian sexuality websites allow evangelicals to feel a sense of liberation about their bodies without leaving their faith. Website users can use these sites to expand what feels good for them sexually, and this also makes them feel good spiritually, emotionally, and relationally. Some are able to find validation for sex acts in which they already engage and take pleasure in but do not know if they should enjoy as devout Christians. Others encounter beliefs that differ from theirs, which encourages them to experiment with their own sexual interests and play. These Christians leverage their bodies—with deeply felt desires that they may feel are beyond their control—to expand their religious faith. Sexual desire is not the same as cognitive knowledge; in the words of anthropologist Annick Prieur, it is "a force on its own."[12] Sex cannot be reduced to the bodies that have it, but the bodies that have it can shape what it means.

It is a familiar finding in the separate literature on the sociology of religion and the sociology of sexuality that people often act in ways that do not neatly line up with their sense of how the world should be. From the time of Alfred Kinsey's monumental study on men's sexual behavior in the mid-twentieth century, research on Americans' sexual practices repeatedly offer similar findings: people are enjoying more sex—and often sex that is kinkier and queerer—than family-values politicians would have us believe.[13] LustyChristianLadies.com bloggers like to mention an unexpected finding from a national survey on sexual behavior: as a group, more married conservative Protestant women report that they always achieve orgasm during sex than any other group.[14] On the surface, LustyChristianLadies.com exists as a belief-versus-action contradiction: a site that helps women to find "sexual freedom" in their marriages while also supporting women's submission to their husbands. Yet this dichotomous distinction between beliefs and practice (a common theme, especially in past research on evangelical women) assumes a relationship that is far too simple.[15] *Christians under Covers* positions religious beliefs—and more specifically, the logic of godly sex produced by conservative evangelical beliefs—in a mediated relationship with the online community that collectively works to construct this religious logic and with the sexual desires and practices of the individuals who create and use Christian sexuality websites.

Whether they describe an evangelical man who enjoys wearing his wife's panties or the housewife whose part-time online business sells erotic toys, the conservative Christians' stories presented in this book repeatedly contradict predominant evangelical sexual stereotypes. Sigmund Freud was perhaps the first researcher to point out the false distinction between *normal* and *perverse*. He wrote, "No healthy person, it appears, can fail to make some addition that might be called perverse to the normal sexual aim; and the universality of this finding is in itself enough to show how inappropriate it is to use the word perversion as a term of reproach."[16] All of us are perverse, claimed Freud, so perversion, it could be argued, is the single trait that unites us all as "normal."

Hundreds of members of BetweenTheSheets.com have posed the question to other users of the site: "Is this normal?" Members ask this about an incredible range of topics, from a man who wondered if the amount of ejaculate he produced was "normal" to a woman who wondered if it was "normal" to want to climax prior to having intercourse with her husband. One long-time moderator of the site, Moonman, responded to these questions. He asked members to "consider whether it MATTERS whether what you are feeling is 'normal.'" He then went on to summarize the principles of his faith that motivate his engagement with BetweenTheSheets.com and explain his sense of sexual "normalness":

> We are Christians. We have freedom in sexuality with our spouses. It matters NOT whether what we desire, or what our spouses desire, is "normal." It is good to learn from other married couples, but please remember that your marriage is unique. What each of you desire is a unique mix, and it does not matter at all whether that is "normal." All that matters is that it is the dynamic in your marriage, and the two of you must seek to please God in His plan. When we have freedom, "normal" is what happens within our marriage. Marriage includes the husband, the wife, and God. Remember that.

An understanding of *normal* as something that can be personalized, as Moonman describes, makes Christian sexuality websites appear accommodating of difference. Although Christian sexuality websites are a collective experience, the stories presented on them are unique to the website users who tell them—these evangelicals find help for *their* individual problems and offer advice based on *their* individual experiences, all of which are equally "normal" so long as website users are devoted to God and His plan.

Despite the appearance that "anything goes" within godly sex, online evangelical discourse is full of exclusions, even within Christian marriages. Some men use their relationships with God and their wives to expand their sexual possibilities, whereas women's sexuality can be stifled by these same relationships. Men may use the logic generated on these sites to guiltlessly engage in gender-deviant, kinky sex acts that challenge what men and women are expected to do sexually. Men who are interested in non-normative sex claim their normalness by citing their devotion to God and the sanctity of (heterosexual) marriage. Women who use the sites, however, tend not to discuss any interest in unusual, extreme, or marginal sex practices and instead talk extensively about the logistics of physical pleasure and learning to orgasm. These discussions construct men's and women's sexuality differently—portraying women as being "stuck" learning to orgasm while men experiment with multiple sexual interests. Christian sexuality websites are places of contradiction, where users draw from unique exchanges that take place online to expand what it means to be evangelical and sexual but also uphold beliefs that give some more choices and power than others.

The tensions revealed on Christian sexuality websites reflect a more widespread effort of conservative Christianity to maintain its distinction from broader culture while adapting to a changing world. How do conservative Christians benefit from modern sensibilities about gender, sexuality, and religion while also rejecting them? Website users see gender as predetermined—natural and mutually exclusive between men and women-but malleable enough to accommodate a diverse array of actions and behaviors. They consider heterosexuality to be a clear line in the sand distinguishing right from wrong but make the boundaries of heterosexuality expansive enough so as to incorporate a diverse arranging of men's and women's bodies to engage in sex acts other than penile-vaginal intercourse. They see Christianity as the exclusive path to salvation yet admit a range of believers devoted to differing Christian doctrines to participate fully in online discussions. Christian sexuality website creators and users present the logic of godly sex to seem simultaneously fixed and changeable.

This construction of godly sex could be described by philosophers as both modern and postmodern. Consider Moonman's definition of *normal*. For him, normal is firmly situated within real identities: the husband and the wife. It is defined by *who* engages in sexual acts, not by *what* they do. Yet his definition of normal also suggests that married couples enact what is normal in every sexual encounter, creating and recreating a sense that they belong, that they are pious, good, and godly. In other words, acting as husband and wife is what creates these identities as we understand them. Because, according to the logic of godly sex, sexual encounters can take many forms, it follows that what is understood as normal can vary. But how much? At what point does technically heterosexual sex in which a woman penetrates a man with a strap-on dildo lose its "straightness"? Or to pose this question another way, could a monogamous gay man penetrated by his husband ever become "normal" and become a part of this "straightness"?

These questions attempt to untangle how gender, marriage, and monogamy matter when it comes to constructing heterosexuality's power. Critical theorists of heterosexuality have described it as a "residual category," meaning that we understand heterosexuality not through some core essence of what it is but rather through the attributes that make it come to be.[17] As these attributes have faced tremendous changes and challenges in recent decades, hegemonic heterosexuality has changed. Historically, marriage gave heterosexuals economic and cultural rewards that were not available to non-heterosexuals. Yet the "one man, one woman" definition of marriage has largely lost its hold in the United States over both attitudes and laws. Marriage as an institution maintains its power to privilege some and not others, but heterosexuality is no longer exclusively attached to it.[18] Activists pursuing the rights of gays and lesbians to marry strategically and successfully worked to separate heterosexuality from Gayle Rubin's "charmed circle of sexuality," involving procreation, monogamy, domesticity, and vanilla sex.[19] Gays, just like straights, can buy homes, have kids, and send out family Christmas cards.

Where marriage, monogamy, domesticity, and sexual decency fail, gender seems to prevail in upholding a clear distinction between heterosexuality and non-heterosexuality. Without a gender binary, heterosexuality—dependent on difference between men and women—seems unable to exist. Yet gender, too, can lose its grip on heterosexuality. This is part of the "gender trouble" that Judith Butler describes, where gender is always falsely stabilized through "the illusion of an interior and organized gender core."[20] Through in-depth interviews with self-identified "straights," sociologist James Joseph Dean argues that looking like a gender-normal man or woman no longer guarantees heterosexual identity in the twenty-first century: "Although a conventional gender performance remains a key way to project a straight status, it no longer promises in any certain terms an unquestionable straight identity for the individual in question."[21] In other words, gender, as a destabilized and fluctuating category, has adapted to a changing world. It remains a necessary but not necessarily sufficient cause of heterosexuality.

Christian sexuality website users work to reconcile this dilemma: that opposite-sex desire is a necessary component of godly sex but that gender cannot automatically secure one's heterosexual status. In chapter five, I argue that they do this not by relying on the gender binary itself—some natural or essential notion of gender difference—but rather on *gender omniscience,* the fact that God and one's spouse possess privileged knowledge about one's gender. This allows men who use these websites to justify engaging in gender-deviant sex, like pegging or cross-dressing, while affirming their masculine and Christian status. This discursive work reveals that the link between gender and heterosexuality is contrived rather than predetermined. For Christian sexuality website users, gender status, and therefore a heterosexuality that is decent and good, depends on the intimate knowledge of an opposite-sexed partner and God. The meaning of sex acts themselves—and the bodies that engage in them—do not create coherent definitions for gender or heterosexuality.

By emphasizing their own understanding of piety and God's rules, Christian sexuality website users can maintain their exclusive hold on a heterosexual definition of *normal* without attending to the discontinuities created by heterosexuality's other familiar attributes: gender, monogamy, and marriage. Separating religion's power from other "intersecting hegemonies" allows conservative Christians to fashion boundaries that separate them from ungodly others while still taking advantage of the pleasures that those ungodly others helped to develop—that is, the pleasures that result from rejecting prescriptive rules restricting sexual expression. The Internet provides a platform for these Christians to combine religious and modern logics: a belief in an uncompromising truth about who can have sex (only married, monogamous heterosexuals) and a belief in subjective sexual experiences that depend upon fluctuating choices and tastes. A question that remains is how Christian sexuality website users may gradually create or continue to close off sexual and religious possibilities for those not like them. Fluctuating boundaries will not eliminate the exclusionary work they do.

In this book's introduction, I quoted queer theorist Michael Warner, who writes about choosing between God and orgasm as an "agony."[22] On the surface, it seems that Christian sexuality websites do the contrary: rather than make the choice between God and orgasm mutually exclusive, they make it mutually affirming. They make visible conversations about topics avoided altogether or only whispered about in church pews. These sites validate existing sexual interests and practices of some users, like one reader of LustyChristianLadies.com who commented on the site's homepage: "My husband and I thought we were weird for loving sex, now we know that you understand this." For many others, the sites themselves are the catalyst for change in their sexual lives. Another LCL reader wrote: "THANK YOU. The love making in my marriage has never been more exciting, and it's definitely thanks to you and your openness in discussing 'taboo' topics." Christian sexuality websites do what other conservative Christian spaces do not: they recognize and affirm sexual feelings and desires that often have a profound impact on who we are—or who we imagine ourselves to be. These sites blend together the practical and ideological tools of achieving sexual pleasure, and in doing so, they mold and extend website users' conservative religious faith.

Yet these sites also expose the ways in which this religious faith inherently limits sexual expression. The shared experience that great sex is *not* easily achieved, even though it is encouraged by God, is what compels the presence and growth of Christian sexuality websites and other forms of Christian sex advice. This elicits a tension between faith and sex: believing in God is not enough to make great sex a reality, and great sex is not necessarily godly. And so website creators and users construct a logic of godly sex that is both permissive and restrictive—permissive enough to allow for married Christians to explore their sexual pleasures and restrictive enough that those pleasures are off limits for those who are not married or not heterosexual. Religion provides the discursive strategies for website users to maintain their beliefs that marriage and heterosexuality are exceptional and natural while participating in the pleasures endorsed by modern sexualized culture.

The ambivalent effects of the logic of godly sex show the ways in which these websites heighten and relieve a tension between religion and sex. Discussions on these sites are actively shaped, but not determined, by gender and heterosexual hegemony and Protestant Christianity. These discussions also make new ways of understanding sexual pleasure from a conservative Christian framework possible, as website users collaboratively define their religious faith and practice it online. The logic of godly sex suggests that religion remains relevant to theories of heterosexuality in contemporary America, even amidst cultural changes that seem to make conservative religious beliefs extraneous. It also suggests that how people make sense of the act of and desire for sex is an important part of theorizing about religion. But perhaps most importantly, the logic of godly sex suggests that religion and sexuality are a unique compound rather than two distinct elements. Together, religion and sexuality are the social forces hard at work in regulating what bodies do, why they do it, and what effect these actions have. Yet their relationship is an unstable one, a push and pull between limits and possibilities that are constantly being constructed and contested.

Like the religious and sexual beliefs that underpin them, Christian sexuality websites are precarious yet resilient spaces. At the time of this writing, BetweenTheSheets.com continues to grow and maintains an active message board where hundreds of comments are posted every day. Lisa still blogs regularly on WeddingNights.com and has committed to turning her blog posts into Bible study curriculum. Yet because many of the blogs, message boards, and online stores in this study were created by evangelicals who have otherwise very full *real* lives—with families, full-time jobs, and church commitments—many sites became too burdensome to maintain. Bloggers on LustyChristianLadies.com and MaribelsMarriage.com have stopped posting. Many sex toy stores, including Samantha's, have closed. Although Samantha's website is no longer active, typing in the old URL reveals a message, "this domain is now available," reminding us that anyone with an Internet connection and a faithful heart can start a site anew: one that will either follow already worn paths of desire or tread new ground.

List of Christian Sexuality Websites

TABLE A-1 Websites Mentioned by Name in the Book

Name	Acronym	Type of site	Creator(s)
AffectionateMarriage.com		Blog	
BetweenTheSheets.com	BTS	Message board	John, Barbara
Corinthians.com		Sex toy store	Ann
FaithfulFantasticFun.com		Blog	Mae
GardenFruit.com		Sex toy store	
GodOfLove.com		Erotic story store	
LovingBride.com		Blog	Barbara
LovingGroom.com		Blog	John
LustyChristianLadies.com	LCL	Blog	Bunny, Chariot, Kitty
MarriageLoveToys.com		Sex toy store	
MaribelsMarriage.com		Blog	Maribel
Samanthas.com		Sex toy store	Samantha
StoreOfSolomon.com		Sex toy store	Holly
WeddingNights.com		Blog	Lisa

Doing Internet Ethnography

My project examines all the websites I could find that I consider to be Christian sexuality websites, determined by two criteria: (1) they were easily identified as Christian (this usually meant that the word "Christian" was displayed prominently on a website's homepage), and (2) their content focused specifically (and explicitly) on positive expressions of sex and sexuality within marriage. Although the Internet is constantly expanding and transforming, at the time of my study, informants told me that my list was exhaustive of these types of sites. I left out websites that focused on broad expressions of sex and sexuality because this would include the large number of websites focusing on "marriage recovery," typically involving pornography addiction, which was beyond the scope of my project. I also excluded a large number of websites that focused generally on enhancing marriages, which sometimes included discussions about sex and sexuality.

I identified three types of sites within the population of Christian sexuality websites: blogs ($n = 16$), online stores ($n = 18$), and message boards ($n = 2$). Blogs were any site with written content that allowed a public readership to comment. Online stores were Christian-owned businesses that sold a range of sex toys, including vibrators, penis rings, massage oils and lubricants, erotic games, and light BDSM toys (such as blindfolds and handcuffs). Two of the online stores in my study sold non-tangible products: one sold personalized erotic stories and the other sold phone counseling sessions with certified Christian sex therapists. The two message boards I observed were organized similarly: users completed a free registration to access all of the site's content and to post on the site. I recorded descriptive information for each site and used purposive and snowball sampling techniques to identify a sample from which to collect in-depth data.

Content Analysis and Online Observation

I analyzed the content of a sample of twelve Christian sexuality websites (one message board, six blogs, and five online stores). Based on observation and interview data, I created a dictionary of keyword search terms and phrases that guided my content analysis of these sites (with the exception of online stores, which are discussed below). This dictionary focused on search terms that would reveal debates and tension over sex acts, which I was particularly interested in because disagreements are often where values are revealed and meaning making takes place. The dictionary included all forms of the following words: *anal, dildo, fetish, gay, homosexuality, kinky, lesbian, pornography, sin,* and *vibrator.*

To perform a standardized search of all websites, I used Google's Advanced Search feature to search the webpages of each blog and message board in my sample.[1] I performed searches for key words within each site. Searches for seven websites (all sites in my sample except online stores) yielded 72,070 results of webpages that included key search terms. Because it was not feasible to analyze the content of each of those webpages, I performed additional keyword searches on the websites to narrow down the results. I relied on the ways in which the sites organized their search results (usually sorting by what was most relevant) to analyze a sample of webpages on each site. Because the amount of content varied greatly across the sites in my sample, I analyzed between ten and fifty webpages per site (about two hundred webpages total). To analyze the content of the sample of online stores, I viewed every product page and documented the types of products sold. The number of products stores sold varied widely, ranging from 5 to over 1,000 items. I also read and analyzed any supplemental webpages on the sites—typically an "About Me" or "About Us" page, which gave personal and professional information about the store owner(s), and a "Frequently Asked Questions" page.

I made real-time online observations of two extremely active websites in my study: BetweenTheSheets.com and LustyChristianLadies.com. Though the process of analysis I used for these sites was similar to the content analysis I described above, online observation is distinct in that I analyzed all content posted to these sites during my observation period (unlike content analysis,

172 · APPENDIX B

in which I used a keyword list to search the sites for specific terms). Carrying out this process of observation over an extended period of time revealed how content was repeated, added, modified, or removed. It allowed me to analyze content that I may not have identified in advance as being meaningful or relevant to the study, but which proved to be meaningful for the users of the websites.

I conducted systematic online observations of both sites for about six months (from October 2010 to March 2011). I received permission from a site administrator to collect data from BetweenTheSheets.com, since some of the content is semiprivate (viewing required free membership). Due to the high number of posts, I conducted a preliminary exploration of the site before my observation period to determine the most active and relevant message board topics for my study. I observed twenty-three board topics, almost half the total topics on the site ($n = 50$).[2] These were the topics that received the most traffic and contained active and often lengthy threads discussing issues related to sex practices. To observe LustyChristianLadies.com, I read new blog posts as they were added (typically four per week) and followed the comments threads during the following week.

Based on content analysis and online observations, I also selected a sample of twelve published Christian sex advice books, one podcast series, and two virtual Bible studies. I used themes derived inductively from website data collection to guide my analysis of this additional print literature and online content.

Online Survey

My Christianity, Sexuality, and the Internet Survey (CSIS) included eighty-seven questions about demographic information, religious affiliation and participation, Internet use, sexual history, and sexual attitudes. The wording of these questions was based on the wording of the questions in the General Social Survey (GSS) and in the National Health and Social Life Survey (NHSLS), the largest and most comprehensive survey on American sexuality to date. Most respondents (89 percent) completed the survey once they started it, a total of 768 respondents. They got to the survey by following links posted on seven Christian sexuality websites (see table B-1)—five blogs, one message board, and one sex toy store. I capped the number of respondents at 150 for each website so that the number of survey respondents would

TABLE B-1 Distribution of completed CSIS by referral website

Website	Type	Number of respondents	Percentage of total sample
LovingBride.com	Blog	150	19.5
LustyChristianLadies.com	Blog	150	19.5
LovingGroom.com	Blog	140	18.2
MaribelsMarriage.com	Blog	124	16.1
BetweenTheSheets.com	Message board	74	9.6
StoreOfSolomon.com	Store	71	9.2
WeddingNights.com	Blog	59	7.7
Totals		768	100

NOTE: Because of rounding, some totals do not equal 100 percent.

not be composed disproportionally of users from a single website. The websites that produced the most survey respondents, LovingBride.com and LustyChristianLadies.com, made up 40 percent of overall survey respondents. The website that collected the least respondents, WeddingNights.com, made up about 8 percent.

To compare the study's survey sample with evangelicals nationally and with the overall population, I used two secondary national data sets: the 2012 GSS and the Pew Forum on Religion and Public Life's 2011 National Survey of Mormons. To compare evangelical Protestants, mainline Protestants, and Catholics, I used GSS data. To differentiate between Protestant denominations, I used the GSS variable "Fundamentalist," which labels certain Protestant affiliations as conservative, moderate, or liberal.[3] I refer to the conservative sample as "evangelical" and to the moderate and liberal sample as "mainline" to maintain consistency with the language I use throughout the book to describe these traditions. To compare demographic information of CSIS Latter-day Saints with a national sample, I used the Pew data set (a sample of over one thousand Mormon respondents) because the GSS does not categorize Latter-day Saints as a distinct religious group. Mormons as represented in the GSS are those respondents who chose "Protestant" as their religious affiliation and then subsequently selected "Mormon" as their denominational affiliation (a sample of only sixteen respondents in 2012). To compare results of the CSIS with national data, I relied exclusively on GSS data because the Pew National Survey of Mormons does not include comparable questions regarding sexual attitudes.

I conducted fifty interviews for this project, most of them online.[4] I interviewed forty-four members and administrators of BTS and LCL, three bloggers on other Christian sexuality sites, two owners of online sex toy stores, and one author of a popular Christian sex advice book. I recruited participants by asking website users who completed the CSIS to volunteer for an online interview, for which they were compensated with an electronic gift card good for twenty dollars. Table B-2 compares the results of the entire CSIS sample with those of specifically the BTS and LCL users whom I interviewed.

The online interviews took place between January and November 2011.[5] They were one-on-one (with one exception), semistructured, lasted about two hours (usually with one five minute break), and produced transcripts between 4,500 and 6,500 words in length. I used online interviews to preserve the original form of social interaction being studied and chose a format that allowed the interviews to take place synchronously (in real time). To do this, I first created a personal website that described my research project and my professional credentials. I then contracted a chat room service to host a private and secure chat room on my site that automatically stored chat room transcripts in a password-protected account. I was able to set a unique password for each chat room session, which ensured that my intended interview participant and I were the only ones with access to each particular session. I conducted the interviews by typing instant messages to respondents, who then typed their responses back to me.

Before starting each interview with a website user or administrator, I reviewed their answers to the CSIS so that I had a general knowledge of their relationship history, religious affiliation, sexual attitudes, and Internet use. During the interviews, I posed detailed questions about how respondents used Christian sexuality websites, asking how they first found the site(s), how often they read and posted content, and what motivated their online participation. I asked how their online activity affected their real-life relationships and whether their real-life relationships included conversations about sex that were similar to those that took place online. I asked them if they used any other resources for information about sex and encouraged detailed responses about what kinds of sources had shaped their beliefs about sexuality. At the end of the interview, I asked any follow-up questions I had from their answers in the CSIS, usually pertaining to their responses to questions about sexual attitudes.

Demographic characteristics for interview and survey respondents

	BTS and LCL interview respondents ($n = 44$)		CSIS respondents ($n = 768$)	
	Number of respondents	*Percentage of total sample*	*Number of respondents*	*Percentage of total sample*
Religion				
Evangelical	41	93	553	72
Mainline Protestant	3	7	91	12
Catholic	0	0	25	3
Latter-day Saint	0	0	89	12
Other or none	0	0	1	9
Gender				
Men	19	43	357	47
Women	25	57	406	53
Age				
18–29	12	27	229	30
30–49	23	52	387	50
50–64	8	18	139	18
65 and older	1	2	13	2
Race				
White	39	91	705	92
Nonwhite	4	9	61	8
Region				
U.S. West	10	23	194	25
U.S. Midwest	9	21	161	21
U.S. Northeast	4	9	67	9
U.S. South	17	39	250	33
Outside U.S.	4	9	96	12
Education				
College degree	22	50	479	62
No degree	22	50	286	37
Employment				
Full-time	16	36	445	58
Part-time	10	23	142	19
Unemployed	18	40	180	24
Marital status				
Married	42	96	715	93
Not married	2	4	51	7
Children				
Has children	35	79	590	77
Has no children	9	21	177	23

NOTE: Because of rounding, some totals do not equal 100 percent. Also, due to the fact that some CSIS respondents did not answer all survey questions, some of the totals given are less than the total number of survey respondents. Respondents were included in analyzed data if they completed 90 percent of the survey.

Through interviews, online observations, and content analysis of websites, I identified real-life events whose speakers promoted beliefs similar to those I had found online (i.e., that God wants for married couples to experience sexual pleasure). With permission from event organizers, I observed three face-to-face Christian sexuality events. I chose these events, all of which were advertised online, because they all targeted different Christian audiences. The first was geared toward married couples, who attended the event together. The second was for women only. The third was for any Christian—single or married, man or woman—who wanted to learn about sexuality. I took detailed field notes at all three events and used a template to format and compare my observations.

The first event I attended for my study was a two-day conference that took place in October 2010, organized and hosted by administrators of BetweenTheSheets.com. I observed all sessions of the conference (except a session that was for men only) and talked informally to all conference participants (a total of eighteen people, including the organizers). The Intimate Issues Conference was the second event I observed, in January 2011. This women-only conference, based on the best-selling evangelical sex advice book of the same name, which is geared towards women, takes place biannually in churches across the country. Five hundred and fifty women attended the conference, and I talked casually with about six of them during the conference. I observed all sessions of the two-day conference (except for a session geared toward single women; I chose to attend an alternate session for married women that took place at the same time). I interviewed one of the authors of *Intimate Issues*, who was also a speaker at the conference. The third conference I observed was a one-day event called Love Life, which was part of Pastor Mark Driscoll's book tour for his most recent book, *Real Marriage: The Truth about Friendship, Sex, and Life Together*. I observed the entire conference and chatted informally with protestors outside of the conference and with young adults working at the merchandise table.

DISCLOSURES

I am not straight or religious, but I was once both. As a teenager, I was intensely involved in a Southern Baptist church community—I attended youth group and Sunday school, volunteered for Vacation Bible School, and committed myself to abstinence at a True Love Waits conference. I sang in a Christian rock band that performed at local churches. All of my friends also did these things, and this gave me a necessary sense of purpose and belonging during tumultuous teenage years. But ultimately, unlike the users of Christian sexuality websites, I was unable to reconcile my sexuality with my faith. I stopped participating in organized religion around the same time I stopped dating men.

I never intentionally deceived the participants of this study, though as I learned, deception becomes quite complicated in a culture in which heterosexuality and love for Jesus is compulsory. Participants frequently expressed gratitude and appreciation that I was making this side of Christianity visible—a side that is pro- rather than antisex, which is often overshadowed by both secular and religious depictions of evangelicals. Underlying this appreciation was an assumption that I was like them—that I, too, believed that God wants straight, married Christians to have great sex and that part of my job was to spread the word! I never told participants if I shared their religious beliefs, though I did answer questions about my religious upbringing honestly. I also attempted to answer questions about my marital status honestly, if evasively, and confirmed that I was married. I did not disclose that my partner is not a man, but no one asked me directly whether this was the case. These are the ethnographic anxieties not easily taught or described in field guides or research methods textbooks and I did my best, however spontaneously, to follow my ethical compass during the research process.

I have my own gut reactions to the messages presented on Christian sexuality websites, and my positionality certainly colors my analysis. As Dawne Moon writes simply in her ethnography of church congregations: "I, too, am a social creature."[6] As a feminist sociologist, I believe the only understanding of the people I study is a subjective one. I do not pretend to achieve neutral scientific objectivity, but I think this enhances my research rather than detracts from it. My identity—not just as a queer person, but also as a parent, a lover, and someone in constant negotiation with those with whom I have relationships—did not disappear while I read message board threads and blog posts. I know writing this confirms what many evangelicals already believe about academia and its liberal and feminist bias. Yet as a researcher, these parts of myself offered unexpected value—not just in my ability to critique, question, and challenge (which I do believe is the task of sociology) but also to sympathize and humanize.[7]

There were many instances during the research process where I found surprising common ground between myself and the users and creators of

Christian sexuality websites. I related to them about their struggles with their relationships and their bodies and admired their sincere efforts to figure out their own lives and make them better. One day, I came home to find *Passionate Marriage* by David Schnarch on my coffee table.[8] The book, not explicitly religious, but implicitly supportive of monogamous, heterosexual matrimony, had been brought up in an interview with a LustyChristianLadies.com reader just days earlier. My partner, an avid reader of pop psychology and self-help books, had borrowed it from a friend. In that moment, my own mental and emotional boundaries between myself and my family (us) and those I study (them) were destabilized. This was an important and recurring lesson I learned as I was reminded of all that we have in common, despite our differences.

I hope I depicted the stories of users and creators of Christian sexuality websites fairly, as this has been my aim. Religious progressives might insist that these evangelicals' interpretations of Christian beliefs are skewed. They might argue for a more inclusive and updated interpretation of scripture—pointing out, for example, that biblical admonitions against homosexuality or premarital sex exist alongside warnings against wearing clothing made of mixed materials, which most evangelicals do quite freely. Yet, as Lynne Gerber writes in the conclusion to her ethnography of evangelical ex-gay and dieting ministries, "the theological case is not mine to make."[9] Avoiding taking a stand on the theological grounds on which evangelicals situate their worldview has not prohibited me from taking a stand on the sociological effects of their messages, what I refer to in this book as the logic of godly sex. This comes from my position as a critical sociologist, whose job it is to complicate a worldview that takes much for granted when it comes to good and bad, right and wrong, moral or sinful.

NOTES

1. All names of websites and their creators and users are pseudonyms. Although all websites included in this book are accessible to the public, I do not list them by name because it could identify users who participated in this study and were promised confidentiality. For additional reading on the ethics of Internet research, see Elizabeth A. Buchanan, *Readings in Virtual Research Ethics: Issues and Controversies* (Hershey, PA: Idea Group, Inc., 2004); Nicole Constable, "Ethnography in Imagined Virtual Communities," in *Romance on a Global Stage: Pen Pals, Virtual Ethnography, and "Mail Order" Marriages* (Berkeley, CA: University of California Press, 2003), 31–62; Donna M. Mertens and Pauline E. Ginsberg, eds., *The Handbook of Social Research Ethics* (Thousand Oaks, CA: SAGE Publications, 2009); and Annette Markham and Elizabeth Buchanan, *Ethical Decision-Making and Internet Research: Recommendations from the AoIR Ethics Working Committee,* Association of Internet Researchers, December 2012, http://aoir.org/reports/ethics2.pdf.

2. Michael Warner, "Tongues Untied: Memoirs of a Pentecostal Boyhood," in *Que(e)rying religion: A Critical Anthology,* ed. Gary David Comstock and Susan E. Henking (New York: Continuum Publishing Company, 1997), 229.

3. Ibid., 229.

4. For a detailed historical overview of the evangelical sex industry, see Amy DeRogatis, *Saving Sex: Sexuality and Salvation in American Evangelicalism* (New York: Oxford University Press, 2015).

5. Erving Goffman, *The Presentation of Self in Everyday Life* (New York: Anchor Books, [1959] 1990).

6. For a critique of Christian sexuality websites and other forms of Christian sex advice, see Dagmar Herzog, *Sex in Crisis: The New Sexual Revolution and the Future of American Politics* (New York: Basic Books, 2008).

7. Feona Attwood, "Sexed Up: Theorizing the Sexualization of Culture," *Sexualities* 9 (2006): 77–94; Anthony Giddens, *Modernity and Self-Identity: Self and Society in the Late Modern Age* (Stanford, CA: Stanford University Press, 1991);

John Santelli et al. "Abstinence and Abstinence-Only Education: A Review of U.S. Policies and Programs," *Journal of Adolescent Health* 38 (2006): 72–81; Robert D. Putnam and David E. Campbell, *American Grace: How Religion Divides and Unites Us* (New York: Simon and Schuster, 2010).

8. *Religion* (and related terms—*Christianity, God, evangelicalism, fundamentalism*) is missing from the indexes of many seminal works in critical heterosexuality studies. For example, Chrys Ingraham writes in the introduction to the anthology *Thinking Straight: The Power, the Promise, and the Paradox of Heterosexuality* (New York: Routledge, 1995), "make no mistake that religions will insert themselves in this debate [over banning same-sex marriage]. They have a long and dramatic investment in dominating private and familial relations for a variety of ideological reasons" (8). Yet, other than a few cursory references to religion, no essay in the anthology elaborates on the religious impact on debates over heterosexuality. See also Jenny Hockey, Angela Meah, and Victoria Robinson, *Mundane Heterosexualities: From Theory to Practices* (New York: Palgrave MacMillan, 2007); Stevi Jackson, *Heterosexuality in Question* (Thousand Oaks, CA: SAGE Publications, 1999); and Diane Richardson, *Rethinking Sexuality* (Thousand Oaks, CA: SAGE Publications, 2000).

9. Dawne Moon makes a similar argument in *God, Sex, and Politics: Homosexuality and Everyday Theologies* (Chicago, IL: University of Chicago Press, 2004), claiming that religious debates over homosexuality often involve language about religion and sexuality, which "worked to naturalize each other" (11), suggesting that religion and (hetero)sexuality become mutually dependent on one another.

10. Melanie Heath addresses the relationship between these cultural changes and heterosexuality in her book *One Marriage under God: The Campaign to Promote Marriage in America* (New York: New York University Press, 2012). By focusing on marriage campaigns, she finds that marriage politics link heterosexuality to gender, race, and social class. Marriage campaigns, Heath argues, create heterosexual and non-heterosexual "outsiders," who are excluded from the American ideology of family, especially gay and lesbian couples and poor, unwed, and usually nonwhite mothers.

11. Herbert Blumer, *Symbolic Interactionism: Perspective and Method* (Berkeley, CA: University of California Press, [1969] 1986); Pierre Bourdieu, *The Logic of Practice* (Stanford, CA: Stanford University Press, [1980] 1990); Goffman, *Presentation of Self*; Michel Foucault, *An Introduction,* Vol. 1, *The History of Sexuality,* trans. Robert Hurley (New York: Vintage, [1978] 1990); George Herbert Mead, *Mind, Self, and Society from the Standpoint of a Social Behaviorist* (Chicago, IL: University of Chicago Press, [1934] 1967).

12. Annamarie Jagose, *Queer Theory: An Introduction* (New York: New York University Press, 1996), 3.

13. Candace West and Don Zimmerman, "Doing Gender," *Gender & Society* 1 (1987): 125–151.

14. Judith Lorber, *Paradoxes of Gender* (New Haven, CT: Yale University Press, 1994).

15. C.J. Pascoe, *Dude, You're a Fag: Masculinity and Sexuality in High School* (Berkeley, CA: University of California Press, 2007); Margot Canaday, *The Straight*

State: Sexuality and Citizenship in Twentieth-Century America (Princeton, NJ: Princeton University Press, 2011).

16. John H. Gagnon and William Simon, *Sexual Conduct: The Social Sources of Human Sexuality* (New Brunswick, NJ: Aldine Transaction, [1973] 2005). See also Kristen Schilt and Laurel Westbrook, "Doing Gender, Doing Heteronormativity: 'Gender Normals,' Transgender People, and the Social Maintenance of Heterosexuality," *Gender & Society* 23 (2009): 440–464.

17. Courtney Bender, *Heaven's Kitchen: Living Religion at God's Love We Deliver* (Chicago, IL: University of Chicago Press, 2003); David D. Hall, ed., *Lived Religion in America: Toward a History of Practice* (Princeton, NJ: Princeton University Press, 1997).

18. Orit Avishai, "'Doing Religion' in a Secular World: Women in Conservative Religions and the Question of Agency," *Gender & Society* 22 (2008): 413.

19. Meredith McGuire draws from social theorist Pierre Bourdieu's work to examine religion as an embodied practice in *Lived Religion: Faith and Practice in Everyday Life* (New York: Oxford University Press, 2008).

20. Mimi Schippers, "Recovering the Feminine Other: Masculinity, Femininity, and Gender Hegemony," *Theory and Society* 36 (2007): 85–102; R. W. Connell, *Masculinities* (Berkeley, CA: University of California Press, 1995).

21. Ariel Levy, *Female Chauvinist Pigs: Women and the Rise of Raunch Culture* (New York: Free Press, 2006), 5.

22. Melissa Burkett and Karine Hamilton, "Postfeminist Sexual Agency: Young Women's Negotiations of Sexual Consent," *Sexualities* 15 (2012): 815–833; Melissa Crawford and Diane Popp, "Sexual Double Standards: A Review and Methodological Critique of Two Decades of Research," *The Journal of Sex Research* 40 (2003): 13–26; Rosalind Gill, "Mediated Intimacy and Postfeminism: A Discourse Analytic Examination of Sex and Relationships Advice in a Women's Magazine," *Discourse and Communication* 3 (2009): 345–369.

23. Adrienne Rich, "Compulsory Heterosexuality and Lesbian Existence," in *Powers of Desire: The Politics of Sexuality,* ed. Ann Snitow, Christine Stansell, and Sharon Thompson (New York: Monthly Review Press, [1980] 1983), 177–205; Gayle Rubin, "Thinking Sex: Notes for a Radical Theory of the Politics of Sexuality," in *Culture, Society, and Sexuality: A Reader,* ed. Richard Parker and Peter Aggleton (Philadelphia: UCL Press, [1984] 1999), 143–178; Judith Butler, *Gender Trouble: Feminism and the Subversion of Identity* (New York: Routledge, [1990] 1999).

24. Schippers, "Recovering the Feminine Other," 91.

25. These intersecting levels of heterosexuality come from Stevi Jackson, who distinguishes between four different levels: the level of social structure, the level of meaning, the level of everyday practices, and the level of embodiment (*Heterosexuality in Question,* 5–6).

26. Carol Vance, "Pleasure and Danger: Toward a Politics of Sexuality," in *Feminist Theory: A Reader,* ed. Wendy K. Kolmar and Frances Bartkowski (New York: McGraw-Hill, [1984] 2013), 335.

27. An early and influential example of a radical feminist interpretation of sex is Kate Millet's *Sexual Politics* (New York: Doubleday, 1970). Millet was among the first feminist thinkers to argue that the slogan "the personal is political" applies to sexual encounters as well as to non-sexual ones. For a pro-sex feminist response, see Rubin, "Thinking Sex."

28. Margot Weiss, *Techniques of Pleasure: BDSM and the Circuits of Sexuality* (Durham, NC: Duke University Press, 2011), 188, 7. *BDSM* refers to bondage and discipline, domination and submission, and sadomasochism. *Scene* is the word used to describe a BDSM sexual encounter.

29. Rubin, "Thinking Sex." I offer an incomplete list of all of the acts Rubin described as existing within and outside of the "charmed circle," due to the fact that norms have changed since "Thinking Sex" was first published in 1984. See Steven Seidman, *Beyond the Closet: The Transformation of Gay and Lesbian Life* (New York: Routledge, 2002).

30. Lisa Duggan, "The New Homonormativity: The Sexual Politics of Neoliberalism," in *Materializing Democracy: Towards a Revitalized Cultural Politics,* ed. Russ Castronovo and Dana D. Nelson (Durham, NC: Duke University Press, 2002), 175–195. See also Michael Warner, *The Trouble with Normal* (New York: Free Press, 1999). Neither Duggan nor Warner celebrates this elevation of gays and lesbians as "normal." Rather, as Warner's title suggests, they find it troubling for queer politics.

31. Janet R. Jakobsen and Ann Pellegrini, *Love the Sin: Sexual Regulation and the Limits of Religious Tolerance* (New York: New York University Press, 2003). See also Tracy Fessenden, *Culture and Redemption: Religion, the Secular, and American Literature* (Princeton, NJ: Princeton University Press, 2007).

32. In her book *Pray the Gay Away: The Extraordinary Lives of Bible Belt Gays* (New York: New York University Press, 2012), Bernadette Barton draws from Foucault's theory of the Panopticon to describe informal and implicit surveillance that polices Bible Belt Christianity through "tight social networks of family, neighbors, church and community members, and a plethora of Christian signs and symbols sprinkled throughout the region" (24).

33. Much research on religion and sexuality focuses on the ways in which religious people (assumed to be heterosexual) express or change their beliefs about homosexuality. Research on religious queers is a relatively recent addition to the sociology of religion. For a study on LGBT Christians, see Melissa M. Wilcox, *Coming Out in Christianity: Religion, Identity, and Community* (Bloomington, IN: Indiana University Press, 2003). For an anthology on LGBT people who practice religious faiths outside of mainstream traditions, see Kath Browne, Sally R. Munt, and Andrew K.T. Yip, eds., *Queer Spiritual Spaces: Sexuality and Sacred Places* (Farnham, UK: Ashgate, 2010). For a study on lesbian and gay evangelical Protestants, see Dawne Moon, "Love and the Authentic Self: Insights from Gay Evangelicals in the 21st Century," presentation, Southern Sociological Society Annual Meeting, New Orleans, LA, March 25–28, 2015.

34. In 2010, Matthew Vines, a young, white, gay evangelical Christian, gave a speech at his local church on why Christians should support homosexuality. The

video went viral and was viewed nearly a million times on YouTube. Since then, Vines started the Reformation Project, a fast-growing network of LGBT evangelical Christians (www.reformationproject.org). Two groups, both called Affirmation, support LGBTQ Methodists and Latter-day Saints, respectively, and their families (www.umaffirm.org and www.affirmation.org); Integrity USA supports LGBTQ Episcopals (www.integretiyusa.org); DignityUSA supports LGBTQ Catholics (www.dignityusa.org); and More Light Presbyterians supports full participation for its LGBTQ members (www.mlp.org).

35. Wilcox, *Coming Out,* 170.

36. Jakobsen and Pellegrini, *Love the Sin.*

37. This definition of ideology as common sense with ruling and oppositional forms comes from Eduardo Bonilla-Silva's book on racial ideology and color-blind racism in contemporary America, *Racism without Racists: Color-Blind Racism and the Persistence of Racial Inequality in the United States* (Lanham, MD: Rowman and Littlefield, 2006). For a study on how gay Christian Black men negotiate the ruling ideology of their religion, see Richard N. Pitt, "'Killing the messenger': Religious Black Gay Men's Neutralization of Anti-Gay Religious Messages," *Journal for the Scientific Study of Religion* 49 (2010): 56–72.

38. Butler, *Gender Trouble,* 41. See also Janet E. Halley, "The Construction of Heterosexuality," in *Fear of a Queer Planet: Queer Politics and Social Theory,* ed. Michael Warner (Minneapolis, MN: University of Minnesota Press, 1993), 82–102.

39. Chris Schilling and Philip A. Mellor, "Cultures of Embodied Experience: Technology, Religion, and Body Pedagogics," *The Sociological Review* 55 (2007): 545.

40. Michael W. Ross, "Typing, Doing, and Being: Sexuality and the Internet," *The Journal of Sex Research* 42 (2005): 344.

41. Aimee Carrillo Rowe, Sheena Malhotra, and Kimberlee Pérez, *Answer the Call: Virtual Migration in Indian Call Centers* (Minneapolis, MN: University of Minnesota Press, 2013), 3.

42. danah boyd, "White Flight in Networked Publics: How Race and Class Shaped American Teen Engagement with MySpace and Facebook," in *Race After the Internet,* ed. Lisa Nakamura and Peter A. Chow-White (New York: Routledge, 2012), 203–222. See also Robert Glenn Howard, *Digital Jesus: The Making of a New Christian Fundamentalist Community on the Internet* (New York: New York University Press, 2011); and Lisa Nakamura, *Digitizing Race: Visual Cultures of the Internet* (Minneapolis, MN: University of Minnesota Press, 2008).

43. There are non-evangelical Christian religious resources for discussing sexual pleasure, though they are much less prevalent than evangelical resources. *Holy Sex: A Catholic Guide to Toe-Curling, Mind-Blowing, Infallible Loving* (New York: Crossroads Publishing, 2008), written by counselor and author Gregory Popcak, is the only readily available contemporary Catholic sex advice book. It has many similarities with its evangelical counterparts, including an emphasis on scripture and an acceptance of sexual practices other than penile-vaginal intercourse (including oral sex and the use of vibrators) within heterosexual marriage. Unlike evangelical authors, however, Popcak opposes contraception and instructs his readers to follow

the "One Rule"—that all sex acts must lead to penile-vaginal intercourse in which a man ejaculates, thereby allowing a possibility of conception. In addition to this book, there are online marriage and family resources geared toward Catholics that sometimes discuss marital sex, usually as it pertains to natural family planning. However, there are no online resources specifically created for married Catholics to discuss having sex for pleasure. Mormons have a wider range of marital sexuality resources available to them, including a small number of sex advice books and websites. Mormons also appear better integrated than Catholics into evangelical culture, which promotes marital sex. Laura M. Brotherson, for instance, the author of *And They Were Not Ashamed: Strengthening Marriage through Sexual Fulfillment* (Boise, ID: Inspire Books, 2004), a Mormon sex advice book, also sells many well-known evangelical sex advice books on her website. Mormon resources, like evangelical ones, are often identified only as "Christian," and therefore additional context is required to establish that they were created by and for Latter-day Saints.

44. John D'Emilio and Estelle B. Freedman, *Intimate Matters: A History of Sexuality in America* (New York: Harper and Row, 1988); Jonathan Ned Katz, *The Invention of Heterosexuality* (Chicago, IL: University of Chicago Press, 1995).

45. Sarah Baringer Gordon, *The Mormon Question: Polygamy and Constitutional Conflict in Nineteenth-Century America* (Chapel Hill, NC: University of North Carolina Press, 2002).

46. Katz, *Invention of Heterosexuality*, 21.

47. D'Emilio and Freedman, *Intimate Matters*. Scholars of twentieth-century American religion note that shifts away from formal religious authority do not necessarily signal a waning in religion's importance in social life but rather an integration of religious and secular cultural values. For instance, the popularity of twentieth-century dieting programs reflected the prevailing Protestant ideology of the time, which emphasized the connection between the health of one's physical body and one's self-worth. Similarly, the rise of the self-help industry in the 1970s and '80s revitalized religious values. See R. Marie Griffith, *Born Again Bodies: Flesh and Spirit in American Christianity* (Berkeley, CA: University of California Press, 2004); and Robert Wuthnow, *Sharing the Journey: Support Groups and America's New Quest for Community* (New York: The Free Press, 1994).

48. Putnam and Campbell, *American Grace*, 13–14. See also Randall Balmer, *Mine Eyes Have Seen the Gory: A Journey into the Evangelical Subculture of America* (New York: Oxford University Press, [1989] 2006). The language academics use to classify conservative Protestant evangelicals requires some caveats. Although conservative Protestant evangelicals today have definitive roots in twentieth-century fundamentalism, evangelicalism as a religious movement predates fundamentalism. Most historians of religion agree that a religious revitalization in the 1730s known as the first Great Awakening introduced America to evangelicalism, a particular strand of Protestantism that emphasized individual responsibility for conversion, abstaining from sin, and proselytizing. Scholars typically divide contemporary Protestants into two groups, distinguishing Black Protestants from mostly white conservative Protestant evangelicals due to their differing historical experiences and

political beliefs, even though their theological beliefs have much in common. In this book, I use the term *evangelical* to refer to those groups dominated by white believers.

49. There is an extensive and motley body of literature on how evangelicals adapt to secular culture. Two ethnographies that showcase the creativity and breadth of evangelical engagement with salient cultural values are Omri Elisha's *Moral Ambition: Mobilization and Social Outreach in Evangelical Megachurches* (Berkeley, CA: University of California Press, 2011) and Amy McDowell's "Warriors and Terrorists: Antagonism as Strategy in Christian Hardcore and Muslim 'Taqwacore' Punk Rock" (*Qualitative Sociology* 37 [2014]: 255–276). For an overview of evangelical reaction to secular media, see Heather Hendershot, *Shaking the World for Jesus: Media and Conservative Evangelical Culture* (Chicago: University of Chicago Press, 2004). For a general overview of evangelical believers in the late twentieth century, see Christian Smith, *Christian America?: What Evangelicals Really Want* (Berkeley, CA: University of California Press, 2000).

50. D'Emilio and Freedman, *Intimate Matters;* Mark D. Jordan, *Recruiting Young Love: How Christians Talk about Homosexuality* (Chicago: University of Chicago Press, 2011).

51. Attwood, "Sexed Up," 78.

52. Robert N. Bellah, *Habits of the Heart: Individualism and Commitment in American Life* (Berkeley, CA: University of California Press, 1985); Micki McGee, *Self-Help, Inc.: Makeover Culture in American Life* (New York: Oxford University Press, 2005); Wade Clark Roof, *Spiritual Marketplace: Baby Boomers and the Remaking of American Religion* (Princeton: Princeton University Press, 1999); Robert Wuthnow, *After Heaven: Spirituality in America since the 1950s* (Berkeley, CA: University of California Press, 1998).

53. Wuthnow, *After Heaven,* 15.

54. Nancy Tatom Ammerman, *Bible Believers: Fundamentalists in the Modern World* (New Brunswick, NJ: Rutgers University Press, 1987); Balmer, *Mine Eyes;* T. M. Luhrmann, *When God Talks Back: Understanding the American Relationship with God* (New York: Alfred A. Knopf, 2012), 56.

55. DeRogatis, *Saving Sex.*

56. Pew Research Center, *Usage Over Time,* Pew Internet and American Life Project, 2012, accessed January 28, 2013, http://pewinternet.org/Static-Pages/Trend-Data-(Adults)/Usage-Over-Time.aspx. Indeed, there has been a proliferation of online communities of virtually every religious tradition, from Chabad Jews to Neopagans. See Oren Golan, "Charting Frontiers of Online Religious Communities: The Case of Chabad Jews," in *Digital Religion: Understanding Religious Practice in New Media Worlds,* ed. Heidi Campbell (New York: Routledge, 2013), 155–163; and Sarah M. Pike, *New Age and Neopagan Religions in America* (New York: Columbia University Press, 2006).

57. Shayne Lee and Phillip Luke Sinitiere, *Holy Mavericks: Evangelical Innovators and the Spiritual Marketplace* (New York: New York University Press, 2009).

58. Hendershot, *Shaking the World.*

59. Mary L. Gray, *Out in the Country: Youth, Media, and Queer Visibility in Rural America* (New York: New York University Press, 2009).

60. James Joseph Dean, *Straights: Heterosexuality in Post-Closeted Culture* (New York: New York University, 2014), 2.

61. According to one survey, white evangelical Protestant support for same-sex marriage shifted from 12 percent in 2003 to 27 percent in 2013, although their support during both years was lower than any other religious group. There is a considerable difference of opinion between age groups, however. In 2013, 43 percent of evangelical Millennials supported same-sex marriage, compared to 22 percent of evangelical baby boomers. See Robert P. Jones, Daniel Cox, and Juhem Navarro-Rivera, *A Shifting Landscape: A Decade of Change in American Attitudes about Same-Sex Marriage and LGBT Issues,* Public Religion Research Institute, February 26, 2014, http://publicreligion.org/site/wp-content/uploads/2014/02/2014.LGBT_REPORT.pdf. See also Linda Bean and Brandon C. Martinez, "Evangelical Ambivalence toward Gays and Lesbians," *Sociology of Religion* 75 (2014): 1–23.

62. The Gospel, Homosexuality, and the Future of Marriage was a conference held October 27–29, 2014, hosted by the Ethics and Religious Liberty Commission of the Southern Baptist Convention (http://erlc.com/conference). The journalist's quote comes from Zack Ford's account of the conference, "Single, Married, Celibate, Sexual, Ex-Gay: The Southern Baptists' Mixed Messages on Homosexuality," ThinkProgress, November 4, 2014, http://thinkprogress.org/lgbt/2014/11/04/3588151/southern-baptists-ex-gay-mixed-messages/. The conference speaker was quoted in Rachel Zoll's article "Southern Baptists Tell Pastors: Hold Line on Gays," *Deseret News,* October 28, 2014, http://www.deseretnews.com/article/765661902/Southern-Baptists-tell-pastors-hold-line-on-gays.html.

63. For guidelines about virtual ethnographies and related methodologies, see Christine Hine, *Virtual Ethnography* (Thousand Oaks, CA: SAGE Publications, 2000). One feminist example of a virtual ethnography that also details the methods is Nicole Constable's *Romance on a Global Stage.*

64. Demographic characteristics for CSIS respondents were comparable for users of all seven websites represented in the survey (five blogs, one message board, and one online store). For more information, see Research Strategy in Appendix B.

65. My experiences in the "field"—both virtual and real life—reflect what Orit Avishai, Lynne Gerber, and Jennifer Randles describe in "The Feminist Ethnographer's Dilemma: Reconciling Progressive Research Agendas with Fieldwork Realities" (*Journal of Contemporary Ethnography* [2012]: 1–33) as a "feminist ethnographer's dilemma," which manifests itself especially when studying conservative communities. For a more detailed description of my methods, see Appendix B: Doing Internet Ethnography.

66. In their book *American Grace,* which documents one of the largest studies to date on American religion, Putnam and Campbell write that they found that

people who attended high-profile nondenominational (but widely identified as evangelical) churches overwhelmingly labeled themselves simply as "Christian."

67. Melinda Bollar Wagner, in "Generic Conservative Christianity: The Demise of Denominationalism in Christian Schools" (*Journal for the Scientific Study of Religion* 36 [1997]), argues that ecumenism, which is not typically used to describe conservative Christian groups, flourishes in Christian schools, where "some of the corners of historical doctrinal differences [are] rounded down" (14).

68. This coalition included the U.S. Conference of Catholic Bishops, the National Association of Evangelicals, the Church of Jesus Christ of Latter-day Saints, the Southern Baptist Convention, and the Lutheran Church Missouri Synod.

69. Mark Chaves, *American Religion: Contemporary Trends* (Princeton, NJ: Princeton University Press, 2011), 82.

70. The CSIS uses the categories constructed by the Pew Research Center to lump together denominations into broader evangelical traditions. See Pew Research Center, *U.S. Religious Landscape Survey*, Pew Forum on Religion and Public Life, 2008, accessed November 11, 2014, http://religions.pewforum.org/pdf/report-religious-landscape-study-appendix2.pdf.

71. For national comparisons, I use two national data sets: the 2012 General Social Survey (GSS) and the Pew Forum on Religion and Public Life 2011 National Survey of Mormons. I use the Pew Forum data to supplement GSS data for Mormon respondents, since the GSS categorizes Latter-day Saints as a subset of Protestants, even though most Mormons believe themselves to be a part of a distinct Christian tradition. The GSS therefore includes an extremely small LDS sample (in 2012, the number of Mormon respondents was sixteen). For more information on these comparisons, see Research Strategy in Appendix B.

72. Twelve percent of CSIS respondents reported that they lived outside the United States. The majority lived in Canada or Europe (each group representing 4 percent of the total sample). Table 2 presents the geographic distribution, by region, of only those respondents living in the United States so that these data can be compared with national data sets. Table B-2 in Appendix B includes the geographic distribution, by region, of all CSIS and interview respondents. All interview respondents living outside the United States or Canada (*n* = 3) were American citizens engaged in missionary work abroad.

73. Mainline Protestant denominations include the United Methodist Church, the Lutheran Church (with the exception of the Missouri and Wisconsin Synod), the Presbyterian Church (U.S.A.), the Episcopal Church, and the United Church of Christ. In *Pray the Gay Away*, Barton notes that, especially in the American South, attitudes about homosexuality are what unite the broad range of Christian groups that comprise what she calls "Bible Belt Christianity." She notes, "while there may be great variation in church norms throughout the Bible Belt [...], most Christian denominations [...], from Baptist to Methodist to Holiness to Catholic to Jehovah's Witness to Mormon to nondenominational, are uniform in their construction of homosexuality as sinful" (13).

1. Tim LaHaye and Beverly B. LaHaye, *The Act of Marriage: The Beauty of Sexual Love* (Grand Rapids, MI: Zondervan Publishing House, [1976] 1998), 11–12.

2. Ibid., 99, 97.

3. Alex Confort's *The Joy of Sex: A Gourmet Guide to Lovemaking,* for example, a sex manual popularized in the 1970s, provided practical advice about having sex, although it maintained an idealized notion of heterosexual pleasure and romance. For a discussion of this book, see Valerie V. Peterson, "The Sex of Joy: A Gourmet Guide to Lovemaking Rhetoric," *Popular Communication* 6 (2008): 3–19.

4. DeRogatis, *Saving Sex.*

5. LaHaye and LaHaye, *The Act of Marriage,* 14.

6. *Premillennial dispensationalism* is the belief that history is divided into seven Biblically inspired dispensations that end with Christ's return and the apocalypse. Dispensationalists believe that the world gets progressively worse as time goes by. This tenet emerged with early twentieth-century fundamentalism, when believers interpreted cultural changes as evidence that the apocalypse was near. For a history of the development of this belief, see Balmer, *Mine Eyes.*

7. In her ethnography of a fundamentalist church, *Bible Believers,* Ammerman points out that fundamentalist Christians use a strict literalist interpretation of the Bible in order to make sense of secular society.

8. Ed Young and Lisa Young, *Sexperiment: 7 Days to Lasting Intimacy with Your Spouse* (New York: Faith Words, 2012), 4.

9. Dillow and Pintus, *Intimate Issues;* Shannon Ethridge, *The Sexually Confident Wife; Connecting with your Husband Mind, Body, Heart, Spirit* (New York: Broadway Books, 2008); Ed Young and Lisa Young, *Sexperiment.*

10. Mark Driscoll and Grace G. Driscoll, *Real Marriage: The Truth about Sex, Friendship, and Life Together* (Nashville, TN: Thomas Nelson, Inc., 2012), xi, 177.

11. Driscoll resigned from Mars Hill Church in the fall of 2014 following controversies related to *Real Marriage* and his authoritative style as lead pastor. In 2013, a radio host questioned Driscoll on air about whether he plagiarized passages from *Real Marriage,* an allegation that he denied at the time. Later, however, he admitted to plagiarism and to paying a marketing firm to purchase copies of the book upon its release to ensure that it reached the *New York Times* best-seller list. These controversies pushed Driscoll further into the spotlight, resulting in a large number of vocal critics but also a number of defenders. Situating *Real Marriage* among other evangelical sex manuals, historian Amy DeRogatis (*Saving Sex,* 68) writes, "while the Driscolls' tone and style might not be palatable to all evangelicals, their approach to biblical sex is consistent with some contemporary evangelical sex manuals." See also Craig Welch, "The Rise and Fall of Mars Hill Church," *Seattle Times,* September 13, 2014, accessed October 30, 2014 www.seattletimes.com/seattle-news /the-rise-and-fall-of-mars-hill-church/.

12. LaHaye and LaHaye, *Act of Marriage,* 11; Driscoll and Driscoll, *Real Marriage,* 42.

13. Katelyn Beaty and Marlena Graves, "Q & A: Mark and Grace Driscoll on Sex for the 21st-Century Christian," *Christianity Today,* January 5, 2012, accessed July 15, 2012, www.christianitytoday.com/ct/2012/januaryweb-only/mark-driscoll-sex-marriage.html.

14. Driscoll and Driscoll, *Real Marriage,* 177.

15. LaHaye and LaHaye, *Act of Marriage,* 374; Driscoll and Driscoll, *Real Marriage,* 186, 119.

16. Mark D. Jordan, *The Ethics of Sex* (Oxford: Blackwell Publishers, 2002), 78.

17. Ethridge, *Sexually Confident Wife.*

18. Arguments that hormones like oxytocin are physical evidence that human bodies (particularly women's bodies) are intended for a single sex partner have widely been debunked by the scientific community. See Stacy Schiff, "Sex and the Single-Minded," *New York Times,* January 20, 2007, accessed October 30, 2014, www.nytimes.com/2007/01/20/opinion/20schiff.html.

19. Douglas E. Rosenau, *A Celebration of Sex* (Nashville, TN: Thomas Nelson, Inc., [1994] 2002); Clifford Penner and Joyce Penner, *The Gift of Sex: A Guide to Sexual Fulfillment* (Nashville, TN: Thomas Nelson, Inc., [1973] 2003); Terry Wier, *Holy Sex: God's Purpose and Plan for Our Sexuality* (New Kensington, PA: Whitaker House, 1999).

20. Tony DiLorenzo and Alisa DiLorenzo, *Stripped Down: 13 Keys to Unlocking Intimacy in Your Marriage* (Cary, NC: Past Due Press, 2010).

21. Ibid, 140.

22. Ibid, 142.

23. The survey questionnaire specified that all sex acts in question were between two consenting adults.

24. Their responses to the CSIS suggest that respondents reject beliefs that are increasingly common among mainline Protestants and Catholics, further distinguishing these Christian sexuality sites as evangelical. Support of same-sex marriage among Catholics saw a shift from 40 percent in 2001 to 57 percent in 2014, and mainline Protestants' support went from 38 percent in 2001 to 60 percent in 2014. However, white evangelicals Protestant support remained lower than that of any other religious group, with 13 percent supporting same-sex marriage in 2001 and 21 percent in 2014. For more information and statistics, see Pew Research Center, *Changing Attitudes on Gay Marriage,* Pew Research Center's Religion & Public Life Project, July 29, 2015, www.pewforum.org/2014/09/24/graphics-slideshow-changing-attitudes-on-gay-marriage/. For a historical examinations of Christians' engagement with homosexuality, see Jordan, *Recruiting Young Love.*

25. Most religious Americans, regardless of affiliation, support monogamy and the belief that sex should take place only in a committed relationship. See Edward O. Laumann, John H. Gagnon, Robert T. Michael, and Stuart Michaels, *The Social Organization of Sexuality: Sexual Practices in the United States* (Chicago, IL: University of Chicago Press, 1994).

26. Evangelical abstinence campaigns also reflect the message presented in Christian sex advice—that God wants for married couples to have satisfying sex. In

fact, some of these campaigns use the pleasure of marital sex as a rhetorical strategy to encourage teens to abstain from sex until marriage. See Christine J. Gardner, *Making Chastity Sexy: The Rhetoric of Evangelical Abstinence Campaigns,* (Berkeley, CA: University of California Press, 2011).

27. Young and Young, *Sexperiment,* 4.

28. Ethridge, *Sexually Confident Wife,* 61; see also Kevin Leman, *Sheet Music: Uncovering the Secrets of Sexual Intimacy in Marriage* (Tyndale House Publishers, 2003), 17, 19; Ed Wheat and Gaye Wheat, *Intended for Pleasure: Sex Technique and Sexual Fulfillment in Christian Marriage* (Grand Rapids, MI: Fleming H. Revell, [1977], 2010), 135.

29. The CSIS did not ask respondents specifically if they remained virgins until marriage, so although I infer that respondents who reported a single sexual partner were referring to their spouse, I cannot make claims about whether or not sexual activity took place before marriage.

30. See also Stephen Arteburn, Fred Stoeker, and Mike Yorkey, *Every Man's Battle: Winning the War on Sexual Temptation One Victory at a Time* (New York: Random House, 2000). Antiporn ministries offer filtering software for Christian men who struggle with the temptation to view pornography. The online antiporn ministry XXX Church, for example, offers a software package that allows customers to use the Internet without encountering sexually explicit sites, thereby avoiding the risk of sin.

31. Driscoll and Driscoll, *Real Marriage,* 109. Driscoll also wrote a fifty-nine-page e-book, *Porn Again Christian: A Frank Discussion on Masturbation and Pornography* (Seattle, WA: Mars Hill Church, 2009), that was available for a limited time on the Mars Hills Church website.

32. Emphasizing sexual feelings as sinful is not universal within evangelicalism. Ex-gay groups, for example, distinguish between sexual feelings and sexual actions and are wary of labeling the former as definitively sinful. See Lynne Gerber, *Seeking the Straight and Narrow: Weight Loss and Sexual Reorientation in Evangelical America* (Chicago, IL: University of Chicago Press, 2011).

33. There are many statistics about pornography consumption, but few of them come from reputable scholarly sources. The evangelicals in my study frequently cited research supported by conservative interest groups, such as the Witherspoon Institute, which likely give exaggerated numbers when it comes to how many Americans, especially young men, view pornography. General Social Survey data suggest that, as of 2005, only 14 percent of Americans report having ever viewed sexually explicit material. This number was higher for men, about 25 percent of whom reported having viewed pornography in the past thirty days. See Timothy Buzzell, "Demographic Characteristics of Persons Using Pornography in Three Technological Contexts," *Sexuality & Culture* 9 (2005): 28–48.

34. Some evangelicals focus on heterosexual sex as the standard by which to judge acceptable sexual behavior rather than focusing on heterosexuality as the only acceptable sexual orientation or identity category for Christians. For example, instead of demonizing same-sex attraction, the ex-gay movement encourages participants to talk

openly about their desires and attempt to reconcile the conflict between those desires and their religious beliefs. In fact, scholars of this movement have pointed out its "queerness." Evangelical ex-gays believe that sexuality is fluid, that sexual change is possible, and that there is space beyond the narrow identity categories of homosexual or heterosexual. This allows individuals who fail to meet normative heterosexual standards to still be accepted within a Christian framework. See Tanya Erzen, *Straight to Jesus: Sexual and Christian Conversions in the Ex-Gay Movement* (Berkeley, CA: University of California Press, 2006); and Gerber, *Seeking the Straight and Narrow.*

35. For two examples of evangelical sex manuals that discuss homosexuality and ways to overcome same-sex desire, see Rosenau, *Celebration of Sex;* and Wier, *Holy Sex.*

36. The only evangelical sex manuals examined in this study that do not discuss women's submission to men are Ethridge's *The Sexually Confident Wife* and Bill Farrel and Pam Farrel's *Red, Hot Monogamy: Making Your Marriage Sizzle* (Eugene, OR: Harvest House Publishers, 2006). For scholarly accounts of evangelicals' gender beliefs and practices, see John P. Bartkowski, *Remaking the Godly Marriage: Gender Negotiation in Evangelical Families* (New Brunswick, NJ: Rutgers University Press, 2001); and Sally K. Gallagher, *Evangelical Identity and Gendered Family Life* (New Brunswick, NJ: Rutgers University Press, 2003).

37. Bartkowski, *Remaking the Godly Marriage;* DeRogatis, *Saving Sex;* Lynne Gerber, "The Opposite of Gay: Nature, Creation, and Queerish Ex-Gay Experiments," *Nova Religio: The Journal of Alternative and Emergent Religions* 11 (2008): 8–30.

38. Joseph Dillow et al., *Intimacy Ignited: Conversations Couple to Couple* (Colorado Springs, CO: NAV Press, 2004), 110.

39. Wheat and Wheat, *Intended for Pleasure,* 238.

40. Ibid, 18, 20.

41. Dillow et al., *Intimacy Ignited,* 10, 13.

42. Driscoll and Driscoll, *Real Marriage,* 172; Tremper Longman III, *Song of Songs: The New International Commentary on the Old Testament* (Grand Rapids: Wm. B. Eerdmans Publishing Company, 2001), 195. See also Tommy Nelson, *The Song of Solomon: A Study of Love, Marriage, and Romance,* The Hub Digital Bible Study, 1995.

43. See Driscoll and Driscoll, *Real Marriage;* Ethridge, *Sexually Confident Wife;* and Rosenau, *Celebration of Sex.*

44. Driscoll and Driscoll, *Real Marriage,* 178–179.

45. Marriage is no longer an exclusive privilege of heterosexual unions, as same-sex marriage has been legalized in countries throughout North and South America and Western Europe. Although the CSIS uses the term *marriage* without specifying *heterosexual marriage,* I am confident that, based on their overwhelming opposition to homosexuality, survey respondents interpreted any mention of marriage as a reference to a heterosexual relationship. Statistics on attitudes about oral sex, manual stimulation, and vibrator use are taken from questions asking about a woman performing the act on her husband. There was virtually no difference in attitudes about acts that a man performs on his wife.

46. Gerber, *Seeking the Straight and Narrow*, 89.

47. Wheat and Wheat, *Intended for Pleasure*, 113, 116 (emphasis added).

48. Bartkowski, *Remaking the Godly Marriage;* Gallagher, *Evangelical Identity.*

49. Leman, *Sheet Music,* 25.

50. Wuthnow, *Sharing the Journey,* 18.

51. DeRogatis, *Saving Sex.*

52. Foucault, *History of Sexuality,* 11.

53. Eve Kosofsky Sedgwick, *Epistemology of the Closet* (Berkeley, CA: University of California Press, 1990), 11.

54. David A. Snow, "Extending and Broadening Blumer's Conceptualization of Symbolic Interactionism," *Symbolic Interaction* 24, no. 3 (2001): 367–377.

2. OVERCOMING THE OBSCENE

1. Robert D. McFadden, "New York Hears Words of Hope from Billy Graham," *New York Times,* September 23, 1991, accessed June 11, 2014, www.nytimes.com/1991/09/23/nyregion/new-york-hears-words-of-hope-from-billy-graham.html; "BGEA: Records of the Hour of Decision Radio Program," Billy Graham Center Archives, Wheaton College, accessed June 11, 2014, www2.wheaton.edu/bgc/archives/GUIDES/191.htm.

2. Aaron Smith, "6 New Facts about Facebook," Pew Research Center, February 3, 2014, accessed November 6, 2014, www.pewresearch.org/fact-tank/2014/02/03/6-new-facts-about-facebook/.

3. Jeffrey K. Hadden and Douglas E. Cowan, eds., *Religion on the Internet: Research Prospects and Promises* (London: JAI Press, 2000). See also Heidi Campbell, ed., *Digital Religion: Understanding Religious Practice in New Media Worlds* (New York: Routledge, 2013); Howard, *Digital Jesus.*

4. Of the thirty-six websites in this study, four were created by or for published authors, two by ordained members of clergy, and one by a licensed therapist.

5. Susannah Fox and Lee Rainie, "The Web at 25 in the U.S.," Pew Research Center Internet and American Life Project, February 27, 2014, accessed June 11, 2014, www.pewinternet.org/2014/02/27/summary-of-findings-3/.

6. Bourdieu, *Logic of Practice.* The term *spiritual capital* comes from Bradford Verter, "Spiritual Capital: Theorizing Religion with Bourdieu Against Bourdieu," *Sociological Theory* 21, no. 2 (2003): 150–174. See also David Swartz, "Bridging the Study of Culture and Religion: Pierre Bourdieu's Political Economy of Symbolic Power," *Sociology of Religion* 57, no. 1 (1996): 71–85.

7. Bourdieu, *Logic of Practice.* See also Verter, "Spiritual Capital."

8. Howard and Jeanne Hendricks of the Center for Christian Leadership at the Dallas Theological Seminary endorse Dillow and Pintus' *Intimate Issues.*

9. Some notable titles include Dillow et al., *Intimacy Ignited;* Linda Dillow, *How to Really Love Your Man* (Nashville, TN: Thomas Nelson Inc., 1993); Linda Dillow and Lorraine Pintus, *Gift-Wrapped by God: Secret Answers to the Question "Why Wait?"* (Colorado Springs, CO: WaterBrook Press, 2002); and Lorraine Pintus, *Jump Off the Hormone Swing: Fly Through the Physical, Mental, and Spiritual Symptoms of PMS and Peri-Menopause* (Chicago, IL: Moody Publishers, 2010).

10. James S. Bielo, *Words upon the Word: An Ethnography of Evangelical Group Bible Study* (New York: New York University Press, 2009).

11. Leman, *Sheet Music,* 74.

12. In *Saving Sex,* DeRogatis notes that most evangelical sex manuals are authored by "husband and wife teams," although the "authorial voice throughout the text is generally male" (51).

13. I included eighteen online stores in my study. One store did not include identifying information about the owner(s).

14. In the "Note to the Reader" at the beginning of his book *Sheet Music,* Leman instructs unmarried readers to read chapters one through four and then "stop there—and wait to read the rest until after you're married."

15. Merton's explanation of social deviance in his strain theory suggests that social strains (like poverty) pressure individuals to commit acts of deviance to meet culturally approved goals (like wealth). Innovators rationalize these deviant acts for themselves but not for others. In the case of Christian sexuality websites, social conditions pressure individuals to have *good sex,* and website creators have justified the means through which they achieve it. See Robert K. Merton, "Social Structure and Anomie," *American Sociological Review* 3 (1938): 672–682.

16. Elisha, *Moral Ambitions,* 23 (italics in original).

17. Ibid, 23.

18. Hadden and Cowan, *Religion on the Internet;* Howard, *Digital Jesus.*

3. VIRTUAL AND VIRTUOUS

1. For sociological accounts of community-building, see Kathleen M. Blee, *Democracy in Making: How Activist Groups Form* (New York: Oxford University Press, 2012); and Paul Lichterman, *Elusive Togetherness: Church Groups Trying to Bridge America's Divisions* (Princeton, NJ: Princeton University Press, 2005). For a rich scholarly account of online community, see Tom Boellstorff's virtual ethnography, *Coming of Age in Second Life: An Anthropologist Explores the Virtually Human* (Princeton, NJ: Princeton University Press, 2008).

2. Goffman, *Presentation of Self,* 35.

3. Howard, *Digital Jesus,* 174. For an analysis of the inclusive possibilities for religion online, see Brenda E. Brasher, *Give Me That Online Religion* (San Francisco, CA: Jossey-Bass, 2001).

4. Lichterman, *Elusive Togetherness*, 15. See also Michele Lamont and Virag Molnar, "The Study of Boundaries in the Social Sciences," *Annual Review of Sociology* 28 (2002): 167–195.

5. Although some scholars have noted the ways in which evangelicals have catered to American individualism (for example, see Wuthnow, *After Heaven*), Elisha reflects that "evangelicals go to great lengths to encourage (and enforce) relationalism as a collective ethos that complements and at times complicates individualism" (*Moral Ambition*, 21).

6. A 2012 Pew Research study finds that almost 90 percent of American adults use the Internet and that 72 percent of these users have looked online for health information in the past year. See Susannah Fox and Maeve Duggan, *Health Online 2013*, Pew Research Internet Project, January 15, 2013, accessed November 7, 2014, www.pewinternet.org/2013/01/15/health-online-2013/.

7. The vast majority of CSIS respondents (about 83 percent) attend church at least every week, compared to 56 percent of evangelicals nationally and 31 percent of the overall American population, according to GSS 2012 data.

8. In *Sheet Music*, Leman calls these chapters "For Men Only" and "For Women Only."

9. For a more detailed account of evangelical men who have a low sex drive and use Christian sexuality websites, see Kelsy Burke and Amy Moff Hudec, "Sexual Encounters and Manhood Acts: Evangelicals, Latter-day Saints, and Religious Masculinities," *Journal for the Scientific Study of Religion* 54, no. 2 (2015): 330–344.

10. Half of the website users I interviewed (twenty-two of forty-four) viewed Christian sexuality websites at least daily. The majority of respondents (twenty-five of forty-four) had been following BetweenTheSheets.com or LustyChristianLadies.com for one to five years at the time of their interviews. Of those twenty-five respondents, fifteen still viewed BTS or LCL at least daily. I interviewed seven website users who were long-time followers of the sites (meaning that they had been following the sites for more than five years). Five of these seven respondents still viewed BTS or LCL at least daily.

11. DiLorenzo and DiLorenzo, *Stripped Down*.

12. For a description of LGBT evangelicals, see Moon, "Love and the Authentic Self."

13. Ammerman, *Bible Believers;* Luhrmann, *When God Talks Back*.

14. Virginia Lieson Brereton, *From Sin to Salvation: Stories of Women's Conversions, 1800 to the Present* (Bloomington, IN: Indiana University Press, 1991); Peter G. Stromberg, *Language and Self-Transformation: A Study of the Christian Conversion Narrative* (New York: Cambridge University Press, 1993). I discuss how website users' stories resemble salvation narratives in more detail in chapter four.

15. Goffman, *Presentation of the Self.*

16. Snow, "Extending and Broadening."

17. The social construction of religion is a basic premise of sociology that dates back to one of the founders of the discipline, Emile Durkheim. Durkheim argued that religion is a "representation" of social realities, meaning that communities cre-

ate religion as a way to understand their societies and that religion, in turn, reflects social values. God, for Durkheim, is "nothing else than the clan itself" (206). See Emile Durkheim, *The Elementary Forms of Religious Life,* trans. Joseph Ward Swain (Mineola, NY: Dover Publications, [1915] 2008).

4. SEXUAL AWAKENING

1. Brereton, *Sin to Salvation,* 48.

2. There is a rich body of research investigating how conservative religious women exhibit agency within the constraints of their patriarchal religions. For a review of this literature, see Kelsy Burke, "Women's Agency in Gender-Traditional Religions: A Review of Four Approaches," *Sociology Compass* 6 (2012): 122–133. For an evangelical context, see Brenda E. Brasher, *Godly Women* (New Brunswick, NJ: Rutgers University Press, 1997); and R. Marie Griffith, *God's Daughters: Evangelical Women and the Power of Submission* (Berkeley, CA: University of California Press, 1997).

3. In a BTS thread asking members to share the stories of their sexual awakenings, over a hundred members posted their stories, and all but one were written by or about women.

4. For more on the importance of sexual stories, see Kenneth Plummer, *Telling Sexual Stories: Power, Change, and Social Worlds* (New York: Routledge, 1995). Jill Peterfeso observes how important these stories are for making sense of religious women's sexuality in "From Testimony to Seximony, from Script to Scripture: Revealing Mormon Women's Sexuality Through the Mormon Vagina Monologues," *Journal of Feminist Studies in Religion* 27 (2011): 31–49. In the article, Peterfeso describes how performers draw from the rhetorical form of *The Vagina Monologues* to critique the Mormon Church, celebrate women's sexuality, and still remain devout believers of their Mormon faith.

5. Journalist Ariel Levy argues that the sexualization of women through what she calls "raunch culture" is anti-feminist. According to Levy, the goal of women's liberation—to empower women sexually—never actualized: "The truth is that the new conception of raunch culture as a path to liberation rather than oppression is a convenient (and lucrative) fantasy with nothing to back it up" (*Female Chauvinist Pigs,* 82). A more optimistic reading of the intersection of feminism and pop culture can be found in J. Jack Halberstam's *Gaga Feminism: Sex, Gender, and the End of Normal* (Boston, MA: Beacon Press, 2012).

6. In *Desiring Revolution: Second-Wave Feminism and the Rewriting of American Sexual Thought, 1920 to 1982* (New York: Columbia University Press, 2013), Jane Gerhard outlines the history of second-wave feminism and women's sexual pleasure, arguing that "feminists agreed on little else beyond the shared value of women determining for themselves what they wanted from sex" (8).

7. Burkett and Hamilton, "Postfeminist Sexual Agency"; Gill, "Empowerment/Sexism"; Levy, *Female Chauvinist Pigs.*

8. Michelle Wolkomir, "Giving It Up to God: Negotiating Femininity in Support Groups for Wives of Ex-Gay Christian Men," *Gender & Society* 18 (2004): 739.

9. Gill, "Mediated Intimacy," 33.

10. Wheat and Wheat, *Intended for Pleasure,* 111; Ethridge, *Sexually Confident Wife,* 13.

11. Ethridge, *Sexually Confident Wife,* 106.

12. Ibid, 109, 113, 112.

13. Leman, *Sheet Music,* 91–92, 11.

14. Driscoll and Driscoll, *Real Marriage,* 124.

15. Ibid.

16. DeRogatis, *Saving Sex,* 54.

17. Ethridge, *Sexually Confident Wife,* 108.

18. In *Born Again Bodies,* Griffith argues that the body is central to twentieth-century Christianity. Control of the body (especially in regards to sexuality and diet) has exposed "the complex relationship between the visible body and the invisible soul" (23).

19. Attwood, "Sexed Up," 87.

20. Anthropologist Saba Mahmood's ethnography of women participating in the Egyptian Islamic mosque movement, *The Politics of Piety: The Islamic Revival and the Feminist Subject* (Princeton, NJ: Princeton University Press, 2005), is instructive when considering religious women's ability to make choices when faced with constraints. She writes that religious women's accounts must be analyzed according to "the particular field of arguments" made available by their religious communities and "the possibilities for action these arguments have opened and foreclosed" (183). Mahmood diverges from typical definitions of agency as being defined by free will and instead considers an agency that may be docile and compliant, reflecting the possible choices available to women given their religious circumstances.

21. Stevi Jackson and Sue Scott describe the "sexual sentence," a typical narrative about sexual activity that focuses on vaginal intercourse between a man and woman, leading to mutual orgasm and ending ultimately with a man's ejaculation. "Faking Like a Woman? Towards an Interpretive Theorization of Sexual Pleasure," *Body and Society* 13 (2007): 95–116.

5. WHAT MAKES A MAN

A version of this chapter appears in Kelsy Burke, "What Makes a Man: Gender and Sexual Boundaries on Christian Sexuality Websites," *Sexualities* 17 (2014): 3–22.

1. Many news outlets emphasized the fact that Weiner was married at the time of these incidents, but the scandalous nature of his exploits did not draw solely from the fact that they were extramarital. Instead, media pundits focused excessively on the deviant nature of exchanging sexually explicit photographs online. Lance

Dodes, "Is Anthony Weiner a Sex Addict?" *Psychology Today,* June 22, 2011, accessed April 9, 2014, www.psychologytoday.com/blog/the-heart-addiction/201106/is-anthony-weiner-sex-addict. See also Joshua Gamson, "Normal Sins: Sex Scandal Narratives as Institutional Morality Tales," *Social Problems* 48 (2001): 185–205.

2. Guy Hocquenghem, *Homosexual Desire,* trans. Daniella Dangoor (Durham, NC: Duke University Press, 1993), 101.

3. Jackson and Scott, "Faking Like a Woman?"

4. David Kyle Foster, "The Divine Order to Marriage," Focus on the Family, accessed April 9, 2014, www.focusonthefamily.com/marriage/gods_design_for_marriage/marriage_gods_idea/the_divine_order_to_marriage.aspx. See also Attwood, "Sexed Up"; Fausto-Sterling, *Sexing the Body;* Giddens, *Modernity and Self-Identity.*

5. The word *pegging* comes from a 2001 poll conducted by sex advice columnist Dan Savage, who asked his readers, "What we should call it when a woman fucks a man in the ass with a strap-on dildo?" Over 12,000 readers voted and the word *peg* received the most votes. According to the reader who proposed the term, the word originates from boy prostitutes, who were sometimes called "peg boys." Pegging gradually became a part of American sexual vernacular. Dan Savage, "Let's Vote," *Savage Love,* May 24, 2001, accessed November 11, 2014, www.thestranger.com/seattle/SavageLove?oid=7446; Dan Savage, "We Have a Winner!" *Savage Love,* June 21, 2001, accessed November 11, 2014, www.thestranger.com/seattle/SavageLove?oid=7730.

6. I analyzed nine blog posts and message board threads that mentioned cross-dressing; thirteen that mentioned pegging explicitly; and thirty that mentioned male anal play but did not use the word *pegging.* Of the eighteen Christian-owned online sex toy stores in my study, ten sold products explicitly intended for anal play. Of the eighteen online message boards and blogs included in my study, twelve discussed (though did not necessarily endorse) anal sex. I performed in-depth content analysis on a sample of twelve websites in my study to examine discussions about non-normative sex acts, which included, but were not limited to, anal sex. In order to gauge the content of the remainder of the sites in my study, I performed a content search using the word *anal,* since anal sex was the most frequently discussed (and most easily labeled) non-normative sex act on the sites. Anal sex, when discussed on Christian sexuality websites, almost always describes an act in which a man penetrates a woman.

7. W. Bradford Wilcox, *Soft Patriarchs, New Men: How Christianity Shapes Fathers and Husbands* (Chicago: University of Chicago Press, 2004). See also Bartkowski, *Remaking the Godly Marriage;* Michael A. Messner, "'Changing Men' and Feminist Politics in the United States," *Theory and Society* 22 (1993): 723–737; Melanie Heath, "Soft-Boiled Masculinity: Renegotiating Gender and Racial Ideologies in the Promise Keepers Movement," *Gender & Society* 17 (2003): 423–444; Gerber, *Seeking the Straight and Narrow.*

8. Burke and Moff Hudec, "Sexual Encounters and Manhood Acts."

9. Connell, *Masculinities,* 79; Douglas Schrock and Michael Schwalbe, "Men, Masculinity, and Manhood Acts," *Annual Review of Sociology* 35 (2009): 277–295;

Jane Ward, "Dude-Sex: White Masculinities and 'Authentic' Heterosexuality Among Dudes who have Sex with Dudes," *Sexualities* 11 (2008): 414–434; Michelle Wolkomir, "Making Heteronormative Reconciliations: The Story of Romantic Love, Sexuality, and Gender in Mixed-Orientation Marriages," *Gender & Society* 23 (2009): 494–519.

10. Rubin, "Thinking Sex," 163.

11. LaHaye and LaHaye, *Act of Marriage*, 242.

12. Bartkowski, *Remaking the Godly Marriage*, 39.

13. Leman, *Sheet Music*, 165.

14. Hebrews 13:4, King James Version.

15. Ethridge, *Sexually Confident Wife*, 185.

16. Forums on BetweenTheSheets.com fall into one of three categories: (1) those related to specific sex acts (e.g., "Oral Sex" and "Masturbation in Marriage"); (2) those related to non-specified sex (e.g., "Sexual Attitudes" and "Prayer"); and (3) those that discuss what I call *theoretical sex,* which deal with hypothetical scenarios and general beliefs about sex (e.g., "Science and Sex" and "The Bible and Sex"). Twelve percent of threads related to specific sex acts are found in the "Anal Delights" and "Out of the Box" forums, though non-normative sex is also mentioned in all other forums.

17. The wording used in figure 15 is different from the wording that appeared in the CSIS questionnaire. The CSIS asked respondents if they consider active or passive anal intercourse to be "not at all appealing," "not very appealing," "somewhat appealing," or "very appealing." I coded the responses by gender to summarize attitudes about anal sex in which a man is penetrated versus anal sex in which a woman is penetrated.

18. "The Playboy Advisor," *Playboy Magazine,* February 1999, 39; Rachel Hills, "Sex Talk Realness: What Men Think about Pegging," *Cosmopolitan,* November 20, 2014, www.cosmopolitan.com/sex-love/news/a33467/sex-talk-realness-what-men-think-about-pegging/.

19. Hocquenghem, *Homosexual Desire;* Lynne Segal, *Straight Sex: Rethinking the Politics of Pleasure* (Berkeley: University of California Press, 1994).

20. This logic is similar to that used by some practitioners of BDSM to justify sex play that draws from cultural trauma like rape or slavery by creating boundaries between what can happen in a sexual scene and the violence and inequalities of the "real world" (see Weiss, *Techniques of Pleasure*). Users of Christian sexuality websites and some members of the BDSM community both present consensual sex as unique and exceptional, attempting to create fissures between the sexual and non-sexual world. In her ethnography of San Francisco's BDSM community, *Techniques of Pleasure,* Weiss argues that sex acts are best understood as "circuits," never entirely removed from the social world and its embedded structures of privilege and inequality.

21. Lynne Gerber makes a similar argument about ex-gay evangelicals, who talk about gender using nature (biological differences between males and females) as well as a subjective understanding of the "creator," who is responsible for such differences.

"The Opposite of Gay: Nature, Creation, and Queerish Ex-Gay Experiments," *Nova Religio: The Journal of Alternative and Emergent Religions* 11 (2008): 8–30.

22. Driscoll and Driscoll, *Real Marriage*, 120.

23. Leman, *Sheet Music*, 45.

24. Wheat and Wheat, *Intended for Pleasure*, 39.

25. Penner and Penner, *The Gift of Sex*, 327; Farrell and Farrell, *Red-Hot Monogamy*, 164.

26. Moon, *God, Sex, and Politics*, 227.

27. The concept I propose of the privileged relationship between the self, one's spouse, and God draws from the triangular nature of certain erotic relationships, most notably described by Eve Sedgwick in *Between Men: English Literature and Male Homosocial Desire* (New York: Columbia University Press, 1985). Sedgwick notes that dyadic erotic relationships are often mediated by a third party. Drawing on the work of René Gerard and Sigmund Freud, she proposes that a man who desires a woman may, for example, desire her because of his rivalry with another man, thereby inadvertently strengthening a (quasi-erotic) bond between himself and that other man. The erotic triangle I present differs from these paradigms, since God is a unique actor in it—desired (at least theoretically) equally by evangelicals and with full awareness by both the self and the spouse. Additionally, the self's relationship with God exists simultaneously with his or her relationship with the spouse; it is neither a cause nor an effect of the primary erotic relationship. Yet, like Sedgwick's erotic triangle, the primary sexual relationship between a man and woman is deeply affected by their relationship with a third party—in this case, God.

28. Luhrmann, *When God Talks Back*, 66.

29. Joshua Gamson, *Freaks Talk Back: Tabloid Talk Shows and Sexual Nonconformity* (Chicago, IL: University of Chicago Press, 1998), 18–19.

30. Gallagher, *Evangelical Identity*. See also Bartkowski, *Remaking the Godly Marriage*; Smith, *Christian America?*; Judith Stacey, *Brave New Families: Stories of Domestic Upheaval in Late Twentieth-Century America* (Berkeley, CA: University of California Press, 1990); and Wilcox, *Soft Patriarchs*.

CONCLUSION

1. William Lidwell, Kritina Holden, and Jill Butler, *Universal Principles of Design* (Beverly, MA: Rockport Publishers, 2003). For another example of how this metaphor has been appropriated in the social sciences, see Laura Nichols, "Social Desire Paths: A New Theoretical Concept to Increase the Usability of Social Science Research in Society," *Theory and Society* 43 (2014): 647–665.

2. Matthew Tiessen, "Accepting Invitations: Desire Lines as Earthly Offerings," *Rhizomes* 15 (2007), accessed April 11, 2015, www.rhizomes.net/issue15/tiessen.html.

3. Peter Berger, *The Sacred Canopy: Elements of a Sociological Theory of Religion* (New York: Anchor Books [1967] 1990). Berger later described secularization theory as "falsified." See Peter Berger, "Secularization Falsified," *First Things,* February

2008, accessed November 6, 2014. www.firstthings.com/article/2008/02/002-secularization-falsified.

4. Luhrmann, *When God Talks Back,* 301.

5. Robert Orsi, "Everyday Miracles: The Study of Lived Religion," in *Lived Religion in America: Toward a History of Practice,* ed. David D. Hall (Princeton, NJ: Princeton University Press, 1997), 3–21. See also Ammerman, *Bible Believers;* Brasher, *Godly Women;* and Griffith, *God's Daughters.*

6. Luhrmann, *When God Talks Back,* 320.

7. Ross, "Typing, Doing, and Being," 344.

8. Sociologist Meredith McGuire explains that "lived religion is constituted by the practices people use to share, enact, adapt, create, and combine the stories out of which they live" (*Lived Religion,* 111). This definition is particularly fitting in the context of Christian sexuality websites. The Internet becomes the "practice" with which users share, create, etc., the stories that influence living a religious life. See Hadden and Cowan, *Religion on the Internet.*

9. Snow, "Extending and Broadening."

10. *The Scofield Study Bible* (New York: Oxford University Press, [1909] 2004).

11. Ann Snitow, Christine Stansell, Sharon Thompson, eds., *Powers of Desire: The Politics of Sexuality* (New York: Monthly Review Press, 1983), 42–43.

12. Annick Prieur, *Mema's House, Mexico City: On Transvestites, Queens, and Machos* (Chicago, IL: University Of Chicago Press, 1998), 40.

13. Kinsey's findings suggested that the majority of American men were either non-monogamous or having sex with other men. While scholars have widely criticized Kinsey's methods and the accuracy of his data, his findings still challenged sexual norms at the time, which suggested that *no* sane, competent man engaged in non-monogamous or homosexual behavior. Even if Kinsey's findings are exaggerated, the fact that they show that many purportedly "normal" men were engaging in "non-normative" behavior suggests that the norm was not grounded in universal behavior. See Warner, *Trouble with Normal.*

14. This comes from *The Social Organization of Sexuality,* Laumann et al., which is, to date, one of the largest and most comprehensive surveys of Americans' sexual attitudes and behaviors.

15. D'Emilio and Freedman, writing about research on the history of sexuality in their book, *Intimate Matters,* note that the dichotomy between *sexual ideology* and *sexual behavior* "assumes too simple and direct a relationship, as well as an opposition, between what individuals believe and what they do" (xv). For related critiques of research assuming a dichotomous relationship between religious women's subordination or empowerment, see Avishai, "Doing Religion"; Sirma Bilge, "Beyond Subordination vs. Resistance: An Intersectional Approach to the Agency of Veiled Muslim Women," *Journal of Intercultural Studies* 31 (2010): 9–28; and Mahmood, *Politics of Piety.*

16. Sigmund Freud, *Three Essays on the Theory of Sexuality* (New York: Basic Books, [1965] 1989), 57.

17. Hockey, Meah, and Robinson, *Mundane Heterosexualities,* 11.

18. As Heath argues in *One Marriage under God,* contemporary debates about marriage reveal the deep connection between marriage, heterosexuality, and American identity. Though these debates persist, straights no longer hold a monopoly over marriage. As of June 2015, same-sex couples have the right to marry throughout the United States. A national survey conducted one year earlier suggests that the majority of Americans (54 percent) support the right of gays and lesbians to marry. See Pew Research Center, *Changing Attitudes.*

19. Rubin, "Thinking Sex." Recent accounts of the gay marriage movement have highlighted the ways in which gays and lesbians pursuing the right to marry already partake in traditions associated with marriage and family life (e.g., weddings, children, middle-class status) while simultaneously resisting being labeled heteronormative assimilationists. See, for example, the essays included in Mary Bernstein and Verta Taylor, eds., *The Marrying Kind?: Debating Same-Sex Marriage within the Lesbian and Gay Movement* (Minneapolis, MN: University of Minnesota Press, 2013).

20. Butler, *Gender Trouble,* 173.

21. Dean, *Straights,* 31.

22. Warner, "Tongues Untied," 229.

APPENDIX B

1. Websites have different formats for displaying search results, which makes it impossible to compare search results from various sites. For example, one site's search engine may count every instance a word is mentioned, returning a high number of results, while another site's may only count each webpage that includes the search term (which could appear multiple times on a page), returning a smaller number of results.

2. My observation excluded board topics that discussed housekeeping and those that excluded regular members, such as boards created for moderators or the site's oversight group.

3. For more information on this classification, see Tom W. Smith, "Classifying Protestant Denominations," *General Social Survey Methodological Report No. 43,* 1987.

4. I asked interview respondents who were affiliated with Christian sexuality websites to participate in online interviews, but I allowed phone interviews for three respondents, all of whom were website administrators. In one case, the respondent was without a computer at the time of the interview and asked if the interview could take place on the phone. In the other two cases, the respondents could only commit to hour-long interviews, so I suggested conducting them by phone, since online conversations typically require more time because people tend to type slower than they talk. I interviewed the sex advice book author face-to-face.

5. I first interviewed members of BTS between January and March 2011. I interviewed LCL readers between October and November 2011. Even though there were

male readers of LCL who completed the CSIS, I limited my interviews with LCL readers to women because the site is geared specifically toward them and because I interviewed a disproportionate number of men from BTS.

6. Moon, *God, Sex, and Politics*, 6.

7. Avishai, Gerber, and Randles describe their quandary as feminist researchers studying conservative subjects, the "dilemma [that] ensues when our feminist political commitments clash with our subjects' worldviews, forcing us to reconcile our perspectives with those of respondents who do not share our understanding and valuation of rights, opportunities, liberation, and constraints, but whose views we have a responsibility to interpret and represent accurately and fairly" ("Feminist Ethnographer's Dilemma," 2).

8. David Schnarch, *Passionate Marriage: Keeping Love and Intimacy Alive in Committed Relationships* (New York: W. W. Norton and Company, 2009).

9. Gerber, *Seeking the Straight and Narrow*, 222.

BIBLIOGRAPHY

Ammerman, Nancy Tatom. *Bible Believers: Fundamentalists in the Modern World.* New Brunswick, NJ: Rutgers University Press, 1987.

Arterburn, Stephen, Fred Stoeker, and Mike Yorkey. *Every Man's Battle: Winning the War on Sexual Temptation One Victory at a Time.* New York: Random House, 2000.

Attwood, Feona. "Sexed Up: Theorizing the Sexualization of Culture." *Sexualities* 9 (2006): 77–94.

Avishai, Orit. "'Doing Religion' in a Secular World: Women in Conservative Religions and the Question of Agency." *Gender & Society* 22 (2008): 409–433.

Avishai, Orit, Lynne Gerber, and Jennifer Randles. "The Feminist Ethnographer's Dilemma: Reconciling Progressive Research Agendas with Fieldwork Realities." *Journal of Contemporary Ethnography* (2012): 1–33.

Balmer, Randall. *Mine Eyes Have Seen the Gory: A Journey into the Evangelical Subculture of America.* New York: Oxford University Press, [1989] 2006.

Bartkowski, John P. *Remaking the Godly Marriage: Gender Negotiation in Evangelical Families.* New Brunswick, NJ: Rutgers University Press, 2001.

Barton, Bernadette. *Pray the Gay Away: The Extraordinary Lives of Bible Belt Gays.* New York: New York University Press, 2012.

Bean, Lydia, and Brandon C. Martinez. "Evangelical Ambivalence toward Gays and Lesbians." *Sociology of Religion* 75 (2014): 1–23.

Beaty, Katelyn, and Marlena Graves. "Q & A: Mark and Grace Driscoll on Sex for the 21st-Century Christian." *Christianity Today,* January 5, 2012. Accessed on July 15, 2012. www.christianitytoday.com/ct/2012/januaryweb-only/mark-driscoll-sex-marriage.html.

Bellah, Robert N. *Habits of the Heart: Individualism and Commitment in American Life.* Berkeley, CA: University of California Press, 1985.

Bender, Courtney. *Heaven's Kitchen: Living Religion at God's Love We Deliver.* Chicago, IL: University of Chicago Press, 2003.

Berger, Peter L. *The Sacred Canopy: Elements of a Sociological Theory of Religion.* New York: Anchor, [1967] 1990.

———. "Secularization Falsified." *First Things,* February 2008. www.firstthings .com/article/2008/02/002-secularization-falsified.

Bernstein, Mary, and Verta Taylor, eds. *The Marrying Kind?: Debating Same-Sex Marriage within the Lesbian and Gay Movement.* Minneapolis, MN: University of Minnesota Press, 2013.

"BGEA: Records of the Hour of Decision Radio Program—Collection 191" Billy Graham Center Archives. Wheaton College. Accessed on June 11, 2014. www2 .wheaton.edu/bgc/archives/GUIDES/191.htm.

Bielo, James S. *Words upon the Word: An Ethnography of Evangelical Group Bible Study.* New York: New York University Press, 2009.

Blee, Kathleen M. *Democracy in Making: How Activist Groups Form.* New York: Oxford University Press, 2012.

Blumer, Herbert. *Symbolic Interactionism: Perspective and Method.* Berkeley, CA: University of California Press, [1969] 1986.

Boellstorff, Tom. *Coming of Age in Second Life: An Anthropologist Explores the Virtually Human.* Princeton, NJ: Princeton University Press, 2008.

Bonilla-Silva, Eduardo. *Racism without Racists: Color-Blind Racism and the Persistence of Racial Inequality in the United States.* Lanham, MD: Rowman and Littlefield, 2006.

Bourdieu, Pierre. *The Logic of Practice.* Stanford, CA: Stanford University Press, [1980] 1990.

boyd, danah. "White Flight in Networked Publics: How Race and Class Shaped American Teen Engagement with MySpace and Facebook." In *Race After the Internet,* edited by Lisa Nakamura and Peter A. Chow-White, 203–222. New York: Routledge, 2012.

Brasher, Brenda E. *Godly Women.* New Brunswick, NJ: Rutgers University Press, 1997.

———. *Give Me That Online Religion.* San Francisco, CA: Jossey-Bass, 2001.

Brereton, Virginia Lieson. *From Sin to Salvation: Stories of Women's Conversions, 1800 to the Present.* Bloomington, IN: Indiana University Press, 1991.

Brotherson, Laura M. *And They Were Not Ashamed: Strengthening Marriage through Sexual Fulfillment.* Boise, ID: Inspire Books, 2004.

Browne, Kath, Sally R. Munt, and Andrew K. T. Yip, eds. *Queer Spiritual Spaces: Sexuality and Sacred Places.* Farnham, UK: Ashgate, 2010.

Buchanan, Elizabeth A. *Readings in Virtual Research Ethics: Issues and Controversies.* Hershey, PA: Idea Group, Inc., 2004.

Burke, Kelsy. "Women's Agency in Gender-Traditional Religions: A Review of Four Approaches." *Sociology Compass* 6 (2012): 122–133.

———. "What Makes a Man: Gender and Sexual Boundaries on Christian Sexuality Websites." *Sexualities* 17 (2014): 3–22.

Burke, Kelsy, and Amy Moff Hudec. "Sexual Encounters and Manhood Acts: Evangelicals, Latter-day Saints, and Religious Masculinities." *Journal for the Scientific Study of Religion* 54, no. 2 (2015): 330–344.

Burkett, Melissa, and Karine Hamilton. "Postfeminist Sexual Agency: Young Women's Negotiations of Sexual Consent." *Sexualities* 15 (2012): 815–833.

Butler, Judith. *Gender Trouble: Feminism and the Subversion of Identity*. New York: Routledge, [1990] 1999.

Buzzell, Timothy. "Demographic Characteristics of Persons Using Pornography in Three Technological Contexts." *Sexuality & Culture* 9 (2005): 28–48.

Campbell, Heidi, ed. *Digital Religion: Understanding Religious Practice in New Media Worlds*. New York: Routledge, 2013.

Canaday, Margot. *The Straight State: Sexuality and Citizenship in Twentieth-Century America*. Princeton, NJ: Princeton University Press, 2011.

Chaves, Mark. *American Religion: Contemporary Trends*. Princeton, NJ: Princeton University Press, 2011.

Connell, R. W. *Masculinities*. Berkeley, CA: University of California Press, 1995.

Constable, Nicole. *Romance on a Global Stage: Pen Pals, Virtual Ethnography, and "Mail Order" Marriages*. Berkeley, CA: University of California Press, 2003.

Crawford, Melissa, and Diane Popp. "Sexual Double Standards: A Review and Methodological Critique of Two Decades of Research." *The Journal of Sex Research* 40 (2003): 13–26.

Dean, James Joseph. *Straights: Heterosexuality in Post-Closeted Culture*. New York: New York University, 2014.

D'Emilio, John, and Estelle B. Freedman. *Intimate Matters: A History of Sexuality in America*. New York: Harper & Row, 1988.

DeRogatis, Amy. *Saving Sex: Sexuality and Salvation in American Evangelicalism*. New York: Oxford University Press, 2015.

Dillow, Linda. *How to Really Love Your Man*. Nashville, TN: Thomas Nelson Inc., 1993.

Dillow, Linda, and Lorraine Pintus. *Intimate Issues: Answers to 21 Questions Christian Women Ask about Sex*. Colorado Springs, CO: Waterbrook Press, 1999.

———. *Gift-Wrapped by God: Secret Answers to the Question "Why Wait?"* Colorado Springs, CO: WaterBrook Press, 2002.

Dillow, Joseph, Linda Dillow, Peter Pintus, and Lorraine Pintus. *Intimacy Ignited: Conversations Couple to Couple*. Colorado Springs, CO: NAV Press, 2004.

DiLorenzo, Tony, and Alisa DiLorenzo. *Stripped Down: 13 Keys to Unlocking Intimacy in Your Marriage*. Cary, NC: Past Due Press, 2010.

Dodes, Lance. "Is Anthony Weiner a Sex Addict?" *Psychology Today,* June 22, 2011. Accessed on April 9, 2014. www.psychologytoday.com/blog/the-heart-addiction/201106/is-anthony-weiner-sex-addict.

Driscoll, Mark. *Porn Again Christian: A Frank Discussion on Masturbation and Pornography*. Seattle, WA: Mars Hill Church, 2009.

Driscoll, Mark, and Grace G. Driscoll. *Real Marriage: The Truth about Sex, Friendship, and Life Together*. Nashville, TN: Thomas Nelson, Inc., 2012.

Duggan, Lisa. "The New Homonormativity: The Sexual Politics of Neoliberalism." In *Materializing Democracy: Towards a Revitalized Cultural Politics,* edited by

Russ Castronovo and Dana D. Nelson, 175–195. Durham, NC: Duke University Press, 2002.

Durkheim, Emile. *The Elementary Forms of Religious Life*. Translated by Joseph Ward Swain. Mineola, NY: Dover Publications, [1915] 2008.

Elisha, Omri. *Moral Ambition: Mobilization and Social Outreach in Evangelical Megachurches*. Berkeley, CA: University of California Press, 2011.

Erzen, Tanya. *Straight to Jesus: Sexual and Christian Conversions in the Ex-Gay Movement*. Berkeley, CA: University of California Press, 2006.

Ethridge, Shannon. *The Sexually Confident Wife: Connecting with Your Husband Mind, Body, Heart, Spirit*. New York: Broadway Books, 2008.

Farrel, Bill, and Pam Farrel. *Red-Hot Monogamy: Making Your Marriage Sizzle*. Eugene, OR: Harvest House Publishers, 2006.

Fessenden, Tracy. *Culture and Redemption: Religion, the Secular, and American Literature*. Princeton, NJ: Princeton University Press, 2007.

Ford, Zack. "Single, Married, Celibate, Sexual, Ex-Gay: The Southern Baptists' Mixed Messages On Homosexuality," ThinkProgress, November 4, 2014. Accessed on November 6, 2014. http://thinkprogress.org/lgbt/2014/11/04/3588151 /southern-baptists-ex-gay-mixed-messages/.

Foster, David Kyle. "The Divine Order to Marriage." Focus on the Family. Accessed on April 9, 2014. www.focusonthefamily.com/marriage/gods-design-for-marriage/marriage-gods-idea/the-divine-order-to-marriage.

Foucault, Michel. *An Introduction*. Vol. 1, *The History of Sexuality*. Translated by Robert Hurley. New York: Vintage, [1978] 1990.

Fox, Susannah, and Maeve Duggan. "Health Online 2013." Pew Research Center's Internet & American Life Project, January 15, 2013. Accessed on November 7, 2014. www.pewinternet.org/2013/01/15/health-online-2013/.

Fox, Susannah, and Lee Rainie. "The Web at 25 in the US." Pew Research Center Internet and American Life Project, February 27, 2014. Accessed on June 11, 2014. www.pewinternet.org/2014/02/27/about-this-report-4/.

Freud, Sigmund. *Three Essays on the Theory of Sexuality*. New York: Basic Books, [1965] 1989.

Gagnon, John H., and William Simon. *Sexual Conduct: The Social Sources of Human Sexuality*. New Brunswick, NJ: Aldine Transaction, [1973] 2005.

Gallagher, Sally K. *Evangelical Identity and Gendered Family Life*. New Brunswick, NJ: Rutgers University Press, 2003.

Gamson, Joshua. *Freaks Talk Back: Tabloid Talk Shows and Sexual Nonconformity*. Chicago, IL: University of Chicago Press, 1998.

———. "Normal Sins: Sex Scandal Narratives as Institutional Morality Tales." *Social Problems* 48 (2001): 185–205.

Gardner, Christine J. *Making Chastity Sexy: The Rhetoric of Evangelical Abstinence Campaigns*. Berkeley, CA: University of California Press, 2011.

Gerber, Lynne. "The Opposite of Gay: Nature, Creation, and Queerish Ex-Gay Experiments." *Nova Religio: The Journal of Alternative and Emergent Religions* 11 (2008): 8–30.

————. *Seeking the Straight and Narrow: Weight Loss and Sexual Reorientation in Evangelical America*. Chicago, IL: University of Chicago Press, 2011.

Gerhard, Jane. *Desiring Revolution: Second-Wave Feminism and the Rewriting of American Sexual Thought, 1920 to 1982*. New York: Columbia University Press, 2013.

Giddens, Anthony. *Modernity and Self-Identity: Self and Society in the Late Modern Age*. Stanford, CA: Stanford University Press, 1991.

Gill, Rosalind. "Mediated Intimacy and Postfeminism: A Discourse Analytic Examination of Sex and Relationships Advice in a Women's Magazine." *Discourse and Communication* 3 (2009): 345–369.

Goffman, Erving. *The Presentation of the Self in Everyday Life*. New York: Anchor Books, [1959] 1990.

Golan, Oren. "Charting Frontiers of Online Religious Communities: The Case of Chabad Jews." In *Digital Religion: Understanding Religious Practice in New Media Worlds*, edited by Heidi Campbell, 155–163. New York: Routledge, 2013.

Gordon, Sarah Barringer. *The Mormon Question: Polygamy and Constitutional Conflict in Nineteenth-Century America*. Chapel Hill, NC: University of North Carolina Press, 2002.

Gray, Mary L. *Out in the Country: Youth, Media, and Queer Visibility in Rural America*. New York: New York University Press, 2009.

Griffith, R. Marie. *God's Daughters: Evangelical Women and the Power of Submission*. Berkeley, CA: University of California Press, 1997.

————. *Born Again Bodies: Flesh and Spirit in American Christianity*. Berkeley, CA: University of California Press, 2004.

Hadden, Jeffrey K., and Douglas E. Cowan, eds. *Religion on the Internet: Research Prospects and Promises*. London: JAI Press, 2000.

Halberstam, Jack J. *Gaga Feminism: Sex, Gender, and the End of Normal*. Boston, MA: Beacon Press, 2012.

Hall, David D., ed. *Lived Religion in America: Toward a History of Practice*. Princeton, NJ: Princeton University Press, 1997.

Halley, Janet E. "The Construction of Heterosexuality." In *Fear of a Queer Planet: Queer Politics and Social Theory*, edited by Michael Warner, 82–102. Minneapolis, MN: University of Minnesota Press, 1993.

Heath, Melanie. "Soft-Boiled Masculinity: Renegotiating Gender and Racial Ideologies in the Promise Keepers Movement." *Gender & Society* 17 (2003): 423–444.

————. *One Marriage under God: The Campaign to Promote Marriage in America*. New York: New York University Press, 2012.

Hendershot, Heather. *Shaking the World for Jesus: Media and Conservative Evangelical Culture*. Chicago, IL: University of Chicago Press, 2004.

Herzog, Dagmar. *Sex in Crisis: The New Sexual Revolution and the Future of American Politics*. New York: Basic Books, 2008.

Hills, Rachel. "Sex Talk Realness: What Men Think about Pegging," *Cosmopolitan*, November 20, 2014. Accessed on September 18, 2015. www.cosmopolitan.com /sex-love/news/a33467/sex-talk-realness-what-men-think-about-pegging/.

Hine, Christine. *Virtual Ethnography.* Thousand Oaks, CA: SAGE Publications, 2000.

Hockey, Jenny, Angela Meah, and Victoria Robinson. *Mundane Heterosexualities: From Theory to Practices.* New York: Palgrave MacMillan, 2007.

Hocquenghem, Guy. *Homosexual Desire.* Translated by Daniella Dangoor. Durham, NC: Duke University Press, 1993.

Howard, Robert Glenn. *Digital Jesus: The Making of a New Christian Fundamentalist Community on the Internet.* New York: New York University Press, 2011.

Ingraham, Chrys, ed. *Thinking Straight: The Power, the Promise, and the Paradox of Heterosexuality.* New York: Routledge, 2005.

Jackson, Stevi. *Heterosexuality in Question.* Thousand Oaks, CA: SAGE Publications, 1999.

Jackson, Stevi, and Sue Scott. "Faking Like a Woman?: Towards an Interpretive Theorization of Sexual Pleasure." *Body and Society* 13 (2007): 95–116.

Jagose, Annamarie. *Queer Theory: An Introduction.* New York: New York University Press, 1996.

Jakobsen, Janet R., and Ann Pellegrini. *Love the Sin: Sexual Regulation and the Limits of Religious Tolerance.* New York: New York University Press, 2003.

Jones, Robert, Daniel Cox, and Juhem Navarro-Rivera. *A Shifting Landscape: A Decade of Change in American Attitudes about Same-Sex Marriage.* Washington, DC: Public Religion Research Institute, February 26, 2014. http://publicreligion.org/site/wp-content/uploads/2014/02/2014.LGBT_REPORT.pdf.

Jordan, Mark D. *The Ethics of Sex.* Oxford: Blackwell Publishing, 2002.

———. *Recruiting Young Love: How Christians Talk about Homosexuality.* Chicago, IL: University of Chicago Press, 2011.

Katz, Jonathan Ned. *The Invention of Heterosexuality.* Chicago, IL: University of Chicago Press, 1995.

LaHaye, Tim, and Beverly B. LaHaye. *The Act of Marriage: The Beauty of Sexual Love.* Grand Rapids, MI: Zondervan Publishing House, [1976] 1998.

Lamont, Michele, and Virag Molnar. "The Study of Boundaries in the Social Sciences." *Annual Review of Sociology* 28 (2002): 167–195.

Laumann, Edward O., John H. Gagnon, Robert T. Michael, and Stuart Michaels. *The Social Organization of Sexuality: Sexual Practices in the United States.* Chicago, IL: University of Chicago Press, 1994.

Lee, Shayne, and Phillip Luke Sinitiere. *Holy Mavericks: Evangelical Innovators and the Spiritual Marketplace.* New York: New York University Press, 2009.

Leman, Kevin. *Sheet Music: Uncovering the Secrets of Sexual Intimacy in Marriage.* Wheaton, IL: Tyndale House Publishers, 2003.

Levy, Ariel. *Female Chauvinist Pigs: Women and the Rise of Raunch Culture.* New York: Free Press, 2006.

Lichterman, Paul. *Elusive Togetherness: Church Groups Trying to Bridge America's Divisions.* Princeton, NJ: Princeton University Press, 2005.

Longman III, Tremper. *Song of Songs: The New International Commentary on the Old Testament*. Grand Rapids, MN: Wm. B. Eerdmans Publishing Company, 2001.

Lorber, Judith. *Paradoxes of Gender*. New Haven, CT: Yale University Press, 1994.

Luhrmann, T. M. *When God Talks Back: Understanding the American Evangelical Relationship with God*. New York: Alfred A. Knopf, 2012.

Mahmood, Saba. *The Politics of Piety: The Islamic Revival and the Feminist Subject*. Princeton, NJ: Princeton University Press, 2005.

Markham, Annette, and Elizabeth Buchanan. *Ethical Decision-Making and Internet Research: Recommendations from the AoIR Ethics Working Committee*. Association of Internet Researchers, December 2012. Accessed on April 14, 2013. http://aoir.org/reports/ethics2.pdf.

McDowell, Amy. "Warriors and Terrorists: Antagonism as Strategy in Christian Hardcore and Muslim 'Taqwacore' Punk Rock." *Qualitative Sociology* 37 (2014): 255–276.

McFadden, Robert D. "New York Hears Words of Hope From Billy Graham." *New York Times,* September 23, 1991. Accessed on June 4, 2014. www.nytimes.com/1991/09/23/nyregion/new-york-hears-words-of-hope-from-billy-graham.html.

McGee, Micki. *Self-Help, Inc.: Makeover Culture in American Life*. New York: Oxford University Press, 2005.

McGuire, Meredith. *Lived Religion: Faith and Practice in Everyday Life*. New York: Oxford University Press, 2008.

Mead, George Herbert. *Mind, Self, and Society from the Standpoint of a Social Behaviorist*. Chicago, IL: University of Chicago Press, [1934] 1967.

Mertens, Donna M., and Pauline E. Ginsberg, eds. *The Handbook of Social Research Ethics*. Thousand Oaks, CA: SAGE Publications, 2009.

Merton, Robert K. "Social Structure and Anomie." *American Sociological Review* 3 (1938): 672–682.

Messner, Michael A. "'Changing Men' and Feminist Politics in the United States." *Theory and Society* 22 (1993): 723–737.

Millet, Kate. *Sexual Politics*. New York: Doubleday, 1970.

Moon, Dawne. *God, Sex, and Politics: Homosexuality and Everyday Theologies*. Chicago, IL: University of Chicago Press, 2004.

———. "Love and the Authentic Self: Insights from Gay Evangelicals in the 21st Century." Presentation given at the Southern Sociological Society Annual Meeting, New Orleans, LA, March 25–28, 2015.

Nakamura, Lisa. *Digitizing Race: Visual Cultures of the Internet*. Minneapolis, MN: University of Minnesota Press, 2008.

Nelson, Tommy. *The Song of Solomon: A Study of Love, Marriage, and Romance*. The Hub Digital Bible Study, 1995.

Orsi, Robert. "Everyday Miracles: The Study of Lived Religion." In *Lived Religion in America: Toward a History of Practice,* edited by David D. Hall, 3–21. Princeton, NJ: Princeton University Press, 1997.

Pascoe, C. J. *Dude, You're a Fag: Masculinity and Sexuality in High School.* Berkeley, CA: University of California Press, 2007.

Penner, Clifford, and Joyce Penner. *The Gift of Sex: A Guide to Sexual Fulfillment.* Nashville, TN: Thomas Nelson, Inc., [1973] 2003.

Peterfeso, Jill. "From Testimony to Seximony, from Script to Scripture: Revealing Mormon Women's Sexuality through the Mormon Vagina Monologues." *Journal of Feminist Studies in Religion* 27 (2011): 31–49.

Peterson, Valerie V. "The Sex of Joy: A Gourmet Guide to Lovemaking Rhetoric." *Popular Communication* 6 (2008): 3–19.

Pew Research Center. *Usage Over Time.* Pew Research Center's Internet Project. Accessed on January 28, 2013. www.pewinternet.org.

———. *U.S. Religious Landscape Survey.* Pew Research Center's Religious & Public Life Project. Accessed on November 11, 2014. http://religions.pewforum.org /pdf/report-religious-landscape-study-appendix2.pdf.

———. *Changing Attitudes on Gay Marriage.* Pew Research Center's Religion & Public Life Project. Accessed on November 21, 2014. www.pewforum .org/2014/09/24/graphics-slideshow-changing-attitudes-on-gay-marriage/.

Pike, Sarah M. *New Age and Neopagan Religions in America.* New York: Columbia University Press, 2006.

Pintus, Lorraine. *Jump Off the Hormone Swing: Fly Through the Physical, Mental, and Spiritual Symptoms of PMS and Peri-Menopause.* Chicago, IL: Moody Publishers, 2010.

Pitt, Richard N. "'Killing the Messenger': Religious Black Gay Men's Neutralization of Anti-Gay Religious Messages." *Journal for the Scientific Study of Religion* 49 (2010): 56–72.

"The Playboy Advisor." *Playboy Magazine,* February 1999, 39.

Plummer, Kenneth. *Telling Sexual Stories: Power, Change, and Social Worlds.* New York: Routledge, 1995.

Popcak, Gregory. *Holy Sex: A Catholic Guide to Toe-Curling, Mind-Blowing, Infallible Loving.* New York: Crossroads Publishing, 2008.

Prieur, Annick. *Mema's House, Mexico City: On Transvestites, Queens, and Machos.* Chicago, IL: University Of Chicago Press, 1998.

Putnam, Robert D., and David E. Campbell. *American Grace: How Religion Divides and Unites Us.* New York: Simon and Schuster, 2010.

Rich, Adrienne. "Compulsory Heterosexuality and Lesbian Existence." In *Powers of Desire: The Politics of Sexuality,* edited by Ann Snitow, Christine Stansell, and Sharon Thompson, 177–205. New York: Monthly Review Press, [1980] 1983.

Richardson, Diane. *Rethinking Sexuality.* Thousand Oaks, CA: SAGE Publications, 2000.

Roof, Wade C. *Spiritual Marketplace: Baby Boomers and the Remaking of American Religion.* Princeton, NJ: Princeton University Press, 1999.

Rosenau, Douglas E. *A Celebration of Sex.* Nashville, TN: Thomas Nelson, Inc., [1994] 2002.

Rosenfeld, Dana. "Heteronormativity and Homonormativity as Practical and Moral Resources." *Gender & Society* 23 (2009): 617–638.

Ross, Michael W. "Typing, Doing, and Being: Sexuality and the Internet." *The Journal of Sex Research* 42 (2005): 344.

Rowe, Aimee Carrillo, Sheena Malhotra, and Kimberlee Pérez. *Answer the Call: Virtual Migration in Indian Call Centers.* Minneapolis, MN: University of Minnesota Press, 2013.

Rubin, Gayle. "Thinking Sex: Notes for a Radical Theory of the Politics of Sexuality." In *Culture, Society, and Sexuality: A Reader,* edited by Richard Parker and Peter Aggleton, 143–178. Philadelphia: UCL Press, [1984] 1999.

Santelli, John, Mary Ott, Maureen Lyon, Jennifer Rogers, Daniel Summers, and Rebecca Schleifer. "Abstinence and Abstinence-Only Education: A Review of U.S. Policies and Programs." *Journal of Adolescent Health,* 38 (2006): 72–81.

Savage, Dan. "Let's Vote." *Savage Love,* May 24, 2001. Accessed on November 11, 2014. www.thestranger.com/seattle/SavageLove?oid=7446.

———. "We Have a Winner!" *Savage Love,* June 21, 2001. Accessed on November 11, 2014. www.thestranger.com/seattle/SavageLove?oid=7730.

Schiff, Stacy. "Sex and the Single-Minded," *New York Times,* January 20, 2007. Accessed on October 30, 2014. www.nytimes.com/2007/01/20/opinion/20schiff.html.

Schilling, Chris, and Philip A. Mellor. "Cultures of Embodied Experience: Technology, Religion, and Body Pedagogics." *The Sociological Review* 55 (2007): 545.

Schilt, Kristen, and Laurel Westbrook. "Doing Gender, Doing Heteronormativity: 'Gender Normals,' Transgender People, and the Social Maintenance of Heterosexuality." *Gender & Society* 23 (2009): 440–464.

Schippers, Mimi. "Recovering the Feminine Other: Masculinity, Femininity, and Gender Hegemony." *Theory and Society* 36 (2007): 85–102.

Schnarch, David. *Passionate Marriage: Keeping Love and Intimacy Alive in Committed Relationships.* New York: W. W. Norton and Company, 2009.

Schrock, Douglas, and Michael Schwalbe. "Men, Masculinity, and Manhood Acts." *Annual Review of Sociology* 35 (2009): 277–295.

The Scofield Study Bible. New York: Oxford University Press, [1909] 2004.

Sedgwick, Eve Kosofsky. *Between Men: English Literature and Male Homosocial Desire.* New York: Columbia University Press, 1985.

———. *Epistemology of the Closet.* Berkeley, CA: University of California Press, 1990.

Segal, Lynne. *Straight Sex: Rethinking the Politics of Pleasure.* Berkeley, CA: University of California Press, 1994.

Seidman, Steven. *Beyond the Closet: The Transformation of Gay and Lesbian Life.* New York: Routledge, 2002.

Smith, Aaron. "6 New Facts about Facebook." Pew Research Center, February 3, 2014. Accessed on November 6, 2014. www.pewresearch.org/fact-tank/2014/02/03/6-new-facts-about-facebook/.

Smith, Christian. *Christian America?: What Evangelicals Really Want.* Berkeley, CA: University of California Press, 2000.

Smith, Tom W. "Classifying Protestant Denominations." *General Social Survey Methodological Report No. 43,* 1987.

Snitow, Ann, Christine Stansell, and Sharon Thompson, eds. *Powers of Desire: The Politics of Sexuality.* New York: Monthly Review Press, 1983.

Snow, David A. "Extending and Broadening Blumer's Conceptualization of Symbolic Interactionism." *Symbolic Interaction* 24, no. 3 (2001): 367–377.

Stacey, Judith. *Brave New Families: Stories of Domestic Upheaval in Late Twentieth-Century America.* Berkeley, CA: University of California Press, 1990.

Stromberg, Peter G. *Language and Self-Transformation: A Study of the Christian Conversion Narrative.* New York: Cambridge University Press, 1993.

Swartz, David. "Bridging the Study of Culture and Religion: Pierre Bourdieu's Political Economy of Symbolic Power." *Sociology of Religion* 57, no. 1 (1996): 71–85.

Tiessen, Matthew. "Accepting Invitations: Desire Lines as Earthly Offerings." *Rhizomes* 15 (2007). Accessed on April 11, 2015. www.rhizomes.net/issue15/tiessen .html.

Vance, Carol. "Pleasure and Danger: Toward a Politics of Sexuality." In *Feminist Theory: A Reader,* edited by Wendy K. Kolmar and Frances Bartkowski, 335–340. New York: McGraw-Hill, [1984] 2013.

Verter, Bradford. "Spiritual Capital: Theorizing Religion with Bourdieu Against Bourdieu." *Sociological Theory* 21, no. 2 (2003): 150–174.

Wagner, Melinda Bollar. "Generic Conservative Christianity: The Demise of Denominationalism in Christian Schools." *Journal for the Scientific Study of Religion* 36 (1997): 13–24.

Ward, Jane. "Dude-Sex: White Masculinities and 'Authentic' Heterosexuality among Dudes who Have Sex with Dudes." *Sexualities* 11 (2008): 414–434.

Warner, Michael. "Tongues Untied: Memoirs of a Pentecostal Boyhood." In *Que(e)rying Religion: A Critical Anthology,* edited by Gary David Comstock and Susan E. Henking, 223–231. New York: Continuum Publishing Company, 1997.

———. *The Trouble with Normal.* New York: Free Press, 1999.

Weiss, Margot. *Techniques of Pleasure: BDSM and the Circuits of Sexuality.* Durham, NC: Duke University Press, 2011.

Welch, Craig. "The Rise and Fall of Mars Hill Church." *Seattle Times,* September 13, 2014. Accessed on October 30, 2014. www.seattletimes.com/seattle-news /the-rise-and-fall-of-mars-hill-church/.

West, Candace, and Don Zimmerman. "Doing Gender." *Gender & Society* 1 (1987): 125–151.

Wheat, Ed, and Gaye Wheat. *Intended for Pleasure: Sex Technique and Sexual Fulfillment in Christian Marriage.* Grand Rapids, MI: Fleming H. Revell, [1977] 2010.

Wier, Terry. *Holy Sex: God's Purpose and Plan for Our Sexuality.* New Kensington, PA: Whitaker House, 1999.

Wilcox, Melissa M. *Coming Out in Christianity: Religion, Identity, and Community.* Bloomington, IN: Indiana University Press, 2003.

Wilcox, W. Bradford. *Soft Patriarchs, New Men: How Christianity Shapes Fathers and Husbands.* Chicago, IL: University of Chicago Press, 2004.

Wolkomir, Michelle. "Giving It Up to God: Negotiating Femininity in Support Groups for Wives of Ex-Gay Christian Men." *Gender & Society* 18 (2004): 735–755.

———. "Making Heteronormative Reconciliations: The Story of Romantic Love, Sexuality, and Gender in Mixed-Orientation Marriages." *Gender & Society* 23 (2009): 494–519.

Wuthnow, Robert. *Sharing the Journey: Support Groups and America's New Quest for Community.* New York: The Free Press, 1994.

———. *After Heaven: Spirituality in America since the 1950s.* Berkeley, CA: University of California Press, 1998.

Young, Ed, and Lisa Young. *Sexperiment: 7 Days to Lasting Intimacy with Your Spouse.* New York: Faith Words, 2012.

Zoll, Rachel. "Southern Baptists Tell Pastors: Hold Line on Gays." *Deseret News,* October 28, 2014. Accessed on November 4, 2014. www.deseretnews.com /article/765661902/Southern-Baptists-tell-pastors-hold-line-on-gays.html.

INDEX

Brereton, Virginia, 110
Brotherson, Laura M., 186n43
BTS. *See* BetweenTheSheets.com
Butler, Judith, 8, 10, 164

Campbell, David, 13, 188n66
Catholics, 20–23, 92–94, 174, 185n43, 191n24
A Celebration of Sex (Rosenau), 63 *fig.*
Chaves, Mark, 20–21
Christian hegemony, 9
Christianity, Sexuality, and the Internet Survey (CSIS): attendance at religious services, 22, 87; demographic characteristics of respondents, 21–25, 176 *table;* marriage, use of term, 193n45; and men's privilege, 135; methodology, 18–19, 173–74; number of sexual partners, 50; oral sex rates, 50; religious affiliations, 21, 93; sex toy purchases, 104; sexual attitudes, 23–24, 39–42, 46–48, 52, 84, 123–24, 141
Christian sex advice books, 15, 29–33; Catholic, 185n43; explicit language and images, 61–63, 78; male authors, 66; Mormon, 186n43; as out of date, 86; religious authority, 58–59; on women's pleasure, 112–14, 121
Christian sex toy stores: anal play products, 199n6; description of, 171; list of, 169 *table;* purchases at, 104; and secular pornography, 56–60, 73–74; women creators, 1–2, 66, 68–69
Christian sexuality websites, 1–5; as alternative path to religious beliefs about sex, 155–57; anonymity on, 86, 94, 102, 105, 158; and construction of sexuality, 10–12, 153; content analysis, 172–73; creators, 55–58, 63–80, 92–95, 175; ethnographic research on, 17–20, 169 *table;* etiquette, 93–95; explicit language on, 59–63; frequency of use, 196n10; and logic of godly sex, 52–53, 78–80 (*see also* godly sex); message boards, 81–82; as ministry, 68–70; online communities, 27–28; online observation, 172–73; as places of

emergence, 53; social norms, 94; types of, 171–72; unknowable audience, 75–77; warnings about pornography, 41. *See also* BetweenTheSheets.com; LustyChristianLadies.com; online religious communities; sexual awakening stories
Christian sexuality workshops, 19–20, 36–37, 177; BTS conference, 37, 42, 90–91, 177; Intimate Issues conferences, 36–37, 45, 90, 177; Love Life conference, 177
Church of Jesus Christ of Latter-day Saints (LDS). *See* Latter-day Saints
cisgender/cissexual, 6
community, 81–82. *See also* online religious communities
complementarianism: gender, 42, 49–50, 118, 137, 142–43; sexual, 137, 142–43
Concerned Women for America, 30
confidentiality, xiii–xiv, 181n1
Comfort, Alex, 190n3
Connell, R. W., 136
consent, 49, 146–47, 200n20
conservative Christians, 4–5, 9; attitudes toward sexuality, 43; political activism, 20; use of term, 20–21. *See also* evangelical Christians
conversion narratives. *See* salvation narratives
1 Corinthians 6:12, 45
Corinthians.com, 68–69, 169 *table*
Cowan, Douglas, 55
cross-dressing, erotic, 28, 134, 137, 140, 142, 144–52, 165, 199n6
CSIS. *See* Christianity, Sexuality, and the Internet Survey
cultural capital, 58

Dallas Theological Seminary, 194n8
Dean, James Joseph, 16, 164
D'Emilio, John, 202n15
DeRogatis, Amy, 190n11, 195n12
desire paths/lines, 155–56
Deuteronomy 22:5, 138
deviant sex. *See* gender-subversive sex; non-normative sex
DignityUSA, 185n34

Dillow, Joseph, *Intimacy Ignited* (Dillow et al.), 42, 44, 126

Dillow, Linda, 36–37, 44–47, 66; *Intimate Issues* (Dillow and Pintus), 30–31, 59

DiLorenzo, Tony and Alisa, *Stripped Down*, 38, 91

disclosure of identity, 67–68

discourse, 52–53

dispensationalism, 190n6

dispositions, 58, 80

Driscoll, Grace, 118

Driscoll, Grace and Mark, *Real Marriage*, 31–33, 41, 44–46, 145, 177, 190n11

Driscoll, Mark, 42; *Porn Again Christian*, 192n30

Duggan, Lisa, 9

Durkheim, Emile, 196n17

dwelling-oriented spirituality, 14

ecumenism, 189n67

Elisha, Omri, 80

Episcopal Church, 189n73

Episcopalians, 21, 185n34, 189n73

erotica, customized, 73–74

ethnographic research: cultural access, 20, 177–79; disclosures, 177–79; ethics in, xiii, 188n65; feminist, 178, 188n65, 204n7; on the Internet, xiii–xiv, 17–20, 171–79, 181n1; participant observation of real-life events, 177

Ethridge, Shannon, 39, 66, 123–24, 139; *The Sexually Confident Wife*, 31, 112–13, 193n36

evangelical Christians: authentic identities, 55, 58, 77, 82–83, 94–105, 150, 159; choice, as value, 48, 52; and history of heterosexuality, 13–17; masculinity, 135–36; messages about sex, 3–5, 15–17, 35–36, 43, 52–53, 86–87; prescriptive sex advice, 33, 53, 58, 86, 114, 136, 155–57 (*see also* Christian sex advice books); self-identification, 20; white, 20–21, 186n48. *See also* Christian sexuality websites; godly sex

evangelicalism, history of, 13–16, 186n48

ex-gay movement, 135, 137, 192n32, 192n34, 200n21

Exodus International, 135

extramarital sex. *See* unmarried sex

Facebook, 11, 31–32, 88; BGEA page, 54–55

FaithfulFantasticFun.com, 73, 169 *table*

Falwell, Jerry, 30

Farrell, Bill and Pam, 148; *Red, Hot Monogamy*, 193n36

feelings, as basis of moral arguments, 148–49

femininity, performance of, 6. *See also* gender

feminism, 6, 111–12, 122, 197n5

feminist theory, 5, 8–9, 153

Focus on the Family, 133; radio program, 30, 31, 59

Foucault, Michel, 7, 52–53, 184n32

Freedman, Estelle B., 202n15

Freud, Sigmund, 162

fundamentalists, 7, 13, 160, 190n6

Gagnon, John H., 6

Gallagher, Sally, 154

Gamson, Joshua, 153

GardenFruit.com, 41, 169 *table*

gays and lesbians: Christian, 10, 184n33, 185n34; and identity categories, 192n34; media depictions of, 16; and social norms, 9. *See also* homosexuality; queer theory; same-sex marriage

gender: essentialist perspectives on, 32–33, 152, 163; and homosexuality, 136–39; social construction of, 5–9, 11, 156–57, 160

gender binary, 6, 10, 137–38, 164–65

gender differences, 135; and heterosexuality, 42–43, 163–65; and sexual pleasure, 28, 32–33, 87; and viewing pornography, 57

gender-equal language, 50, 66, 110, 112, 135, 145, 153–54

gender hegemony, 6–8, 111, 135–37, 166

gender inequality, 4, 7, 12, 146–47, 153–54

gender normalcy, 5–6, 28, 134, 137, 143–44, 147, 150, 152, 164

gender omniscience, 134, 144–48, 152, 165

gender roles, 12, 42–43, 49–52, 144–48

Intimacy Ignited (Dillow et al.), 42, 44, 126
Intimate Issues (Dillow and Pintus), 30–31, 59
Intimate Issues conferences, 36–37, 45, 90, 177

Jackson, Stevi, 131, 183n25
Jagose, Annamarie, 6
Jordan, Mark, 34
The Joy of Sex (Comfort), 190n3

Katz, Jonathan Ned, 13
Keller, Tim, 32
kinky sex. *See* non-normative sex
Kinsey, Alfred, 14, 161
Krafft-Ebing, Richard von, 13

LaHaye, Beverly and Tim, *The Act of Marriage,* 29–33, 86, 137
Latter-day Saints (LDS), 197n4; as CSIS respondents, 21–26; marital sexuality resources, 186n43; national datasets on, 189n71; participation on Christian sexuality websites, 92–93; polygamy, 12; sexual attitudes, 46
Laumann, Edward O., 202n14
LCL. *See* LustyChristianLadies.com
Lee, Shayne, 15
Left Behind (LaHaye and Jenkins), 30
Leman, Kevin, 50, 139, 146; *Sheet Music,* 14, 66, 70, 87
Levy, Ariel, 7, 197n5
LGBT (lesbians, gays, bisexuals, and transgender persons). *See* gays and lesbians; homosexuality; same-sex marriage
liberal, use of term, 20–21
Lichterman, Paul, 83
lived religion, 7, 80, 158, 160
logic of godly sex. *See* godly sex
Longman, Tremper, III, 44
Lorber, Judith, 6
Love Life conference, 177
Loveline with Dr. Drew, 32
LovingBride.com, 94, 169 *table,* 174
LovingGroom.com, 17, 63 *fig.,* 169 *table*
Luhrmann, T. M., 152, 157–58

LustyChristianLadies.com (LCL): CSIS respondents, 174; as field research site, 17–19, 169 *table;* godly sex, discussions on, 41–42, 46, 60–61; interviews, 175–76; non-normative sex, discussions on, 134, 136, 139–40, 143, 145–46, 149, 166; online community members, 68, 74, 77, 83–85, 88, 91, 103, 105–7, 167; online observation, 172–73; viewing frequency, 196n10; women's sex appeal, discussions on, 136; women's sexual pleasure, discussions on, 108–9, 116–19, 123, 126–29, 161
Lutheran Church, 189n73

Mahmood, Saba, 198n20
mainline Protestants, 21–24, 174, 189n73, 191n24
MaribelsMarriage.com, 17, 93, 116, 167, 169 *table*
marital exceptionalism, 58, 63, 70–75, 78–79, 152, 158
marriage: and gender omniscience, 144–48; intimacy in, 124–29, 146; as marker of heterosexuality, 5, 12, 164–65; and sexual awakening, 110 (*see also* sexual awakening stories); sexual pleasure in, 29–34, 130–31; use of term, 193n45. *See also* godly sex; same-sex marriage
marriage campaigns, 182n10
MarriageLoveToys.com, 70, 169 *table*
Mars Hill Church, 32, 190n11
masculinity, 6, 133–39, 153–54, 165; evangelical, 135–36
masturbation: attitudes on, 46–47, 123–24; by men, 123–24; by women, 105–7, 122–24, 127, 129, 156
Matthew 5:28, 41, 56
McGuire, Meredith, 202n8
mediated religion, 54–55
men: gender-subversive acts, 28, 134–35, 140–54, 162–65; headship, 32, 42, 118, 128, 137, 154; masturbation, 123–24; privileged status, 112, 135, 147, 153; sex appeal, 136; sexual desires, 50, 111, 115, 131, 135; as sexually dominant, 112–14, 130–31, 136, 142. *See also* gender; masculinity

purity, sexual, 34
Putnam, Robert, 13, 188n66

queer politics, 184n30
queer theory, 5, 8–9, 153

Randles, Jennifer, 188n65, 204n7
reality television, 5
Real Marriage (Driscoll and Driscoll),
    31–33, 41, 44–46, 145, 177, 190n11
Red, Hot Monogamy (Farrell and Farrell),
    193n36
Reformation Project, 185n34
regulatory systems, 5–6, 156
relational intimacy, 124–29
religion: boundaries of, 53; embodied, 7;
    integration with secular cultural
    values, 186n47; social construction of,
    7, 9–12, 160, 196n17; and social
    construction of heterosexuality, 5,
    10–11, 162–65
religious authority, 55–58, 63, 66, 80
religious communities, 54–55, 80, 86–87.
    See also online religious communities
religious knowledge. *See* spiritual capital
Religious Right, 4
restrictive sexual attitudes, 24, 46, 49, 111,
    156, 165–66
Rich, Adrienne, 8
Robertson, Pat, 31
role-playing, sexual, 150–52
Rosenau, Douglas, *A Celebration of Sex,*
    63 *fig.*
Ross, Michael, 11, 158
Rowe, Aimee Carrillo, 11
Rubin, Gayle, 8, 9, 137, 162, 184n29

salvation, 92, 96–98
salvation narratives, 97–98, 109–10,
    119–20, 130
Samanthas.com, 1–2, 69, 78–80, 167, 169
    table
same-sex marriage: legalized, 164, 193n45,
    203n18; opposition to, 20; support for,
    16. *See also* gays and lesbians;
    homosexuality
1 Samuel 2:3, 75
Satan, 97; and sexual pleasure, 3, 37, 119

Savage, Dan, 199n5
Schnarch, David, *Passionate Marriage,* 179
Scofield, Cyrus, 160
Scofield Reference Bible, 160
Scott, Sue, 131
scripture: interpretation of, 159–60, 179;
    on sexual pleasure, 44. *See also* Bible
secular culture: messages about sex, 29–31,
    103–4; and religion, 33–34, 156,
    186n47; and women's sexuality, 6,
    111–12, 116, 197n5
secularization, 157
Sedgwick, Eve, 53, 201n27
seeker-oriented spirituality, 14–15
self-improvement and self-help, 14–15, 52,
    130, 186n47
selflessness, female, 111, 127–28
The 700 Club, 31, 32, 59
Sexperiment (Young and Young), 31, 39
sex toys: stores purchased at, 104. *See also*
    Christian sex toy stores; vibrators
sexual abuse survivors, 99–100, 116–18
sexual awakening stories, 28, 109–12;
    achieving pleasure, 121–25; body as
    obstacle, 115–20; God's role in, 125–27;
    men's, 110–11; spiritual and relational
    intimacy, 124–29
sexual complementarianism, 137, 142–43
sexual confidence, 136
sexual desires, 161; fantasies, 71–74; men's,
    50, 111, 115, 131, 135; women's, 50, 110–12,
    115, 128 (*see also* sexual awakening
    stories)
sexuality: "charmed circle" of, 9, 164,
    184n29; distinction between feelings
    and actions, 192n32, 192n34; social
    construction of, 5–12, 160. *See also*
    godly sex, logic of; inhibition paradox;
    "normal" sexuality
sexualized culture, 14, 32–33, 80, 166
The Sexually Confident Wife (Ethridge), 31,
    112–13, 193n36
sexual norms. *See* non-normative sex;
    "normal" sexuality
sexual partners, number of, 50
sexual pleasure: gender differences, 28,
    32–33, 87; women's entitlement to, 52,
    111–13, 121–22, 127, 130